AN INTRODUCTION TO COMPUTER SCIENCE USING C

RECENT COMPUTER SCIENCE TITLES FROM PWS PUBLISHING COMPANY

AN INTRODUCTION TO COMPUTER SCIENCE USING C

Roger Eggen

University of North Florida

Maurice Eggen

Trinity University

PWS PUBLISHING COMPANY

Boston

PWS PUBLISHING COMPANY
20 Park Plaza, Boston, MA 02116-4324

PWS Publishing Company is a division of Wadsworth, Inc.
I(T)P ™
International Thomson Publishing
The trademark ITP is used under license.

 This book is printed on recycled, acid-free paper.

Library of Congress Cataloging-in-Publication Data

Eggen, Roger.
　　An introduction to computer science using C / Roger Eggen, Maurice Eggen.
　　　p. cm.
　　ISBN 0–534–93888–4
　　1. Computer science. 2. C (Computer program language) I. Eggen, Maurice II. Title.
　　QA76.E3532 1993　　　　　　　　　　　　93–34246
　　005.1—dc20　　　　　　　　　　　　　　　CIP

Sponsoring Editor: *Michael J. Sugarman*
Editorial Assistant: *Ken Morton*
Developmental Editor: *Susan M. Gay*
Production Coordinator: *Elise S. Kaiser*
Production: *Editorial Services of New England, Inc.*
Interior Designer: *Robert Sugar*
Cover Designer: *Elise S. Kaiser*
Cover Art: *Silkscreen "Dimension-10-J" by Masaaki Noda. Used with the permission of the artist.*
Marketing Manager: *Nathan Wilbur*
Manufacturing Coordinator: *Lisa Flanagan*
Compositor: *Pine Tree Composition, Inc.*
Cover Printer: *New England Book Components, Inc.*
Text Printer and Binder: *Arcata Graphics/Martinsburg*

Printed and bound in the United States of America.
　　94 95 96 97 — 10 9 8 7 6 5 4 3 2

Contents

PREFACE

This text is intended for a one-semester or two-quarter course introducing the discipline of computer science to those students who have had no computing experience, but need a foundation in the concepts of computing. The text provides a gentle introduction to computer science for students pursuing degrees as well as those with a more general interest. The text distinguishes itself by stressing the concepts of computing using C as the vehicle of communication, rather than being a manual of C language specifics. Software engineering concepts are used to enhance, motivate, and nurture the problem-solving process throughout. The "Problem, Analysis, Design, Code, and Test" paradigm is used in each example to reinforce and illustrate the problem-solving and implementation process. Rigor and preciseness are not sacrificed by the friendly and informal style used to present the concepts.

Prerequisites

Mathematical sophistication equivalent to high school algebra is sufficient to understand the concepts presented in this book. No computing experience is required or expected.

Pedagogy

The text provides an introduction to the following knowledge units recommended by Computing Curricula 1991 reported by the ACM/IEEE-CS Joint Curriculum Task Force:

AL1 Basic Data Structures
AL3 Recursive Algorithms
AL4 Complexity Analysis
AL6 Sorting and Searching
AL8 Problem-Solving Strategies
AR3 Machine Level Representation of Data

PR1　Introduction to a Programming Language
SE1　Fundamental Problem-Solving Concepts
SE2　The Software Development Process

While the text is designed primarily as an introduction to computer science concepts, it also provides the reader with a background in the C programming language. C is a language capable of supporting the concepts demonstrated and is robust enough to be used for a wide variety of applications beyond the first course. Because C is a general-purpose programming environment that supports a wide range of applications, businesses, educational institutions, and research agencies are moving toward C.

The concepts of data representation, control flow, and software design are stressed throughout the text. The array concept is introduced as simply another storage referencing technique. Subscripted variables are natural extensions of identifiers, and thus can be introduced casually without concern for looping, addressing, or other complications associated with arrays. Students learn by referencing arrays, adding the complicating factors as they become comfortable with the notation.

The text should not be considered a language reference manual, since it is not designed to address intricate language features, but rather uses C as the support tool for computing concepts. To master C, the reader is encouraged to study any of the fine texts designed specifically to address language features.

The style of the text is informal and conversational. Its readability allows students to easily grasp computing concepts. This text provides a firm foundation for continued study in the computing field. While a number of operating system concepts and considerations appear in the text, the basic approach is independent of any particular system. The programming examples have been tested in the DOS, Macintosh, and UNIX environments.

Exercises at the end of each section reinforce the concepts presented. Numerous laboratory projects at the end of each chapter give practical experience analyzing, designing, coding, and testing solutions to problems. The types of exercises vary from mathematical to engineering and business disciplines.

All sample programs given in the text are complete, tested programs with expected input and output clearly indicated. Programs are available on diskette and via electronic mail. The *Instructor's Manual*, available from the publisher, suggests presentation and organization techniques, and includes a set of transparency masters. Chapters 1 through 5 should be covered in order since they provide the basis of the computing concepts. Chapter 6, 7, and 8 are independent and can be chosen selectively as time permits.

Acknowledgments

The authors wish to thank Mike Sugarman, acquisitions editor, and many other people at PWS for their assistance and encouragement in producing this manuscript. Without their patience and perseverance this manuscript might have never appeared. The authors also wish to thank their wives, Vicki and Karen, for their continuing love and support during the long hours of work that went into producing this text. The authors also thank the many reviewers who took time and effort to examine the manuscript and offer many constructive suggestions:

Richard J. Botting
*California State University
San Bernardino*

Linda J. Elliott
La Salle University

Ronald J. Gould
Emory University

Peter Hintenaus
Kent State University

John A. Lewis
Villanova University

J. Michael McGrew
Ball State University

Lanny J. Mullens
Northern Arizona University

Ali R. Salehnia
South Dakota State University

Sharon Salveter
Boston University

Dean Sanders
Illinois State University

Suzanne Sever
Wayne State College

David L. Spooner
Rensselaer Polytechnic Institute

Robert A. Walker
Rensselaer Polytechnic Institute

Raymond F. Wisman
Indiana University Southeast

*Roger Eggen
Maurice Eggen*

CHAPTER

1

Introduction to Computer Science

CHAPTER TOPICS

General Computer Organization

Memory Organization and Information Representation

Processor Capabilities

Algorithms and Problem Solving

INTRODUCTION

There are several different approaches to the art and science of introducing computer science. One approach focuses on the programming language—that is, the medium of communication with the computing hardware. Just as people must have some method of communication with one another, so we must have some method of communicating with the computer. Historically, we communicated with the computer in its language, which consists of nothing more than a sequence of zeros and ones. While the computer is perfectly happy with this language, people are not particularly enthralled with typing thousands of ones and zeros to direct the computer's operation. Computer users would like to be able to formalize ideas and concepts in something closer to the English language or some other high-level language. While focusing on the language is acceptable in one context, focusing on the language alone is insufficient when the *discipline* is the issue to be discussed. An analogy would be focusing on the symbolism of mathematics rather than the mathematical concepts.

Another approach to the art and science of computing concerns the ideas and concepts that make up the body of knowledge of computer science. As an analogy, consider a discussion of psychology conducted in English, Spanish, Russian, or any other language with which the participants are comfortable. The language of communication is not the issue — psychology is. In the same way, the concepts associated with computer science can be discussed among the participants in any computing language that is known or can be readily learned by all of the participants, both human and computer. These languages include BASIC, Pascal, FORTRAN, C, LISP, and several others that are not as common.

The approach used in this book is a conceptual one. Just as it is impossible to discuss psychology without using some spoken language, it is also impossible to convey the concepts of computing without using a computing language. Virtually any computing language would do (some are better than others), but we have chosen the C programming language as our vehicle to convey the concepts of computing science. C is our language of communication just as English can be used to discuss psychology. As a result, a certain amount of programming must be taught —

without it the participants in the discussion are severely handicapped, learning about problem solving without solving problems. Additionally, it must be a language known to all—even the computer. C is, for our purposes, the most appropriate language to use. Thus, this book contains all of the concepts commonly associated with an introduction to computer science, including an introduction to programming, information representation, variables, arrays, sequence, selection, repetition and looping, functions and procedures, algorithms, character strings, stacks, records and structures, linked lists, trees, and sequential and random files. It also provides the reader with some foreshadowing of computer science topics. Concepts of computer science that will be taught in detail in subsequent courses are briefly considered. Upon completion of study from this book, the reader should have an overview of what computer science is all about, as well as a good foundation in programming skills.

Despite all of this discussion, we still haven't answered the question, what is computer science? While it is impossible to give a definition of the discipline that will satisfy everyone, most professionals agree that computer science is a scientific study of a variety of topics including computer design, computer programming, information processing, algorithm design, and computability. It is a study of problems and methods of solution for those problems, but with a specific goal in mind. Most notably, persons interested in computer science are interested in problem solving, but they are interested in more than just solving the problem —they are interested in developing algorithms (methods of solution) that are mechanizable, that is, algorithms that are solvable by a machine (the computer). So, the student of computer science is like the student of mathematics—both are interested in the science of the discipline, but the job of the student of computer science is more akin to the student of applied mathematics. Just proving the existence of a solution, which is satisfactory in certain areas of mathematics, is not enough. The solution must be implementable, that is, we must be able to apply the solution by the use of computing technology. Much of this book will be devoted to problem-solving techniques that are geared specifically toward implementing solutions to problems on the computer. More than that, however, the book will prepare the student for advanced study in computer science.

In this chapter you will learn computer organization, number bases, processor capabilities, variables, and an introduction to programming. The introduction to programming is important since it sets the tone for the discussions in subsequent chapters. The techniques of programming described have proven successful in helping the first-time programmer construct meaningful programs. You are encouraged to study Chapter 1 carefully before proceeding to subsequent chapters.

1.1 GENERAL COMPUTER ORGANIZATION

SECTION TOPICS

Computer Organization

Note of Interest

What is a computer? How does a computer do its work? What are the various parts of a computer and how are they fastened together? Why did the Beatles break up? These questions and many more will be considered in this first chapter, which contains an introduction to the remainder of the text. If you wish to become proficient in the concepts and ideas associated with computers and computing, we suggest that you thoroughly study this material. Without it, you may find it difficult to accomplish the goals and objectives in the remainder of the book.

A computer is a machine, a tool to help people accomplish tasks. A common misconception exists concerning computers. The very name of the machine—*computer*— suggests that it is used for only one thing, to process numbers; that is, to compute, to add and subtract. But the computer is much more. It is a helpmate, an information-processing, idea-producing, information-organizing workstation that many persons, both professionals and laypersons alike, would find very difficult to do without. Just as automobiles take us from one location to another, computers also take us from one intellectual plateau to another. The computer is one of the few tools designed to perform "mental" tasks, that is, to help us think. Like the automobile, a computer must be told exactly what to do and how to do it. The computer cannot solve problems for you any better than your car can take you from your house to school without the proper guidance. You must tell the computer exactly what to do in precise language that enables it to solve problems. In effect, you have to *solve* the problem and direct the computer to *carry out your solution*. Remember, since the computer is a machine it must be told exactly what to do, but after being told, it will carry out your instructions tirelessly. A program consists of the set of instructions, following a predetermined syntax, that guides the computer to follow your solution of a problem. You construct the solution in a computer language as a finite sequence of instructions that ultimately solves the problem.

Computer Organization

A computer consists of a central processor (the computer's brain), internal memory, and any peripheral devices that may be attached to it, including auxiliary (secondary) memory, printers, video display terminals, keyboards, disk drives, plotters, scanners, voice synthesizers, music boxes, and other similar devices. The central processing unit (CPU) consists of the computer's logic units, providing the ability to do arithmetic and to communicate with its internal memory. The memory and peripherals enable the processor to solve problems. In part, they help get information into and out of the computer so human/computer communication can occur. The computer's CPU does its work using binary digits (0s and 1s), while humans commonly think using the decimal system. Thus, some of the peripheral devices must translate our input to the computer into a language it can understand. How all this gets done will be the topic of subsequent courses (operating systems, systems programming, and compilers). In general, the operating system controls the operation of the computer and a compiler translates a high-level language like C to the 1s and 0s the computer actually uses. The compiler and the operating system are just a series of programs used by the computer, programs similar to the ones you will learn to write in this book.

As Figure 1.1.1 shows, there is an intimate connection between the CPU and primary memory, as shown by the double lines in the figure. The CPU can communicate with primary memory much faster than it communicates with its input and output devices, which include the computer's keyboard and monitor as well as its auxiliary or secondary memory, including, among other things, disk, CD ROM, and/or tape drives.

While the CPU is an active component of the computer, memory is primarily passive. Think of memory as a file or a notebook. You write into it and read from it, but the notebook essentially doesn't do anything

Figure 1.1.1   Computer Organization

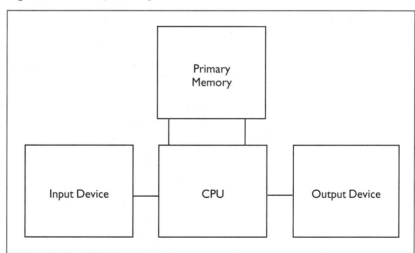

on its own. A notebook is a storage device that contains information. The computer's memory functions similarly, holding data and programs until they are needed. Computers are very good at writing and reading their memory, which comes in two forms: external and internal. As the words indicate, internal memory—primary memory—is that which is inside the computer and is directly accessible to the CPU. External memory can be outside, distant from the computer, perhaps in another cabinet or location. Examples of external memory are disk drives and tape drives. Disk drives are often found in the same cabinet with the internal memory in a personal computer, but reside in a separate cabinet in larger computers. External memory is often called *secondary memory,* while the main memory directly accessible to the processor is called *primary memory.* The basic difference is speed and size. Main memory is measured in thousands or millions of characters (bytes), while secondary memory is measured in millions and billions of characters (bytes) of capacity. Data in main memory can be delivered to the processor faster than data stored in secondary memory.

Floppy disk drives and hard (fixed) disk drives may physically exist inside the computer case, but these devices are considered to be external, based on the method of transferring data to and from the processor rather than the physical location of the device. The role of the monitor is to display results to the user. The keyboard is the mechanism for giving instructions and data to the computer.

Note of Interest

Work is being done to provide a more convenient method of communicating with the computer. One aspect of a field of study called Artificial Intelligence (AI) is a study of methods to allow us to provide data and commands to the computer by speaking in a natural language. Due to the ambiguities in English and other natural languages, this type of communication has proven difficult. Expert systems, vision, logical deduction, and many other areas belong to the AI field of study.

Each section normally concludes with a set of exercises, but because we are just beginning the text, we have provided a list of questions that will be answered by the instructor. These contain information you need to know to successfully begin your study of computing. These questions make you aware of the environment in which you are working. When you can answer them, you will already be more "computer literate"!

1. Name the CPU on the computer you will be using for your study.

2. Name the programming environment you are using.

3. Know the capacity in characters (bytes) of the floppy disks you will be using to store your programs and data for your study, if you

are using a personal computer. If you are using a larger, central computer, find out the amount of secondary storage available in your partition or section of disk.

4. Name the amount of primary memory in the computer you will be using for your study.

5. If you are using a personal computer, name the kind of monitor it has.

6. Explain the difference between primary memory and secondary memory.

7. List the peripherals attached to your computing system.

1.2 MEMORY ORGANIZATION AND INFORMATION REPRESENTATION

SECTION TOPICS

Binary and Hexadecimal Number Systems

Number System Conversions

Negatives and Two's Complement

Hexadecimal Arithmetic

This section discusses processor and memory organization, including different techniques used to store character, integer, and floating-point data.

The energy used to power the computer comes from electricity. Internally, the devices (such as switches) that store information are in only one of two positions: closed or open. Because of this, the memory units used by the computer to store data can be described as *two-state devices*. There are several ways of conceptualizing two-state devices, including presence or absence of power, yes or no, on or off, 1 or 0. Consequently, since the computer stores all its information using these switches, it must do all its work by determining if a switch is closed or open. Because the binary number system consists of two symbols representing the two states of a switch, this system is used as the representation of data stored inside the computer. To effectively understand internal data representation we must also become proficient with the binary number system. The numbers we enter as data into the computer can be in the form of base ten numbers—the numbers we use every day. But to understand how the internals of the computer work, we must know the representation used, which is why we study the binary number system.

Binary and Hexadecimal Number Systems

The binary number system consists of the numbers 0 (first state) and 1 (second state). One binary digit is commonly called a *bit,* for BInary digiT. A group of 8 bits is a *byte.* A group of 16 binary digits is called a *half-word,* and a group of 32 binary digits is called a *word.*

Since there are only two symbols, 0 and 1, arithmetic computation is arguably easier in the binary number system. There are only two choices when faced with an arithmetic problem—the answer can be only 0 or 1 for each computation. Other than that, since number systems are fully understood and have been around for centuries, the rules for the binary number system are the same as for the decimal system. Unfortunately, since we are comfortable with the decimal system, most people think in terms of base 10 numbers. Therefore, until we become proficient with binary, we must learn to convert from decimal to binary and back again. Moreover, since there is a close relationship between binary numbers and hexadecimal numbers (base 16), and because it is difficult to keep track of long sequences of binary digits, we must also learn the hexadecimal number system. Since the system with base 16 must have 16 symbols, the digits 0,1,2,3,4,5,6,7,8, and 9, along with the first six uppercase letters of the alphabet, A,B,C,D,E, and F, are commonly used to represent the digits of the hexadecimal number system. Figure 1.2.1, which contains the first 16 numbers in binary, hexadecimal, and the familiar decimal system, will introduce you to these number systems.

Figure 1.2.1   Decimal, Binary, and Hexadecimal Number Systems

DECIMAL	BINARY	HEXADECIMAL
0	0000	0
1	0001	1
2	0010	2
3	0011	3
4	0100	4
5	0101	5
6	0110	6
7	0111	7
8	1000	8
9	1001	9
10	1010	A
11	1011	B
12	1100	C
13	1101	D
14	1110	E
15	1111	F

Number System Conversions

We represent the binary numbers in groups of four because of the relationship between binary and hexadecimal. Since $2^4 = 16$, each group of four binary digits represents one hexadecimal digit. Conversion from binary to hexadecimal may be accomplished by arranging the binary number in groups of four binary digits and writing the hexadecimal equivalent of each group. For example, the binary number 100101001010010101011 has the following hexadecimal equivalent:

0001	0010	1001	0100	1010	1011
1	2	9	4	A	B

The leading zeros have no effect on the magnitude of the number, and are added to provide a group of four binary digits. The spaces were added for readability. Conversion from hexadecimal to binary is similar, writing a group of four binary digits for each hexadecimal digit. The binary equivalent of the hexadecimal number BEEF is

B	E	E	F
1011	1110	1110	1111

The process of converting from one number system to another depends on our knowledge of the positional representation of numbers. In the same way as the decimal number 342 means $300 + 40 + 2$, which is $3*10^2 + 4*10^1 + 2*10^0$ (the base of our number system is 10), the hexadecimal number 3AB2 must mean

$$3*10^3 + A*10^2 + B*10^1 + 2*10^0$$

where the symbol 10 represents the base of the number system, which is (decimal) 16 in this case. Thus, to convert the hexadecimal number to decimal, we simply replace each symbol by its decimal equivalent, and obtain

$$3*16^3 + 10*16^2 + 11*16^1 + 2*16^0 = 15026$$

Conversion of binary numbers to their decimal equivalents is done in exactly the same way. We write the number in its expanded form, substitute the decimal equivalents of all the symbols, and multiply and add as appropriate. The binary number 10011100 has as its decimal equivalent

$$1*2^7 + 0*2^6 + 0*2^5 + 1*2^4 + 1*2^3 + 1*2^2 + 0*2^1 + 0*2^0 = 156.$$

One method of conversion from decimal to binary involves division. This makes sense, since conversion from binary to decimal involves multiplication. Thus, to convert from decimal to binary, perform successive divisions by 2 and gather the remainders, which will form the binary number. For example, to convert the decimal number 342 to binary, we divide as indicated in Figure 1.2.2.

Figure I.2.2 Conversion from
Decimal to Binary

```
342 ÷ 2 = 171 remainder 0
171 ÷ 2 =  85 remainder 1
 85 ÷ 2 =  42 remainder 1
 42 ÷ 2 =  21 remainder 0
 21 ÷ 2 =  10 remainder 1
 10 ÷ 2 =   5 remainder 0
  5 ÷ 2 =   2 remainder 1
  2 ÷ 2 =   1 remainder 0
  1 ÷ 2 =   0 remainder 1
```

The binary equivalent of the decimal number 342 is obtained by reading the remainders bottom to top from the figure, yielding 1 0101 0110 (with the spaces added for readability). We must read up the column because the digits are generated in a low-to-high-order sequence. We can confirm that our calculation gives the correct result by converting the number back to decimal by the methods outlined above.

$$1*2^8 + 0*2^7 + 1*2^6 + 0*2^5 + 1*2^4 + 0*2^3 + 1*2^2 + 1*2^1 +$$
$$0*2^0 = 256 + 64 + 16 + 4 + 2 = 342$$

Equivalently, we could convert the binary number to hexadecimal, obtaining 156 hexadecimal, and then convert the hexadecimal number to decimal writing it in its expanded form.

$$156 = 1*16^2 + 5*16^1 + 6*16^0 = 256 + 80 + 6 = 342 \ (\text{decimal})$$

You should be aware that the division process outlined above is not restricted to base 2 and base 10; it could be used to convert any number from any base to any other base. The example in Figure 1.2.3 illustrates conversion of 342 decimal to hexadecimal. Reading bottom to top as before, we obtain the hexadecimal number 156. Thus, 342 (dec) = 156 (hex).

Why is understanding the binary number system important? Computers use the binary number system for all calculations. The interface with the computer (the operating system) will convert our base 10 numbers to base 2 for use in the computer, but in order for us to understand

Figure I.2.3 Conversion from
Decimal to Hexadecimal

```
342 ÷ 16 =  21 remainder 6
 21 ÷ 16 =   1 remainder 5
  1 ÷ 16 =   0 remainder 1
```

the internal workings of the computer, we must learn the binary number system. The conversion from base 10 to base 2 is not always a perfect conversion, especially when fractions are present. By understanding the conversion process you will have insight into why some computing results are not perfectly accurate.

Negatives and Two's Complement

Imagine for a moment that you have a new automobile with an odometer that registers the number of miles driven. Only your automobile is unique—it registers miles in binary! Imagine also that the odometer has only four digit positions to register miles traveled. Of course, if the car were new, the odometer would appear as

    0 0 0 0

After driving for one mile, the odometer would be

    0 0 0 1

and after two miles it would be

    0 0 1 0

and so on. After driving for six miles, the odometer would appear as

    0 1 1 0

It would not take very much driving before you ran out of room to store your miles, and this odometer "rolled over" so that it again read all zeros. Also, if the car were new, and you placed the car in reverse and backed up for a mile, the odometer would read

    1 1 1 1

The inescapable conclusion is that this configuration of digits must represent *negative 1* since you backed up for a mile. If we follow this logic for a moment, the configuration 1110 must represent negative 2, 1101 negative 3, etc. (Please remember the hypothesis—there are only four digit positions in which to represent our numeric quantities.) To prove that this number 1110 is in fact negative 2, we rely mathematically on the properties that such a number must have. Specifically, negative 2 is the additive inverse of 2, that is, the number such that when added to 2 gives the sum zero! Thus, adding the numbers 1110 and 0010 together, we see that the result is in fact zero.

```
    0010
+   1110
    0000
```

Remember that there are only four digit positions available to hold the result of an addition. As a result, the carry that occurs from the last position has no place to be stored, and therefore is lost. The resulting sum is zero. Therefore, 1110 correctly represents the negative of 0010 *using four binary digits*. This might appear confusing since in the previous section we indicated 1110 represents the decimal number 13, which is also correct. You must be aware of the context of the discussion. It is important to know whether we are talking about unsigned binary quantities, or whether we wish to include negative (signed) numbers in our discussion. If we are using pure (unsigned) binary numbers to decimal numbers, 1110 is 13, but if we are talking about negative (signed) numbers, then 1110 is negative 2 using our four-digit representation scheme. How do you know which is which? If the sign of the number is important, then the leftmost bit, the 1 in 1110, determines the sign. If the leftmost bit is a 1 and we are concerned about the sign of the number, then the number is negative. If the leftmost bit is a 0, then the number is positive. Many of the modern computers have a *32-bit word,* which means they have a 32-bit *register* to store binary numbers. The same discussion as above for a *four-bit odometer* may be completed for a *32-bit word,* a *16-bit half-word,* an *8-bit byte,* or any other size that is appropriate. The only thing we have to know in order to be able to correctly perform the arithmetic is the size of the storage unit under consideration. The rules are as follows:

Any number with a 1 in its leading digit position is negative.

Any number with a 0 in its leading digit position is positive.

To find the negative (two's complement) of a number, we change all of the 0s to 1s, all of the 1s to 0s, and add 1. To illustrate, consider an 8-bit storage register. The number 2 is 0000 0010. The negative is

```
11111101   (change all zeros to ones and ones to zeros)
      +1   (add one)
11111110   (the correct representation of negative 2 in
           8 bits)
```

To prove that this is in fact the correct representation of negative 2, add the representation of 2 to negative 2 (using exactly eight digit positions) and see that the answer turns out to be 00000000.

As another example, to form the negative of the number 11010101 (which is itself negative in 8 bits since its leading digit is a 1), we change all of the 0s to 1s and all 1s to 0s, yielding 00101010, and add 1, giving 00101011, which is decimal 43. Thus, the number 11010101 must represent negative 43 since negative negative 43 is positive 43.

This arithmetic is exactly what the computer does when it performs its calculations. The process of changing the 0s to 1s and the 1s to 0s is *finding the one's complement or simply finding the complement* of the number. If we complete the process by adding 1 to the result, we are *finding the two's complement or negative* of the number. Technically, the computer does not subtract. The only things the computer does are find the complement and add. The ability to perform these simple operations allows the computer to subtract. Since repeated addition is multiplication and division is merely repeated subtraction, the two simple operations—find the complement and add—allow the computer to perform all elementary arithmetic operations including exponentiation, which is repeated multiplication, which is repeated addition.

Consider the problem of performing the calculation 56 subtract 43 (using 8-bit arithmetic registers):

   56:   00111000
 −43:   <u>11010101 (from above)</u>
(add) 00001101 (no place to store the carry)
00001101 is the (8-bit) binary representation of the decimal number 13

Hexadecimal Arithmetic

Assume for a moment that we wish to work with a computer that has a *32-bit storage device or register.* This means the CPU will use 32 bits every time it performs a calculation. We, as humans, probably cannot consistently write a 32-digit string of 0s and 1s without making an error. As a result, we normally represent 32 bits in hexadecimal rather than in binary because it is easy to convert from hexadecimal to binary and back again, and because it is much easier to write eight hexadecimal digits without making an error. Thus, a new problem arises, that of performing our basic operations, addition and complement, in hexadecimal rather than binary.

To start with, convince yourself that the eight hexadecimal digits (32 binary digits) 0000002B correctly represent the decimal number 43 ($2*16 + 11 = 43$). Each of the hexadecimal digits represents four binary digits. The two's complement (negative) of this number is the number that has the property that when added to 0000002B gives sum zero. The number FFFFFFD5 has the appropriate property. FFFFFFD5 must be negative 43 using 32 binary digits (written in hexadecimal).

        0000002B
(add) <u>FFFFFFD5</u>
        00000000

Using binary digits instead of hexadecimal digits, we would have to represent the above sum as:

```
        0000 0000 0000 0000 0000 0000 0010 1011
(add)   1111 1111 1111 1111 1111 1111 1101 0101
        0000 0000 0000 0000 0000 0000 0000 0000
```

Even with spaces added for readability, we can see that the preceding sums might get hard to deal with if we were forced to use binary digits. Exactly the same information is carried by the hexadecimal representation.

The only difficulty is that we have to learn an additional notation. Since there are only 32 digit positions to represent our quantities, the carry from the last position in the addition is again discarded. This kind of arithmetic makes sense for computer designers, since each of the internal switches can represent only one of two states, 0 or 1. The designers must decide how many switches to place together to represent numbers. Since the string of switches cannot be arbitrarily long, the designers of many modern computers use 32 switches in a row to represent a *full word* quantity. (There are other reasons for using 32 bits, but we shall not go into that here). Since the computer has only a finite amount of space, there must be some practical limit on the size of a word of information. Thus, the scheme we have outlined for you represents a practical way for the central processing unit to do its arithmetic.

► Exercises 1.2

1.2.1   Convert each of the following decimal numbers to binary:

     a) 127   **b)** 255   **c)** 65   **d)** 65535   **e)** 1025

1.2.2   Convert each of the following decimal numbers to hexadecimal:

     a) 127   **b)** 255   **c)** 65   **d)** 65535   **e)** 1025

1.2.3   Convert each of the following binary numbers to hexadecimal:

     a) 0011110100101011   **b)** 1111000011110000   **c)** 100000000000

     d) 1111111111111111   **e)** 1101001010101

1.2.4   Convert each of the following binary numbers to decimal:

     a) 0011110100101011   **b)** 1111000011110000   **c)** 100000000000

     d) 1111111111111111   **e)** 1101001010101

1.2.5   Convert each of the following hexadecimal numbers to decimal:

     a) 127   **b)** FAB   **c)** 12FC   **d)** FEEB   **e)** ABACBBCD

1.2.6   Convert each of the following hexadecimal numbers to binary:

     a) 127   **b)** FAB   **c)** 12FC   **d)** FEEB   **e)** ABACBBCD

1.2.7   Find the 8-bit two's complement binary representation of the decimal number 73.

1.2.8 Find the 16-bit two's complement binary representation of the decimal number 177.

1.2.9 Find the 32-bit two's complement binary representation of the decimal number 1234. Express your answer in hexadecimal.

1.2.10 Find the 32-bit two's complement binary representation of the decimal number −2455. Express your answer in hexadecimal.

1.2.11 The hexadecimal number 5A67 represents a 16-bit two's complement number. Express the same number in 32 bits.

1.2.12 The hexadecimal number FF34 represents a 16-bit two's complement number. Express the same number in 32 bits.

1.2.13 Perform the subtraction 156 − 144 using two's complement binary integer addition and complementation only. Assume 16-bit representation.

1.2.14 Using the binary design described, what is the largest number that can be stored in a 16-bit register? What do you expect will happen if an attempt is made to store a larger number?

1.2.15 Using the two's complement representation scheme for negative numbers, one number can be represented that has the property that its negative cannot be represented in the same number of bits. What is this number?

1.3 PROCESSOR CAPABILITIES

SECTION TOPICS

ASCII

Firmware and Hardware

Input and Output

Variables and Assignment

Arithmetic

Selection — The Computer's Ability to Make Decisions

Iteration — The Computer's Ability to Repeat Tasks

In Section 1.1 we discussed a typical computer configuration with the CPU, main memory, input devices, and output devices. Main memory stores the characters and numbers that are to be manipulated. Section 1.2 described how integers are represented in memory. The physical ability of the computer to store numbers is beyond the scope of this text — for additional information study any good text covering computer architecture. The CPU (central processing unit) is responsible for all work done by the computer—including all additions, subtractions, multiplications, divisions, and data conversion.

American Standard Code for Information Interchange (ASCII)

Each character known to the computer must have a unique numeric code associated with it, since the computer must represent everything using a sequence of 0s and 1s. All the computer scientists all over the world got together in one massive convention and agreed on the representation scheme we now know as the American Standard Code for Information Interchange. (Not really of course.) ASCII evolved because of a need to transmit data economically and in high volumes generated by computers. In 1966 system designs settled on the 7-bit code as the information code to be used. While it is not the only code used, many manufacturers have agreed to use it and therefore it is the de facto standard.

The letters ASCII are usually pronounced "askey." It is desirable for all computers to use the same representation for characters since passing information from one computer system to another is much easier when a standard representation is used. The conversion of characters to ASCII representation must be handled by the interface to the computer. When we enter an A, the representation 01100001, which is ASCII for A, must be stored internally. All information the computer uses, whether numeric or alphabetic, is stored numerically in binary. The ASCII table in Appendix B shows the binary representation for all characters stored in the computer. A *bit* is one binary digit, a 0 or a 1. A sequence of eight binary digits is called a *byte*. The ASCII representation scheme assigns a unique byte (sequence of eight binary digits) to store each character that the computer is to use. Since there are 256 possible combinations of eight 0s and 1s, it is possible for the computer to store and use 256 different characters using an 8-bit ASCII representation.

Firmware and Hardware

The instructions that tell the processor how to perform conversions of characters are part of the CPU and are represented in firmware. The hardware comprises the physical metal and silicon parts of the computer. The software is the program instructions that users write to tell the computer how to solve problems. Software is typically written in languages like C, Pascal, COBOL, or FORTRAN. Firmware is typically written in a low-level language specific to a particular computer. It stays in the heart of the computer all the time, assisting in the operation. Firmware allows communication with the monitor, keyboard, and other peripherals. The distinction between

Figure 1.3.1   Five Basic Functions of a Computer

FUNCTION	EXPLANATION
Input/Output	Read in and print out data (numbers and characters).
Assignment	Store and retrieve data. That is, it can save numbers and then later reference the numbers in much the same way as a standard calculator.
Arithmetic	Perform the basic arithmetic operations: addition, subtraction, multiplication, and division.
Selection	Make basic decisions, like determining whether one number is larger than another. Only items in main memory can be compared (characters and numbers).
Iteration	Execute a sequence of instructions repeatedly.

firmware and hardware is not distinct. One computer's processing may perform operations in firmware and another may do the same in hardware. Our purpose is to make a mild distinction between hardware, software, and the software resident in memory that oversees the computer's operation, which is firmware. Hardware comprises the physical components of the computer such as the CPU, memory chips, controller cards, power supply, keyboard, monitor, printer, and tape drives. Firmware comprises the operating system features as a basic input/output system, language translators, the runtime support package, loaders, and data translation. Some do not make a distinction between software and firmware, and the distinction is a subtle one. We are interested in pointing out a separation between the software written by users, like you, and the software that controls the operation of the computer. As you gain experience in constructing software (programs), you too will be able to write firmware to enhance the operation of your computer system.

Our concern is not with the hardware, software, or firmware, but with a rather abstract notion of what a computer is capable of performing. By considering a computer's capability from an abstract point of view, we will gain a conceptual idea of the computer's abilities and its limitations. This consideration will also provide a fundamental understanding of the programming process and allow for expansion of these ideas in subsequent chapters. The computer is capable of performing the five basic functions described in Figure 1.3.1.

Input and Output

In order for the computer to manipulate information, that information must be readily available to the processor. That is, the information must be available in primary memory. Section 1.1 discussed the difference between secondary memory and primary memory. The *input phase* con-

sists of giving the programming language or commercial package instructions for retrieving data from some auxiliary storage device to primary
memory. Programming languages execute a get, read, scan, input, or similar instruction to cause data to be transferred from auxiliary storage. The
data must be available in primary memory before it can be processed.
Thus, the first basic function of a computer is to transfer data to and from
main memory. When in main memory, user constructed computer programs can reference the data. Details on how this is done will be given in
the next section.

After processing data, the results need to be known. The computer
can either write the results to a file, display the results on the screen, or
write the results to a printer, plotter, or other hard-copy device. The user
can specify instructions telling the computer which of the above options
is desired. This is the *output phase*.

Variables and Assignment

Data that has been read into primary memory is accessed by a program by
using a *variable* (at least in procedural programming languages such as
C). Just as in your high-school algebra class, programming languages
commonly use variables for primary memory storage locations. Two
things must be associated with each storage location: the name (address)
associated with that storage location and the contents stored at that address. For example, in C, if we were to write the statements

```
int x;
x = 5;
```

the first statement would cause a storage location (variable) for an integer
to be created at a particular address in main memory, and would associ-
ate the variable name **x** with it. The second would cause the integer value
5 to be placed in that storage location (at that address). In the same way
that a mailbox contains an address on the outside of the box, the name of
the person, and the mail inside the box, a variable location in main memory contains a symbolic name (**x** in the above example), an address in
memory of **x**, and also some mail (illustrated as 5 in Figure 1.3.2). The
decoding of the expression on the right side of the equal sign and placing
the value into the storage location represented by the variable on the left
side of the equal sign is *assignment*.

As shown, **x** is given an appropriate amount of storage (2 bytes on
some C personal computing systems and 4 bytes on larger systems) and
the binary representation of 5 is placed in that storage location. This
number 5 is accessed by referencing **x**. We reference a variable by simply
using its name in an expression. For example, the statement

```
y = x + 1;
```

Figure 1.3.2 Mailbox Illustration of a Variable Containing 5

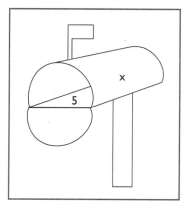

will go to the location indicated by **x**, use the value there to add 1, and store the new value at the location indicated by **y**. The actual technique of retrieving values, the process the computer follows to add the 1, and the storing of the result back in memory is the topic of other courses. Classes dealing with hardware circuits will discuss this topic thoroughly.

Suppose, for example, that we wished to store a character in a variable location. Consider the following C statements:

```
char y;
y = 'a';
```

The first statement causes a one-byte storage location to be allocated and attaches the symbolic address **y** to that location. Since one byte is sufficient to hold the ASCII binary code for one character, the assignment operation in the second statement causes the binary representation of a lowercase 'a' to be placed in that location.

Note that the ASCII representation of the character 'a' is binary 01100001, which is the same as hexadecimal 61 (decimal 97). We could see the different representations of the contents of **y** depending on the particular method we use when we ask the computer for the contents of the memory location **y**. See Figure 1.3.3. The computer correctly interprets the 61 as a character or integer number because we told it that the storage will represent a character.

Variables may also be assigned other variables, as in **w** = **y**. If **y** contained 'a' as in Figure 1.3.3, **w** would also contain 'a'. Since **w** and **y** represent storage locations, a copy of 'a' will be placed in **w**. That is, **w** = **y** causes a copy of the contents of **y** to be placed in **w**. Note that **w** = **y** causes a copy of the data at memory location **y** to be stored in **w** and that **y** is

Figure 1.3.3 Variable with Binary Representation of Character

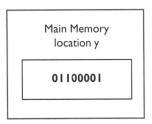

distinct from **w**, so later changing the contents of **y** has no effect on the contents of **w**. See Figure 1.3.4.

In determining variable names, most any name will do, as long as it follows certain rules. However, the selection of a variable name is an important aspect of the programming process. It is extremely important to use variable names that are descriptive of the quantities they contain. Note that we said extremely important! Computer code is difficult to read, to modify, and to maintain unless the particular variable names are appropriately chosen. Figure 1.3.5 shows good variable names.

To summarize, a variable name must begin with a letter or the underscore (_) character, and may be followed by any combination of letters (uppercase and lowercase), numbers (0 through 9), or underscore characters. Most of the difficulty encountered by students in the formation of variable names occurs when they select a reserved word, or mix invalid characters in the variable name. Reserved words may vary slightly from

Figure 1.3.4 The Effect of the Instruction w = y

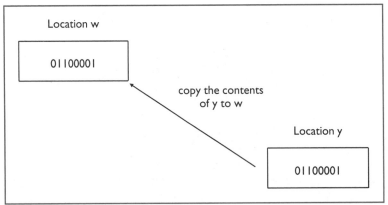

Figure 1.3.5   Good Variable Names

MilesPerGallon	Many programming languages distinguish between uppercase and lowercase characters. If we were to have the computer calculate gas mileage for us, this might be a good variable name.
height	A good variable name to hold a person's height.
x_value	The underscore is an acceptable character in a variable name.
very_long_variable_name	In many programming languages, there is no practical limit to the length of a variable name. However, to make the programmer labor unnecessarily to enter a variable name is counterproductive.
cee3po	Variable names may be a mixture of characters and numbers.
apartment[5]	Variable names may be subscripted. More on this concept will follow, but this allows one name to refrence several storage locations, each distinguished by the value of the subscript.

Figure 1.3.6   Reserved Words in C

auto	break	case	char	const	continue
default	do	double	else	enum	extern
float	for	goto	if	int	long
register	return	short	signed	sizeof	static
struct	switch	typedef	union	unsigned	void
volatile					

installation to installation, but for the most part the words listed in Figure 1.3.6 should not be used as variable names because they mean something special to the C programming environment.

The table in Figure 1.3.7 shows some unacceptable variable names. Study these carefully to avoid problems in name selection.

Arithmetic

The third function the computer is capable of performing is arithmetic. Each computer, independent of brand or software, is capable of doing the fundamental arithmetic operations. All computing languages have in-

Figure 1.3.7   Unacceptable Variable Names

3b2	Letters and numbers are acceptable, but the first character must not be numeric.
Variable Name	A variable name must not contain spaces.
embedded&character	& is an invalid character in a variable name.
v[5]w	Variable names may contain subscripts, but the subscript must be last. A discussion of subscripts will occur later.
char	Reserved words may not be used as variable names.

structions for addition, subtraction, multiplication, and division. Some computing languages include instructions for exponentiation, modulus, integer division, etc. Please study the table in Figure 1.3.8, which contains symbols for the fundamental operations present in the C programming language.

Our concern is that we have an appropriate concept of what takes place when we use a computing language to perform arithmetic. Variables, introduced above, can participate in arithmetic operations. Suppose the following instructions were given to the computer:

```
x = 5;
y = 6;
z = x + y;
```

What will be stored in computer memory location represented by **z**? Your response should be 11, the result of adding the value stored at **x**'s location and the value stored at **y**'s location. Note that the value stored at **x** as well as the value stored at **y** are unaffected by the instruction. Specifically, the instruction **z = x + y** says "go to the storage location whose symbolic address is **x** and retrieve the contents stored there. Then go to the storage location whose symbolic address is **y** and retrieve the contents stored there. Then sum these two quantities, and place the result in the storage location whose symbolic address is **z**." We do not intend to

Figure 1.3.8   Some Arithmetic Operations and Symbols

FUNCTION NAME	SYMBOL	EXPLANATION
Addition	+	The symbol for addition of any two quantities.
Subtraction	−	The symbol for subtraction of any two quantities.
Multiplication	*	Note the use of the asterisk for multiplication.
Division	/	Note that the symbol ÷ is not used for division.
Modulo	%	An integer-based operation, this returns the integer remainder when two integers are divided.

Figure 1.3.9 Find the Sum of Two Quantities

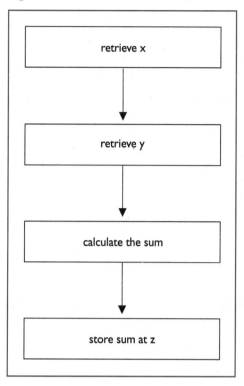

belabor the point since most of this is transparent to the user, but it is important to understand the fundamental concept, as illustrated in Figure 1.3.9.

Selection—The Computer's Ability to Make Decisions

The fourth function the computer can perform is selection. For example, we can ask, is **2 > 4** or is **x > y**? Whether the answer is yes or no will determine the next instruction to be executed. Remember that the computer is like a stupid, but trainable animal. As long as you train it correctly, it is capable of following your instructions. Chapter 3 covers in detail the formation of conditional statements. Data that can be represented in the processor can be compared (integers, real numbers, and characters), but only in decisions that are very carefully formulated. Specifically, only logical instructions that can be answered with "yes" or "no" are appropriate, and only data of the same type, that is, integers and integers or characters and characters, can be compared.

Iteration—The Computer's Ability to Repeat Tasks

The fifth and final basic function appropriate to the computer is iteration or the computer's ability to loop. Programming languages provide instructions that will cause a block of commands to be executed over and over while certain conditions remain true or until certain conditions become true. This concept is typically called repetition, iteration, or looping. The general structure is shown below.

```
LOOP HEAD
      programming
      language
      instructions
RETURN TO LOOP HEAD
```

The above form is very generic and comes in a variety of instructions that will be introduced later. Generally speaking, however, four concepts are associated with the formation of a loop.

1. There must be some sort of initialization.

2. Next, there must be some form of data modification.

3. Statements which make up the body of the loop may include the data modification.

4. Finally, there must be a test for termination of the loop.

If one or more of these parts is missing we may have a loop that executes forever, or a loop that does not execute at all. As an illustration, suppose we wish to remove one of the wheels from our automobile. We might proceed as follows:

1. Jack up the car.

2. Remove a lug nut.

3. If more lug nuts remain, return to step 2.

4. Remove the wheel.

Step 1 is preparation, or initialization. Step 2 is data modification as well as the body of the loop. Step 3 is a test for termination. If we are not through removing lug nuts, we must return to step 2 and continue to remove an additional nut. On a larger automobile with a five-bolt wheel, we would have to execute the loop five times before the wheel would be loose and ready for removal. Anytime a collection of tasks must be repeated, a loop will be involved.

▶ Exercises 1.3

1.3.1   Which of the following variable names are unacceptable, and for what reason?

a) Integer   **b)** float   **c)** variable55   **d)** ShEeP   **e)** five%

f) five_percent   **g)** stuff   **h)** g2b   **i)** [55]xyz

j) TheFirstVariableWhichIsNotASingleCharacter

1.3.2   Name some other exercise, other than removing a wheel from a car, that requires repetition.

1.3.3   The following instructions represent a selection statement that might appear in a program. Write your opinion as to whether this is an appropriate selection statement for a computer program.

```
if (x > 5)  /* the selection, assume an integer value
                 stored in x                             */
      y = 7; /* a simple valid assignment statement      */
```

1.3.4   The following instructions represent a selection statement that might appear in a program. Write your opinion as to whether this is an appropriate selection statement for a computer program.

```
if (color is red)       /* the selection */
     use red paint;      /* do some action */
```

1.4 ALGORITHMS AND PROBLEM SOLVING

SECTION TOPICS

Problem Solving

Problem-solving Methodology

This section introduces the thinking process required to *solve problems* on the computer. A *solution strategy* will be a sequence of instructions directing the computer to perform certain steps in a specified order to get the computer to solve a specific problem. The process of getting the computer to solve problems for us generally involves a procedure called *pro-*

gramming the computer. You might program the alarm system on your car or program the security system on your home. Each of these consists of giving the environment a sequence of steps it is to perform. In the same way, the programming process for a computer involves giving the computer a sequence of steps in a language it understands that will solve a problem.

Problem Solving

The programming process is like any other problem-solving situation. Thus, the emphasis here is on the general *problem-solving process*. This problem-solving process is the same, whether we are students of computer science, mathematicians, automobile repair persons, or advisors to the president of the United States. Each of these individuals may be faced with a problem and needs a methodology to be used in the problem-solving process. G. Polya, in his landmark book *How to Solve It,* written in 1945, identified four steps to be used in any problem-solving process. The problem-solving methodology identified by Polya is just as fresh today as when it was written. These steps are:

1. *Understand the problem.* It makes no sense to attempt a solution to a problem without understanding what is required.

2. *Devise a plan.* One must certainly decide what is to be done first, second, third, and so on in order to solve a particular problem.

3. *Carry out your plan.* Actually carry out your solution. Perform the steps decided upon in the second step to accomplish your goal.

4. *Look back.* Examine your solution to see if the results make sense in light of your original understanding of the problem. Too many times we get an answer and never stop to look at it to see if it is reasonable.

When we phrase the problem-solving steps in the language of computer science, we use slightly different terminology than that used above, but the *process* is the same, whether we are talking about computers or not. The problem-solving process when dealing with computers is similar to that above and is as follows:

1. *Analysis.* We study the statement of the problem until we are sure we understand exactly what is to be done.

2. *Design.* The next step is to design a computer *algorithm* to perform the required tasks. An algorithm is merely a sequence of steps that must be performed to accomplish the solution to the problem. The steps of the algorithm will be presented using the five basic things the computer can do. Specific design tools include *pseudo-*

code, which is a carefully structured English statement of the sequence of steps to solve the problem. Pseudocode is not computer code, but is a statement of the algorithm in a language which is easily transferred to computer code. Other design techniques include American National Standards Institute (ANSI) flowcharts and structured flowcharts.

3. *Code.* The algorithm decided upon in step 2 of the problem-solving process must be implemented in a language that the computer can understand. That is, the computer must be given careful instructions for carrying out the design of the solution to the problem.

4. *Test.* The *look back* phase of the problem-solving methodology consists of executing your program code on the computer with a carefully selected set of test cases designed to ensure that the computer code correctly implements the solution you have decided upon. This field of software testing has received considerable interest from computing professionals in recent years.

Now, when you hear persons talking about the Analysis, Design, Code, and Test methodology, you know that they are simply applying problem-solving strategies to specific computer problems.

Problem-solving Methodology

To illustrate the problem-solving strategies outlined above, we shall consider several examples. Many of the examples are very simple, but the emphasis is on the problem-solving strategy, not on the problems themselves.

▶ **PROBLEM**   Suppose we want the computer to find the average of 5 numbers.

ANALYSIS   To be sure we understand the problem, we make some assumptions concerning the solution to be delivered. Assume for simplicity that the numbers are integers and that the average is to be an integer as well. We will discard the fraction portion of the average. Since this problem is one we are all familiar with, the analysis portion of the problem-solving process is simplified.

DESIGN   To enable the computer to solve this problem we have to think in terms of the capabilities of the computer. What must be done to solve the problem? Our algorithm for solving the problem comprises the following steps—our first attempt at pseudocode for the solution to the problem:

1. The 5 numbers must be brought into main memory of the computer.
2. The sum of the 5 numbers must be found.

    3.   The sum divided by 5 computes the average.

    4.   The resulting average is then displayed.

The programs you write should always begin with a list of instructions similar to the four you have just seen. These assist you in isolating what must be done by the computer to solve the given problem. These pseudocode sentences are part of the design phase of the problem-solving process. The first pseudocode we write may be quite rough, providing us only a general overview of the problem. Then, as we identify where the difficulties are, we make our pseudocode more specific, and provide more detail concerning the problem solution. This process, of successively providing more detail in our description of the problem in pseudocode, is called *stepwise refinement.* We admit that the current problem is quite simple, but for example purposes we continue with the next refinement of our pseudocode.

    1.   Read the first number.

    2.   Read the second number.

    3.   Read the third number.

    4.   Read the fourth number.

    5.   Read the fifth number.

    6.   Calculate Sum = FirstNumber + SecondNumber
        + ThirdNumber + FourthNumber + FifthNumber.

    7.   Calculate Average = Sum divided by 5.

    8.   Display Average, the average of the five numbers.

As suggested in the problem-solving description, once the problem solution has been designed in enough detail, the pseudocode used in the design should be easily transferred to computer code.

CODE   We realize that you may not understand the computer code presented in Figure 1.4.1, but we include it here for completeness. The next step in the problem-solving process is to take our refined pseudocode and implement it in a language that the computer understands. In this case, we present a C program to solve the problem.

If you examine the C computer code written to implement the pseudocode, you can see that there is a close relationship between the actual computer code and the refined pseudocode presented in Figure 1.4.1. If the solution is correctly designed in pseudocode, there should be a very close relationship between the actual code and the pseudocode used to design the computer solution to the problem. Note that no selection or iteration was performed in the solution. Input and output, assignment, and arithmetic alone were necessary to solve this problem. In many of our elementary examples we will request that the computer perform

Figure 1.4.1   Average of Five Numbers in C

```
#include <stdio.h>
main()
{
    int
         firstno, secondno, thirdno, fourthno, fifthno, sum, average;
    printf("Enter first number: ");
    scanf("%d",&firstno);
    printf("enter second number: ");
    scanf("%d",&secondno);
    printf("enter third number: ");
    scanf("%d",&thirdno);
    printf("enter fourth number: ");
    scanf("%d",&fourthno);
    printf("enter fifth number: ");
    scanf("%d",&fifthno);
    sum = firstno + secondno + thirdno + fourthno + fifthno;
    average = sum/5;
    printf("The average of the five entered numbers is %d \n",average);
}
```

input and output, since we wish to provide input to the programs we write and wish to see the results of the calculations performed by the computer.

TEST   We must now find a computing environment, enter the code presented for the solution, and try it on several examples to make sure it performs as expected. Of course, we can easily check the program since it is an easy task to calculate the average of five numbers.

▶ **PROBLEM**   Consider now the problem of finding the average of 50 integers rather than just 5 as in the previous problem.

ANALYSIS   This problem is certainly related to the preceding problem, except we have more numbers to deal with. Since we understand the concept of average, we proceed to the design phase of the problem-solving methodology.

DESIGN   What additional difficulties are presented by the fact that there are 50 numbers rather than 5? Certainly we do not want to use 50 variable names, firstno, secondno, thirdno, and so on, since we would become very unhappy attempting to enter all these variable names. Moreover, if we could enter all 50 variable names, someone will change the problem to 500 or even 5000, and then we will be at a loss unless we can design a more sophisticated solution to this rather elementary problem. The design consists of the following sequence of steps:

```
1. Initialize a sum to zero.
2. Initialize a counter to zero.
3. Read a number.
4. Add the number to the sum.
5. Add one to the counter.
6. If the counter is less than 50, return to step 3.
7. The sum now includes the sum of all 50 numbers.
   Calculate the average which is the sum divided by 50.
8. Display the average.
```

The beauty of this design is that it is not really dependent upon the number of numbers to be entered. In fact, the only change necessary to get the algorithm to work for 500 or 1000 numbers is to change each occurrence of 50 to 500 or 1000. This design includes a loop, the statements 3 through 6. The algorithm executes the loop 50 times, with each pass of the loop reading a number, adding the number to the sum, and increasing the value of the counter by one. In this way, when the counter reaches 50, the sum has accumulated the total of all 50 numbers. Then the average is readily calculated.

CODE   For completeness, the C program code for this example follows:

```c
#include <stdio.h>

main()
{
    int
        sum,average,counter,number;

    counter = 0;
    sum = 0;
    do
    {
        printf("please enter number: ");
        scanf("%d",&number);
        sum = sum + number;
        counter = counter + 1;
    } while (counter < 50);

    average = sum/50;
    printf("the average is %d\n",average);
}
```

TEST   In order to adequately test this program, several test collections of 50 numbers should be entered, in each case checking the program to make sure that the program yields correct results.

▶ PROBLEM   As another example of the development process, consider the problem of finding the largest of a sequence of five integers.

ANALYSIS   Several possible methods of solving this problem are available. Specifically, we would read all the numbers into the computer, and then later look through them to find the largest one. Or, we could read them one at a time and continually keep track of the largest one found so far. After having read all the numbers, the maximum would be known. Both are viable solutions, but the second is slightly easier, so we present it first.

DESIGN   As before, we outline our solution using stepwise refinement. (Actually, we have already started the stepwise-refinement process in the analysis stage.)

```
 1. Read in the first number.
 2. Let maximum be the first number.
 3. Read in the second number.
 4. If the second number is larger than maximum, replace
    maximum with the second number.
 5. Read in the third number.
 6. If the third number is larger than maximum, replace
    maximum with the third number.
 7. Read in the fourth number.
 8. If the fourth number is larger than maximum, replace
    the maximum with the fourth number.
 9. Read in the fifth number.
10. If the fifth number is larger than maximum, replace
    the maximum with the fifth number.
11. Display maximum, the largest of the five numbers.
```

Looking at the outline of the solution we have presented, it appears that some sequence of tasks is being repeated over and over again. This suggests that we should make use of the computer's iterative capability, its ability to perform a loop. But how do we set up a framework for the iterative process? We notice one thing—we need some variable that will simply count to five to tell us when we are to stop looping. We need another variable to hold the current number being tested, and a third variable to hold the largest number found so far.

```
1. Initialize the value of the variable Index with zero.
2. Read the first number into Number.
3. Let Maximum = Number.
4. Increase the value of Index by 1.
```

5. Read the next number into Number.
6. If the value of number is larger than Maximum,
   replace Maximum with Number.
7. If the value of Index is 4, go to the next line, else
   go back to step 4.
8. Display the value of the variable Maximum.

Notice that a loop is again involved in the implementation of the algorithm.

CODE   The code for the problem looks (as it should) very much like the pseudo-code presented earlier. The rules and regulations governing the programming process will be covered completely in the following chapters.

```c
#include <stdio.h>

main()
{
    int
        index, number, maximum;

        index = 0;
        printf("Please enter number: ");
        scanf("%d",&number);
        maximum = number;
        while (index < 4)
        {
            index = index + 1;
            printf("Please enter number: ");
            scanf("%d",&number);
            if (number > maximum)
                maximum = number;
        }
        printf("The maximum of the values entered is %d\n",
                maximum);

}
```

TEST   When the program is executed, the results might be similar to the following. The values entered could be any integers, and the program should correctly choose the maximum.

```
Please enter number: 55
Please enter number: 34
Please enter number: 78
Please enter number: 12
Please enter number: 34
The maximum of the values entered is 78
```

Notice that our solutions to all these problems consist of a sequence of steps taken from the five basic instructions that represent the capabilities of the computer. You have to formulate each solution within these five basic capabilities. Elementary algorithm development is much like solving a puzzle. The design of a problem solution is like a puzzle to be solved and the five basic functions of the computer are the pieces available for constructing your solution. In completing a puzzle, you have the constraints imposed by the problem such as crossword puzzles that require letters to fit appropriately, or jigsaw puzzles that require pieces to fit together. The colors, shapes, and a picture are tools used in finding the solution. Problem solving on the computer is like solving the jigsaw puzzle. You have a problem formulated by some task needing to be done, and you have the tools provided by the computing language and problem-solving skills learned through experience to guide you to a solution. You have to construct a solution using the experience (to be gained here) and computer language features (also gained in this course) to assist in the construction of the set of instructions given to the computer that represent a solution.

▶ Exercises 1.4

1.4.1 The Greatest Common Divisor (GCD) of two positive integers is defined to be the largest positive integer which divides (evenly) both of the given integers. For example, 4 is the GCD of 12 and 16, since 4 evenly divides both 12 and 16, and no integer larger than 4 has this property. An algorithm for finding the GCD of two integers consists of successively subtracting the smaller number from the larger, replacing the larger with the difference (this algorithm is based on Euclid's algorithm for division). This subtraction is continued until the difference is zero. The previous difference is the GCD. For example, to find the GCD of 12 and 16, we calculate:

$$16 - 12 = 4$$
$$12 - 4 = 8$$
$$8 - 4 = 4$$
$$4 - 4 = 0. \text{ Thus the GCD is 4.}$$

Using Polya's problem-solving methodology, design an algorithm for the solution to the problem of finding the GCD. Your algorithm should be presented in pseudocode.

1.4.2 A positive integer is prime if its only divisors are one and itself. One method of determining whether a given positive integer is prime is to successively divide it by numbers smaller than itself to see whether any of these divide it evenly. Using Polya's problem-solving methodology, design an algorithm for the solution to this problem. Your algorithm should be presented in pseudocode.

1.4.3   A computer network has transmitted a body of text (ASCII characters) to our computer. In the transmission some additional spaces have been sent. Using the problem-solving methodology, write the steps necessary to look through the text and eliminate any multiple spaces which occur. Your algorithm should be presented in pseudocode.

1.4.4   Three integers are entered in random order into the computer. Your task is to display the numbers in ascending order. Using the problem-solving methodology, present an algorithm for ordering three numbers. Your algorithm should be presented in pseudocode.

▶ Key Words

arithmetic (+, −, *, /, %)	internal devices (CPU, memory)
ASCII	iteration (while, do, for)
assignment (=)	memory
CPU	reserved words in C
external devices (disk, display, keyboard)	selection (if)
hardware, firmware, and software	software engineering and problem solving (problem, analysis, design, code, test)
input/output (scanf, printf)	
internal data representation (two's complement)	variables (x, y)

▶ Chapter Concepts

1.1   C is the language used for the purpose of discussing computer science concepts. Other languages could have been used, but C is an appropriate language containing a mixture of power and structure suitable for the task.

1.2   The components of a computer, such as hardware, software, firmware, and peripheral devices are considered. Examples of hardware components consist of the monitor, hard drive, floppy disk, internal memory, and external memory. Firmware consists of the operating system (which controls the computer's operation), device drivers (which control disks and printers), editors (for entering and modifying programs and data sets), and language translators (used to change high-level language like C to an executable form). Software is the problem-solving program we will construct as examples throughout this text. Programs that solve specific problems such as sorting, searching, matrix multiplying, circuit analysis, word processing, or spreadsheets are typically considered software.

1.3 Binary numbers, including two's complement arithmetic, present an information representation technique used to store integers in computer's memory. Number bases are important since we need to understand how information is represented when and if errors in calculations occur. Errors may occur due to inexact number translations from base 10 to base 2. Not all base 10 fractions have an exact binary representation.

1.4 When solving problems on a computer using a procedural language such as C, we have the following basic tools to use:

Input/Output—allows information to be brought into the computer for manipulation and computation and the results displayed on a terminal, file, or paper.

Assignment—sometimes called storage or the storing of a value, the computer provides the ability to assign values to variables causing that value to be stored in the computer's primary memory. Variables are not typically stored in secondary memory, rather files or records are normally written to disk storage.

Arithmetic—standard operations of add, subtract, multiply, and divide are basic operations provided by the computer. Other mathematical functions are often built in by including a mechanism for calculating the values. Examples included are trigonometric sine, cosine, tangent, arcsine, arccosine, arctangent, secant, cosecant, cotangent, square root, exponential, and logarithm with base 2, e, or 10.

Selection—the ability to make decisions by comparing like values held in variables. Standard comparison operators are equal (==), not equal (!=), greater than (>), less than (<), less than or equal (<=), and greater than or equal (>=).

Iteration—the ability to perform sequences of instructions over and over. The instructions **While, Do ... While,** and **For** are provided in C.

1.5 Basic software engineering for problem solving is also developed in this chapter. You should gain some insight to the thought processes required to solve problems and implement their solution on the computer. The analysis, design, code, and test paradigm is used throughout to reinforce good program design through software engineering concepts.

CHAPTER 2

Implementation of Complete Programs

INTRODUCTION

This chapter will explain the basics of entering and executing programs written in the C programming language. Computer science concepts detailed in this chapter include editor fundamentals, program execution, source code versus object code, and operating systems. After you finish reading this chapter you should be comfortable using the computer when entering and executing programs. This chapter also introduces the fundamental control structures: pretest and posttest loops, decision structures, input and output, and arithmetic. These fundamental control structures will be covered in greater detail in later chapters.

2.1 UNDERSTANDING C

SECTION TOPICS

The C Language Philosophy

C Functions and C Libraries

Introduction to Programming in C

Assignment

Arithmetic

While the emphasis of this text is *not* on the C programming language per se, we do need some language for communicating the ideas and concepts that embody the collection of material commonly known as "Computer Science I." Therefore, we will have to discuss a certain amount of C programming. The reader is encouraged to pick up any one of the excellent books on the C programming language for a thorough treatment of all of the "bells and whistles" of the rich and powerful C programming environment. We will discuss only that subset of the language necessary to adequately communicate the concepts and ideas essential to a first course in computer science.

The C Language Philosophy

The philosophy behind the C programming language is somewhat different from other programming languages. C itself is a small language, since it does not contain any facilities for input/output processing, mathematical functions, or string processing, for example. There are no *read* or *write* statements commonly found in languages for data transfer to and from the memory of the computer, and no built-in file accessing statements. Since we have learned that these capabilities are essential to the computer, the C programming language must provide these tools. C performs these functions by invoking special library routines, selectively added to the language.

C Functions and C Libraries

C relies on an extensive collection of libraries that contain C functions that may be selectively included in your program or project. Being able to selectively include the features you wish has several advantages, most notably that it keeps the size of the language to a minimum and provides the programmer with an environment in which only features needed on a regular basis will be used. Reducing the size of a programming environment is essential since size and speed are important considerations in the performance of your programming projects. With the work of the American National Standards Institute (ANSI), which provided a standard for the C programming language, a collection of standard libraries was defined which provide most of the functions needed for common programming tasks. Another advantage to this approach is that, once the language and the libraries have been constructed, the implementation is independent of any particular computing hardware. Perhaps you have heard that "C is a transportable language," which means that a C program written for an Apple Macintosh™ will most often run unaltered on an IBM™ computer. Thus, whether you are using the Macintosh or the IBM, programming in C is *programming in C*. One is as good as (but no better than) the other.

There are some inconsistencies in C in that some function calls operate differently on one machine than another. Each of the built-in functions in the standard libraries must be constructed to work on the target machine. Since each machine has its own peculiarities, the result of these functions can vary slightly. Because of its evolution and because C was not designed as a teaching language, some of the features will seem illogical to you. Try to make a note of those instances and remember the "backward" features the next time you use them. Nonetheless, C has gained tremendously in popularity in recent years because it is a rich and powerful programming environment and because it has proven to be an effective medium of expression for a wide variety of programming applications.

Introduction to Programming in C

We wish to get you started as quickly as possible as a C programmer. You saw some C programs in Chapter 1, but they were presented without explanation. The only way to learn a programming language is to practice it. In much the same way that you can't learn to hit your backhand in tennis without going onto the tennis court, you can't learn to write C programs without actually entering them from the keyboard and seeing what they do. Reading all of the books in the public library about hitting a backhand would be worthless without practice.

Thus, in C, a program to print a message

```
The sun is shining clearly
my attitude is bright . . .
when I think of schoolwork
my gloom is dark as night!
```

on the terminal screen would appear as shown in Figure 2.1.1.

Just how to enter and execute this program depends on the system you are using. However, an explanation of the features included in this example is in order. The **#include** statement says that this example requires the standard input/output library, and tells the project manager (the compiler) to include the prototype of these necessary functions. The **#** must be on the left margin (column 1) for this statement to work correctly.

Every C program consists of a collection of functions prepared by the programmer or included from one of the many standard or user-created libraries. One and only one of these functions must be named **main**. Note

Figure 2.1.1　A C Program Example

```c
#include <stdio.h>

main()
{
    printf("The sun is shining clearly\n");
    printf("my attitude is bright . . .\n");
    printf("when I think of schoolwork\n");
    printf("my gloom is dark as night!\n");
}
```

also that C is *case sensitive*—this means that **main** is the appropriate function name, not **MAIN, Main,** or any of the other possibilities. The parentheses following **main**() indicate that this particular function call takes no arguments. Functions may have several arguments or they may have none, but a function may return only one value. This seems unnecessarily restrictive at this point, but we shall see later that, in fact, we have a tremendous amount of flexibility in the things we can ask our functions to do.

Each of the **printf** statements is a call to the library function **printf,** which is found in the standard input/output library. That is why we have included the **<stdio.h>** header file.

For each call to the function **printf**, the text, or literal expression, must be included in double quotes. Each of the **'\n'** characters tells **printf** to go to a new line when it is finished printing. Each of the statements must terminate with a semicolon. The body of the main program is enclosed in braces { }. All functions, even the main function, have their body contained in braces { }.

Assignment

Evaluating expressions is fundamental to programming. In C, we evaluate an expression on the right side of the assignment operator, and the value of the expression is placed in the variable on the left side of the assignment operation. For example, to calculate the expression

```
c = (5/9)*(f - 32);
```

we retrieve the value of the variable **f**, subtract 32, and multiply by 5/9. This value is placed in the variable **c**. The assignment operator is the equal sign. This statement does not say these two quantities are equal, but rather performs the operation of calculating the right side and assigning it to the left side. Because of this, expressions like

```
x = x + 1;
```

make perfectly good sense, since we retrieve the value of **x**, add one, and place it back in **x**.

Arithmetic

General purpose programming languages allow the capability of performing standard arithmetic operations. Addition, subtraction, multiplication, and division, as well as many other fundamental arithmetic operations, are all supported. In C, because of the small-language philosophy, the standard arithmetic operations are all part of the kernel of the language. If we wish to perform more sophisticated mathematical operations, we must include the library that contains these mathematical routines. For example, if we wished to perform mathematical operations with the trigonometric functions of sine or cosine, we would tell the compiler to include the prototype of the relevant functions from the math library by stating

```
#include <math.h>
```

in our program. Standard arithmetic operations include addition (+), multiplication (*), subtraction (–), and division (/). On our UNIX™ system we must compile the program using math functions with the -lm option. This instructs the linker/loader to actually include the instructions for computing the math function in the executable form of the program. For example, the program in Figure 2.1.2 demonstrates the use of the sine function to compute the sine of 30 degrees or $\pi/6$, which is 0.523599 radians.

Assuming the instructions are stored in a file called **sine.c,** the above program is compiled using the following instruction:

```
gcc sine.c -lm
```

This is the instruction to compile the program. We need to now execute the program with the instruction

```
a.out
```

The **-lm** option specifies the linker/loader to include the code for the math function. In this example, **cc** can be substituted for **gcc** if desired. The result of the program is

```
the sine of 0.523599 is 0.500000
```

The result is to be expected since the sine of $\pi/6$ is 0.5. The program runs in the Turbo C 2.0 environment provided the directories option includes Turbo's "lib" directory so that its linker can find the math functions.

Figure 2.1.2   Math Function

```
#include <stdio.h>
#include <math.h>

main()
{
    double y = 0.5235988; /* like float, but more storage allocated to double */
                        /* double demanded by sin function in math library */
    printf("the sine of %lf is %f\n",y, sin(y)); /* lf is long float for sin */
}
```

▶ Exercises 2.1

Note: the following programs are to be attempted as a "first effort" at constructing computer solutions. You are not expected to execute them on a computer at this time.

2.1.1   Describe the output from the following C program:

```
#include <stdio.h>
main()
{
    printf("This is a message\n");
    printf("generated by this program.\n");
}
```

2.1.2   Write a C program that will print your home address as it would appear on an envelope.

2.1.3   Write a C program that will calculate and print the number of seconds in a 24-hour day.

2.1.4   Write a C program that will print the result of converting a given Fahrenheit value to Centigrade. Your program should begin with

```
#include <stdio.h>
main()
{
    int faren = 75; /* 75 degrees fahrenheit */
    .
    .
    .
```

2.1.5   Write a C program that will print the following pattern:

2.1.6   What will be printed by the following program if the user types in "4" in response to the prompt?

```
#include <stdio.h>
#define pi 3.14159265

float Circum(float diameter);
```

```
main()
{
    float
        diameter, circumference;
    printf("Please enter the diameter of the circle\n");
    scanf("%f",&diameter);
    circumference = Circum(diameter);
    printf("the circumference of a circle");
    printf(" of diameter %f is %f",diameter, circumference);
}
float Circum(float diameter)
{
    return (diameter * pi);
}
```

2.1.7 Using the following program:

• What instruction is used to compile the following program if you are working in the UNIX environment?

• What will be printed by the program?

• What instruction will execute the program if you are working in the UNIX environment?

```
#include <stdio.h>
#include <math.h>

main()
{
    double y = 0.5235988;

    printf("the sine of %lf is %f\n",y, sin(y));
}
```

2.2 OPERATING SYSTEMS

SECTION TOPICS

Editors and Compilers

Source Code

Object Code

Regardless of the system you have chosen to use when learning computer science concepts, several things remain consistent across the various kinds of hardware and software environments.

Figure 2.2.1 The Role of the Editor and Compiler

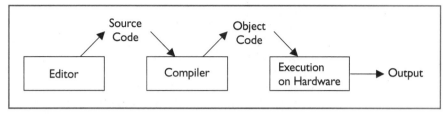

Editors and Compilers

Most notably, each system will require you to use an editor to enter the source code and a compiler which will translate the *source code* into *object code*. The object code, after being loaded into memory and executed, will hopefully produce the desired output. Many of the C programming environments have an integrated editor which interacts directly with the operating system to allow program modification and execution in the same environment. Others require the programmer to use an external editor to create the source code that must be compiled by the system to produce the object code. Each of these steps is a set of distinct instructions to the operating system. Many programming systems have an integrated editor which provides the user more flexibility since an integrated editor can catch some of the syntactic programming mistakes. See Figure 2.2.1.

The editor creates an environment that allows the user to enter text, symbols, and commands. Many different editors are available, but all will allow the user to electronically correct mistakes, enter information, move blocks of characters, save to disk, and print the contents of a file. A file can be thought of as an electronic sheet of paper used to store programs and data. The editor, which consists of a set of commands, is used to enter the source code for computer programs.

Source Code

The source code is that collection of symbols (characters representing instructions to the computer) that represent commands to the computer to perform specific tasks. The file containing the source code is called a *source file*. An example of C source code entered using an editor is shown in Figure 2.2.2. This code prints the numbers from 0 through 9 inclusive on the terminal screen. While this program may not make sense to you, you should attempt to understand what the instructions are requesting the computer to do. This text is dedicated to the concepts that will enhance your understanding of the program, but we now regress slightly to discuss each statement in turn.

The numbers at the left edge of the program are not part of the source code but are used for reference purposes only. Line 1 allows the program to perform input and/or output. It causes the compiler to include header files necessary for input/output. Line 2 marks the beginning of the actual program. Line 3 is a grouping symbol that matches the symbol in line 12. These grouping or blocking symbols must always match. Lines 4 and 5 work as a team to set up integer storage for a variable called **i**. Line 6 places 0 at the storage location represented by **i**. Line 7 marks the beginning of a loop; the loop will be entered if the storage represented by **i** has a value less than 10, which it does initially. Line 8 marks the beginning of the block of statements that make up the body of the loop. The brace at line 8 matches line 11, which marks the end of the loop. Remember, for each opening brace { there must be a closing brace }. Line 9 causes the value of **i** to be displayed on the screen. The function **printf** on line 9 performs output, and **%d** is a control character indicating integer output (the characters between the two quotation marks are formatting information that indicates how the output is to appear). In this example, the program expects an integer followed by a blank to be printed. The **i** following the **",** matches the **%d**. The value stored at the location represented by **i** is printed. Line 10 increases the value stored at the location represented by **i** by 1. Lines 11 and 12 have been discussed in relation to lines 8 and 3, respectively.

A few additional comments. Each statement in C ends with a semi-colon. Statements are not totally obvious, but basically those instructions that appear in the body of a block are statements and therefore need a semicolon. The **#include <stdio.h>** is a compiler directive (and therefore not a statement) so it does not need a semicolon and **main** is the start of a function, thus not a statement and therefore no semicolon. The

Figure 2.2.2   A C Source Code Example

```
1   #include <stdio.h>      /* the standard I/O library            */

2   main()                  /* the start of the main routine       */
3   {                       /* begin the main block                */
4       int                 /* set up integer storage              */
5           i;              /* for a variable called i             */
6       i = 0;              /* put 0 in that storage location      */
7       while (i < 10)      /* iterate while i contains < 0        */
8       {                   /* mark the beginning of the block     */
9           printf("%d ",i); /* print (display) the value of i     */
10          i = i + 1;      /* increase i by 1                     */
11      }                   /* end of the "while" block            */
12  }                       /* end of the "main" block             */
```

{ and } are not statements; they only block sections of code. The /* and */ are comments designed for people. They are ignored by the computer and are included to assist users in understanding a program. You should include comments describing your program and instructions that might cause confusion. These comments are included to assist your understanding, and therefore, are at a lower level and more detailed than typically included in a program. Most systems do not allow comments within comments. You must again be careful in that each /* must have a corresponding */.

Enter the program in Figure 2.2.2 in your computing environment and watch the results of program execution. This program shows looping, arithmetic, assignment, and output, four fundamental capabilities of the computer. The compiler, provided by the programming environment, takes the source code and translates it into a form that the CPU can understand. Of course, the CPU is not human so we would not expect it to understand our language. Thus, the source code must be changed into what is ordinarily a collection of binary digits (1s and 0s) that are meaningful to the CPU. We do not read its language and it does not read ours. Consequently, some translation must take place.

Object Code

When the source code is submitted to the compiler, the result produced by the compiler is called *object code*. The source code is the collection of commands and symbols we enter with an editor, while the object code is the source code translated into the language that can be loaded into the CPU and executed. Generally, the object code consists of the computer's language, which is represented as nothing more than a collection of 0s and 1s. We should not attempt to print this code as ordinary text, since the information contained in such a file would not be printable/readable characters. Often, the object code is called the executable form of our computer program. When we tell our computer to run the program, the object code is loaded into *main* or *primary memory* so that the CPU can access it for processing. When results are produced, they must again be changed into a form that can be read by people and presented on the terminal screen, on the printer, or captured in a file which may be viewed later. Ordinarily, the details of these processes are specific to the computer system being used. The output produced is translated for the user by the specific program commands entered in the source code.

We must keep in mind that the computer is nothing but a box with some wires, switches, and circuits, and as such has not one ounce of intelligence. It will do exactly as we tell it through our source code, nothing more, nothing less. So, when the computer does not behave as we expect, it is not the computer's fault—it is just doing what we told it to do.

But how do we tell it what to do? What is involved in the programming process? How is the source code created? To answer these questions, please consider again the material of Chapter 1 where the problem-solving process was introduced. In order to provide the solution to a particular problem, we must carefully consider the problem-solving steps. Given a problem-solving situation, the programming process consists of the following:

1. Understand what it is you wish to accomplish. Carefully specify the task. Perform the analysis necessary for this understanding.

2. Create an algorithm solving the problem. The design of the algorithm could be done in several ways, all of which might be acceptable. An algorithm is a sequence of specific steps that must be followed to get the computer to produce the solution to the problem.

3. Code the algorithm in C. That is, use an editor to prepare the C source code that implements the algorithm developed in the previous step.

4. Test the source code by compiling it to object code, and submitting the object code to the computer for processing (run the program). This may be an iterative task, since upon studying the output from the program, you may discover it is not what you expected, in which case you must return to step 2, modify the algorithm, make appropriate changes in your C source code, recompile the program, and again run it and study the output to see if design or coding errors were made. You must continue until the desired results are obtained.

▶ Exercises 2.2

2.2.1 What is the purpose of a translator, the program in computing typically called a compiler or interpreter?

2.2.2 What is the name of your editor?

2.2.3 What is the purpose of an editor?

2.2.4 Using the source code editor for your programming environment, how do you:

- delete a line of source code?
- add a line of source code?
- delete a character?
- insert a character?
- move a line of source code from one place in the file to another?
- search for a character or word in the file?

This information should be available to you either from the computer center by way of a handout or from manuals that accompany the system used. For example, there are several manuals that discuss these topics when a system is purchased, such as Borland's Turbo C.™

2.2.5 How do you tell the computing system to save the editing file?

2.2.6 How do you start the editor in your system?

2.2.7 Once you have created the source code for your programming problem, how do you compile this code into object code?

2.2.8 How do you cause the execution of the object code? (How do you run your program?)

2.3 PROGRAMMING FUNDAMENTALS

SECTION TOPICS

Sequence

Selection

Repetition

Those who study the theory of computer science have shown that any well-posed programming problem can be solved in computer code by using three fundamental programming constructs: sequence, selection, and repetition. We studied selection and repetition in a general setting in Section 1.3.

Sequence

We learned in Section 1.4 that the basic problem-solving process consists of four steps: analysis, design, coding, and testing. In the design of the algorithm, any well-posed programming problem can be solved using the three fundamental programming constructs. The first of these is sequence. The word *sequence* means precisely what it implies. Tasks will be executed in sequence, one following another. The instructions could be input instructions, assignment instructions, arithmetic instructions, output instructions, function calls, more input instructions, and so on. Pictorially, sequence is represented as in Figure 2.3.1.

Sequence implies the computer's ability to execute one instruction following another. As indicated in Chapter 1, these statements might be simple arithmetic statements, requests for input, or displays of results.

Figure 2.3.1
Sequence

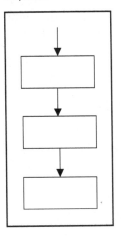

Selection

Selection is the computer's ability to make decisions. Without the ability to make decisions, the computer programs we could generate would be rather uninteresting entities consisting of one instruction following another, with no room for anything creative. Pictorially, selection is represented as in Figure 2.3.2.

Selection gives the computer the ability to make decisions in the form of **if** statements allowing the computer to execute one set of instructions or another set. In each case, one or many tasks or instructions may be performed.

In the design of your source code, we recommend a certain style to

Figure 2.3.2   Selection

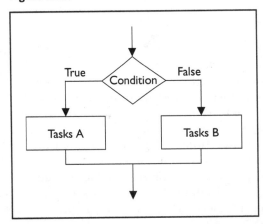

make your programs more readable and to make the process of finding your errors easier. Some consider the process of finding errors—debugging—an art. Some are much better at it than others. But with certain good habits you can make your source code much easier to debug. Specifically, when creating an **if-then-else** sequence as pictured in Figure 2.3.2, we recommend the structure

```
if(condition)
{
    program statements
    program statements
    ...
}
else
{
    more program statements
    more program statements
    ...
}
```

There is no universal agreement concerning the appearance of the code, but the recommendation has certain advantages. Most notably, if the **if**, the opening brace, the closing brace, the **else**, the opening brace, and the closing brace all line up as pictured, then the extent of the **then** block of the **if-then-else** construct can be easily identified, as can the extent of the **else** block. Moreover, one of the problems a beginning programmer has is leaving out a brace to mark the beginning or the ending of a block. If several **if-then-else** blocks are contained in a program, and if there are blocks contained in blocks contained in blocks, which **else** goes with which **if** can become a problem of identification. If the suggested structure is used, these problems can be minimized. If programs are easy to read, they are easier to debug—the primary reason for suggesting this style of program appearance.

As an example of the **if-then-else** construct consider the following program:

```
#include <stdio.h>
main()
{
    int x;
    printf("enter an integer \n");
    scanf("%d",&x);
    /*-------------------------------*/
    /* the decision statement is next */
    /*-------------------------------*/
```

```
if (x > 0)
{
    printf("the number you entered is positive\n");
}
else
{
    printf("the number you entered is negative or zero\n");
}
}
```

This brief example demonstrates the use of the comparison. The value entered, **x**, is an integer and is compared to an integer value, initially 0. If the value stored in **x** is greater than 0, the comparison is true and the statements immediately following the **if** are executed. Otherwise, the **else** portion is executed. Keep in mind that, in general, only like quantities should be compared. That is, float values should be compared to float values, integers to integers, and characters to characters.

Repetition

Repetition (looping or iteration) allows the computer the ability to perform a collection of tasks over and over again, until some specific condition arises that causes the repetition to stop, allowing the computer to continue its execution with other instructions. Each loop contains essentially three parts: data initialization, test for termination, and data modification, which ordinarily takes place within the body of the loop. Also, there are essentially two types of loops: pretest and posttest loops. The type of loop used depends on where the various parts of the loop are placed. A pretest loop may be envisioned pictorially as in Figure 2.3.3.

Figure 2.3.3   Pretest Loop

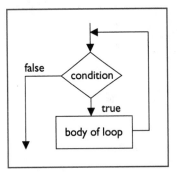

A pretest loop continues to execute *while* a certain condition remains true. Consequently, as control flows into the pretest loop construct, the condition is tested, and the body of the loop is executed if the condition is true. Interestingly enough, if the condition tests false initially, the body of the pretest loop *will never be executed at all!* For the pretest loop, we recommend a structure similar to that recommended above; that is, we recommend that the body of the loop be clearly identifiable.

```
while (condition)
{
    loop statements
    which make up
    the body of the loop
    ...
}
```

By aligning the **while**, the opening brace, and the closing brace, the body of the loop is clear to the reader/programmer and the program code is clearly identified. This means that all statements in the body of the loop are indented. Even if they contain other loop statements, **if-then-else** constructions, or any other program statements, they are still indented appropriately.

The only difference between the pretest loop and the posttest loop is the placement of the test for the termination. Naturally, for a pretest loop the test for termination is at the top of the loop. For a posttest loop the test for termination is at the end of the loop, as shown in Figure 2.3.4.

Figure 2.3.4 Posttest Loop

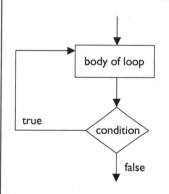

Structurally, we recommend that the code for a posttest loop be presented similar to the following:

```
do
{
    statements which
    make up the
    body of the posttest loop
    ...
} while (condition);
```

This structure is not required by the computer but is recommended to enhance readability and error detection. The C programming environment does not care how the code is submitted. It finds the end of statements by locating the semicolon, and has specific rules for how the code is translated. These suggestions for presenting the code are exactly that — suggestions. But we believe that particularly the beginning programmer will have an easier task if these rules are carefully followed.

Consider the following fundamental examples of pretest and posttest loops. The loops execute similar to one another, but the second loop is ensured of executing once, whereas the first may never execute.

```
#include <stdio.h>
main()
{
    int
        x;
    x = 5;
    /*------------------*/
    /*  pretest loop    */
    /*------------------*/
    while (x > 0)
    {
        printf("x is %d \n",x);
        x = x - 1;
    }
}
```

The output of the above program is

```
5
4
3
2
1
```

The **x** = **5** is the initialization for the index variable **x**. The statement

while(x > 0) is the test for completion and **x = x − 1** is the modification of the index variable that allows the loop to eventually stop.

A similar example follows for posttest loop:

```
#include <stdio.h>
main()
{
    int
        x;
    x = 5;
    /*------------------*/
    /*  posttest loop   */
    /*------------------*/
    do
    {
        printf("x is %d \n",x);
        x = x - 1;
    } while (x > 0);
}
```

The output of the above program is

```
5
4
3
2
1
```

With these rules for program structure in mind, consider the following example of C program source code. Can you determine which tasks are to be performed when?

```
main()
{
    /* variable declarations */
    if (condition1)
    {
        do
        {
            statement
            statement
            if (condition2)
            {
                statement
                statement
                while (condition3)
```

```
                {
                    statement
                    statement
                    statement
                }
            }
            else
            {
                statement
                statement
            }
        } while (condition4)
    else
    {
        statement
        statement
        statement
    }
}
```

One might simply lay a ruler down alongside the program code in order to find out which statements are included in what block. Each of the indents should be uniform, and should be large enough to set off the program statements but not so large that the blocks contained within blocks are pushed off the page to the right. (This might happen anyway, depending upon the complexity of the program decision structure.)

We do not believe it is necessary to comment on every line of program code as some suggest, since the sheer volume of program internal documentation detracts from the program's readability. At the beginning of each block, comment lines should be included to indicate the function of that particular block. User-defined functions should be documented more thoroughly since program enhancement occurs through function modification.

Please study Figure 2.3.5. While it is not necessary for you to structure your C programs this way, a consistent pattern and style of program development will make your programming tasks easier.

The goal of this section is to show you a complete program's structure. Some of the instructions are not used in all programs, and you are not expected to understand all the statements provided. This figure simply gives you the complete picture of a program. You will understand each component thoroughly as you study this course.

In the first area of the program, place all of the #include statements. In this way, if a particular library is needed, you can easily check to see if it was made a part of your particular project. You may also include internal documentation describing exactly which libraries were included and why they were made a part of this particular project. Below those, place

Figure 2.3.5 C Program Structure

```
/* all included files and defines go here */
#include <stdio.h>
#define MaxInt 32767

/* all function prototypes go here */
float FunctionName (int x, float y);

/* all global variables go here */
int ArrayName[50][20];

/* the main function goes here */
main()
{
    /* main's variable declarations go here */
    int
        x,y;
    /* body of main function comes next */
}

/* definitions of user-defined functions go here */
float FunctionName(int x, float y)
{
    /* variable declarations go here */
    float
        p,q;
    /* body of the function comes next */
}
```

all of the **#defines** (if any are needed or desired). Comments may be included anywhere in a C program, as long as they begin with the sequence **/*** and end with the sequence ***/**, and remember the rule that there may be no comments within comments. You have to be careful; at times commenting out sections of code during debugging is useful, and if these sections have comments already in them, the first ***/** seen will finish all comments causing errors to occur if an additional ***/** appears. Note: some programming environments allow comments within comments. Borland's C++ environment is an example of a system that allows nested comments.

The next section of the program should include prototype function calls for all user-defined functions in the program. Placing the prototype in this area of the program or project gives the function appropriate visibility. The general structure for a function prototype is

```
return_type function_name(parameter type list);
```

In Figure 2.3.5, the function prototype indicates that the function is to return a float (real) value, and that it requires two arguments, the first of type `int` (integer) and the second of type **float** (real). The variable names **x** and **y** in the prototype definition are not necessary, but are often included in a prototype as a kind of internal documentation for the user/programmer. Function prototypes are desired by most versions of ANSI C, but not required.

In C, a function call can occur before the function is actually defined, as we have indicated in Figure 2.3.5. By providing a prototype function definition, we inform the compiler of the number and type of specific arguments to be passed to the function. Moreover, the user/programmer is also informed concerning the requirements for a particular function. Good structured programming practices require the declaration of variable names before their use. Prototyping functions is consistent with this philosophy and therefore you should acquire the habit of prototyping your functions, even if they are going to return an `int`, which is the default return type.

Next we include global variable definitions. A variable is *global* if it is known to all of the functions/blocks in the program definition. By placing the global variable declarations in this location, they can easily be modified or recognized by the programmer. Good programmers keep the use of global variables to a minimum. It is not considered good programming practice to use too many global variables.

Next the definition of the main function should be provided. As we have noted, C is case sensitive, which means that the main function must be named precisely that—**main()**. If the main function is to contain any arguments they must be included in the parentheses. Further discussion will be included later. Concentrate for a moment on the structure of a C program. There may be several other blocks, function calls, and arithmetic statements inside the **{ }** for the main function. What and how these are placed in the main function will be the subject of subsequent discussions concerning program structure and design.

Finally, in this program structure, the definitions of all of the user-defined functions are provided. The header for each of the functions should agree exactly with that given in the prototype function definitions.

As an example of the above program structure, the program in Figure 2.3.6 will calculate the area of a circle given the radius.

A sample execution of the program might produce the following output:

```
Please enter the radius of your circle: 4.41
A circle with radius 4.41 has area 61.0980
```

Figure 2.3.6 Area of a Circle

```
/*--------------------------------------------------------------*/
/* Includes and defines go here                                 */
/*--------------------------------------------------------------*/
#include <stdio.h>
#define PI 3.14159265
/*--------------------------------------------------------------*/
/* function prototypes go here                                  */
/*--------------------------------------------------------------*/
float AreaOfACircle(float radius);
/*--------------------------------------------------------------*/
/* no global variables in this example                          */
/*--------------------------------------------------------------*/
/*--------------------------------------------------------------*/
/* the main function comes next                                 */
/*--------------------------------------------------------------*/
main()
{
   float
      area,radius;
   printf("Please enter the radius of your circle: ");
   scanf("%f",&radius);
   area = AreaOfACircle(radius);
   printf("\nA circle with radius %6.2f has area %8.4f\n",radius,area);
}
float AreaOfACircle(float radius)
{
/*--------------------------------------------------------------*/
/* this is a user-defined function which will                   */
/* calculate the area of a circle                               */
/*--------------------------------------------------------------*/
   return (PI*radius*radius);
}
```

The important thing from a programming point of view is not that you understand all of the code, but that you understand what goes where when a C program is entered. Moreover, not all C programmers agree concerning the best way to present a C program. We recommend this structure since it is easy to follow. You may develop your own style as you become more comfortable in the C programming environment.

▶ **Exercises 2.3**

2.3.1 What is the result of the following decision structure (a test of your self-image)?

If I am good looking
  I will attract others
else
  I will be rich

2.3.2 Write the decision structure that will print the larger of a value stored in variable **x** compared to the value stored in variable **y**.

2.3.3 Write the decision structure that will print "this is a large class" if the class is over 20 students or will print "this is a small class" otherwise.

2.3.4 Write the decision structure that will print "the men outnumber the women" if there are more men than women or will print "the women outnumber the men" if there are more women than men, and will print "this is an outstanding class" in either case.

2.4 WRITING YOUR FIRST PROGRAMS

SECTION TOPICS

Program Development

ANSI Flowcharts

Structured Flowcharts

In this section we develop some techniques to help you construct your own computer programs. Several fundamental principles associated with the software engineering discipline should be followed, even in the most elementary programming problems. These techniques should help you construct quality programs from beginning to final execution.

Program Development

Perhaps the most fundamental of all program development techniques is that of modularity. We assume that you are applying the four fundamental problem-solving steps described in Chapter 1. We also assume that you understand the problem fully—the analysis phase of the problem-solving methodology has been completed. We wish to develop some techniques that will help in the design of effective algorithms for solutions to problems.

The first step in the design process is an identification of the major tasks in the problem. What are you required to do? Referring to the analysis phase, identify in English (or some other suitable language) the processes that must be completed in order to effect a solution to the problem. Write these steps down in an ordered list. For example, if we wish to calculate an average, we might write:

1. Enter the data.
2. Calculate the sum.
3. Calculate the average.
4. Present the data to the user.

This list of statements represents a "macro level" flow of control through your problem. This phase of the algorithm design is necessarily very coarse. It merely outlines the major tasks, without providing much detail as to how each of the tasks will be accomplished.

The second phase involves studying the interrelationships of the tasks to be performed. Specifically, what must be done first? What must be done second? Is the completion of task 5, for example, dependent upon the completion of task 11? In other words, you must decide upon a hierarchy of task completion. A chart might be completed, as illustrated in Figure 2.4.1, to identify those tasks that may be completed independently, and on lower levels identify those tasks whose completion is dependent upon the tasks above them in the hierarchy.

The third phase involves refining each of the tasks identified in step 1. Each step in the refinement must bring the statement of the algorithm closer to the language of the computer. Each module or task is studied, using one of the design tools, to provide program structure. Specifically, suppose we were to reconsider the problem of calculating an average. One of the tasks outlined in our macro flow was that of entering the data. A pseudocode refinement of that task might be:

1. Initialize a counter.
2. Enter a number.
3. Increment the counter.
4. Are all numbers entered? If not, return to step 2; if so, proceed to step 5.
5. Display the counter, the number of elements entered.
6. Continue with the remainder of the program.

By providing additional steps for the task, we say we have *refined* the macro flow of the program. This process of *stepwise refinement* should be continued until each of the tasks in the algorithm has been

Figure 2.4.1   Hierarchy Chart

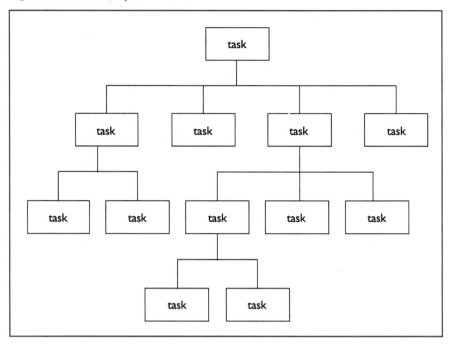

developed in sufficient detail so that coding in a computer language is straightforward. The final step is coding the refined tasks in the chosen computing language.

At some stage in the process of stepwise refinement described above, we may wish to make use of other design techniques. It may be helpful to use structured flowcharts or ANSI flowcharts, rather than the structured English advocated above. Flowcharts allow you to visually see the flow of control through your algorithm. We have used flowcharts earlier in this text with the tacit assumption that they were well known and self explanatory. However, a word of explanation is in order.

ANSI Flowcharts

Since any well-posed programming problem can be solved using three fundamental constructs, we need only describe these three constructs in flowcharting symbols, shown in Figure 2.4.2.

These fundamental symbols describe each of the basic programming constructs, providing a mechanism for describing the algorithm. Figures 2.3.1, 2.3.2, 2.3.3, and 2.3.4 described sequence, if-then-else, and two looping

Figure 2.4.2 ANSI Flowcharting Symbols

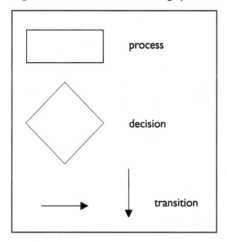

constructs using only the three symbols. At some stage in the design process, you may wish to describe your algorithm using the symbols.

Structured Flowcharts

Some professionals advocate the use of structured flowcharts for compact algorithm description. Using structured flowcharts, the three fundamental constructs are represented as shown in Figure 2.4.3. To illustrate the use of each of these design tools, consider the problem of finding the average of a sequence of numbers. In our earlier discussion, we have written much of the structured English (pseudocode) for the problem. We would like to present a structured flowchart in Figure 2.4.4 and an ANSI flowchart in Figure 2.4.5 for this problem.

Figure 2.4.3 Structured Flowcharting Symbols

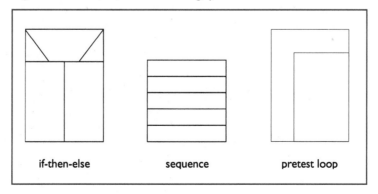

Figure 2.4.4   Structured Flowchart
for Computing the Average

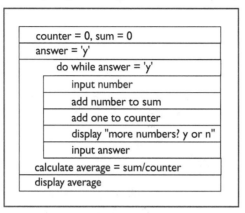

Using a structured flowchart, it is easy to see the extent of the loop as well as a decision structure. It is also clear that the sequence of program steps must flow in the top of the structure and flow out the bottom. Our sequence of execution is always from top to bottom. If the algorithm design uses structured flowcharts, we know acceptable programming constructs are being used.

Both structured and ANSI flowcharts help develop an algorithm since they provide a visual representation of the process interrelationships in the design. We do not advocate one over the other. We simply present them as design tools that may be used to assist the algorithm development process.

Whether we choose structured English (pseudocode), structured flowcharts, or ANSI flowcharts, the algorithm development process remains the same. We continue to refine the algorithm design until it can be easily converted to computer code.

CODE   Assuming our design of the average program is correct, it should be a simple matter to convert the design into program code. Thus, realizing that many of the specific commands will be covered in detail in later chapters, we present the computer code for the average problem.

```c
#include <stdio.h>

main()
{
    float
        sum,average,number,counter;
    int
        answer;
    sum = 0;
```

```
            counter = 0;
            answer = 0;
            while (answer == 0)
            {
                printf("Please enter number ");
                scanf("%f",&number);
                sum = sum + number;
                counter = counter + 1;
                printf("Would you like to stop entering numbers?
                        (1=yes,0=no) ");
                scanf("%d",&answer);
            }
            average=sum/counter;
            printf("The average of the %f numbers you entered is
                    %f\n",counter,average);
        }
```

TEST A sample execution of the program might produce the following output:

```
Please enter number 123
Would you like to stop entering numbers? (1=yes,0=no) 0
Please enter number 234
Would you like to stop entering numbers? (1=yes,0=no) 0
Please enter number 345
Would you like to stop entering numbers? (1=yes,0=no) 0
Please enter number 456
Would you like to stop entering numbers? (1=yes,0=no) 1
The average of the 4.000000 numbers you entered is
        289.500000
```

Once again, we emphasize the importance of the problem-solving paradigm illustrated in these examples. Considering the four phases—analysis, design, coding, and testing the final solution—the most important phases of the problem-solving process are analysis and design. It is impossible to design an elegant, efficient solution to a problem if one does not understand what is to be accomplished. Thus, when allotting time to the problem-solving process, make sure that enough time is allocated for the analysis phase. Too many times, when receiving a programming assignment, the student will proceed directly to the computer terminal and begin typing computer code, without careful consideration of the problem and its requirements. The student should instead begin with a sheet of paper and pencil, and carefully study the problem from every possible point of view to make sure all aspects of the problem have been considered.

When designing the solution, initially make general statements that represent the various steps that the program must accomplish. These

Figure 2.4.5   ANSI Flowchart for Computing
the Average

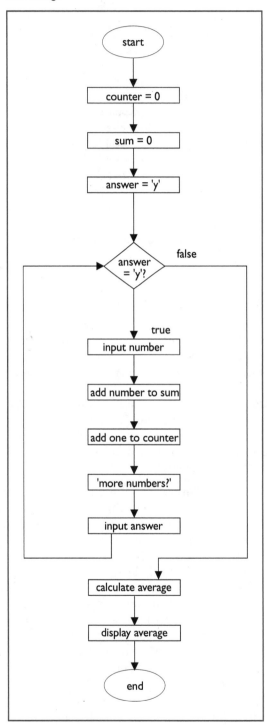

should be independent of one another, so that each can be refined and detailed as subsequent passes through the refinement process are accomplished. The design phase of the problem-solving process is virtually as important as the analysis phase. If the solution is designed correctly, the actual conversion of the design to program code is a relatively simple matter. For many programming applications the language used to implement the design is not of consequence. We agree that some programming languages are more suited to specific applications than others, but for general-purpose programming applications, the language is relatively unimportant. Good program design might be implemented in C, in Pascal, or in BASIC if the programmer wishes.

▶ **PROBLEM**   As a second example of the program development process, suppose you are working for a computing firm that is going to attempt to write the best desktop-publishing package in the entire world. The company has assigned you, their top programmer, to help create the best spell checker and best thesaurus possible for their package. Your task is to write a program that will report the number of vowels in a body of text. Since you are highly paid you cannot refuse this assignment. How can you solve this problem, developing a solution that will allow the computer to report the desired results?

ANALYSIS   The analysis phase of the problem-solving methodology attempts to make sure we understand the problem, and that we know what is required of us before we begin designing our solution. In this case, we know that we are going to be given a body of text. We must report the number of occurrences of a, e, i, o, and u. The program should produce output of the form

```
There are __ a's in the text.
There are __ e's in the text.
There are __ i's in the text.
There are __ o's in the text.
There are __ u's in the text.
```

DESIGN   The design phase of the problem-solving methodology begins with the realization that the computer is capable of reading in data, writing results, doing arithmetic, making decisions, storing intermediate results, and repeating tasks. We will ultimately formulate our solution in terms of these tools. Before we do, however, we will begin our stepwise refinement with essentially the same three steps as in the last example.

```
1. read text
2. count vowels
3. print results
```

When forming solutions to problems it helps to consider what has to be read into the program. In this case we will be reading a series of alphabetic characters. The important characters are the vowels, a, e, i, o, and u. We must increment a counter each time a vowel is encountered. It also helps to consider what the program must produce:

```
1. we must read a body of text character by character
   until there are no more characters to read.
2. we must decide if the character read is one of the
   important characters.
3. if the character is one of the important characters,
   then count it.
4. when all the data is read and counted, the program is
   to report its results.
```

The above list is the first pass at trying to solve the problem. It outlines the tasks required in solving the problem with an eye to writing each task in the manner the computer can understand. We list the possible next step in the refinement of the solution to the problem:

```
1. while there is more data to be read
2. read in the next data item
3. decide if the data item is an a,e,i,o,u
4. count the appropriate a,e,i,o,u (remember we want the
   number of each letter)
5. report the results
```

As our final refinement, consider the following structured English pseudocode. This code is similar to program code, and it illustrates the steps necessary to implement the solution in C:

```
read in the first character
while there is more data to be read
      decide if the data item is an a, if it is count it
      decide if the data item is an e, if it is count it
      decide if the data item is an i, if it is count it
      decide if the data item is an o, if it is count it
      decide if the data item is a u, if it is count it
      read in the next character
end while
when no more data, report the count of each character
```

Notice that an initial read has been added before the start of the loop and that the read inside the loop has been moved to the bottom of the loop. The initial read "seeds" the while loop so that the question asked in the condition makes sense. To set the end-of-file signal, the read needs to be last. If it were at the top of the loop, it would try to read the last time realizing there was no more data, but finish executing the body of the loop before the test for completion was made. Thus, an additional execution of the loop body would occur after the data was exhausted. The last character would be counted twice if it were a vowel. A careful design will help identify these "boundary" conditions allowing you to construct an accurate program.

CODE   For the actual implementation, we must have storage for the counters and each character read in. The program in Figure 2.4.6 will implement the pseudocode.

Figure 2.4.6   Vowel-Counting Program

```c
#include <stdio.h>

main()
{
    int
        counta,counte,counti,counto,countu,i,eof;
    char
        text;

    counta=0;
    counte=0;
    counti=0;
    counto=0;
    countu=0;

    eof = scanf("%c",&text);
    while(eof == 1)
    {
        if (text == 'a') counta = counta + 1;
        if (text == 'e') counte = counte + 1;
        if (text == 'i') counti = counti + 1;
        if (text == 'o') counto = counto + 1;
        if (text == 'u') countu = countu + 1;
        eof = scanf("%c",&text);
    }
    printf("the number of a's are: %d\n",counta);
    printf("the number of e's are: %d\n",counte);
    printf("the number of i's are: %d\n",counti);
    printf("the number of o's are: %d\n",counto);
    printf("the number of u's are: %d\n",countu);
}
```

TEST   If we executed the program and entered the text

```
Now is the time
for all good
persons to come
to the aid of
your party
```

from the keyboard, the results would appear similar to the following:

```
the number of a's are: 3
the number of e's are: 5
the number of i's are: 3
the number of o's are: 10
the number of u's are: 1
```

▶ Exercises 2.4

2.4.1   Perform a stepwise refinement for the problem of calculating the area and perimeter of a rectangle.

2.4.2   Design the solution to the problem of counting the number of words in a body of text. Use pseudocode and stepwise refinement. What are the tasks that must be performed?

2.4.3   Draw a structured flowchart for the problem of determining whether a positive integer is prime. A positive integer is prime if it is divisible only by itself and one.

2.4.4   Draw an ANSI flowchart for the problem of determining whether a positive integer is prime. Compare your flowchart with that obtained in Exercise 2.4.3.

2.4.5   For a given positive integer n, the value of $n!$ (n-factorial) is the product of n with the positive integers less than n. For example, $5! = 5*4*3*2*1$. Draw a structured flowchart that will calculate the value of $n!$ for $n \leq 7$.

2.4.6   The greatest common divisor (GCD) of two positive integers can be found by successively subtracting as follows:

```
larger sub smaller = diff
if diff > smaller then diff - smaller = newdiff
else smaller - diff = newdiff
```

Repeat using newdiff and diff or smaller, whichever is less, until newdiff is 0. The last nonzero difference is the GCD. Create and compare both an ANSI and a structured flowchart for this GCD solution.

2.4.7 Use structured English (pseudocode) and successive refinement to design a solution to the GCD problem of Exercise 2.4.6. Compare the design created using pseudocode with the design created using flowcharts. Which do you prefer?

2.4.8 Division may be performed by continually subtracting the divisor from the dividend and replacing the dividend with the difference, until the dividend becomes smaller than the divisor. The number of subtractions performed is the quotient, and the difference, which is smaller than the divisor, is the remainder. Draw an ANSI flowchart which contains a pretest loop for the design of the solution of this division problem. (Why did we specify a pretest loop for this problem?)

2.4.9 Draw a structured flowchart for the division problem of Exercise 2.4.8.

2.4.10 Using a structured flowchart, design a solution to the problem of removing a wheel from a standard (5-bolt) American automobile.

▶ Key Words

compiler (tcc, gcc, cc, . . .)	repetition (do, while, for)
documentation (hierarchy chart, comments, user manual)	selection (if)
	sequence
editor (tc, vi, . . .)	source code (filename.c)
object code (filename.obj)	structured English (pseudocode)
problem solving	structured flowchart
program execution (a.out, filename.exe, filename)	

▶ Chapter Concepts

2.1 The philosophy of the C language. C provides you with very little as high-level languages go, but C allows a great deal of extension. By adding features desired specifically for your application, C becomes a rich and powerful language. The benefit of this philosophy is that system-dependent features such as input/output can be developed for a specific system. Suppose, for example, that a program is developed on a PC. That program can be copied to a Mac, recompiled and executed, probably without modification. The support routines local to the current system, i/o for example, will be included as necessary. Thus C is considered a "portable language."

2.2 The concept of complete programs and program execution leading to compiling and editing are in this chapter. The editor provides the ability to enter programs while the compiler translates the program into a form suitable for execution by the computer. The editor can be found under a variety of names. Typically the UNIX system uses vi, the DOS system might use vi or an integrated environment where the editor, compiler, and execution are all done within one system. Borland's Turbo C environment is an example; it is started by entering the command tc after moving to the directory where the system resides. Other systems, such as the Macintosh, have their own startup procedure. Check with your instructor or manual to find the proper sequence for editing and program execution.

2.3   Basic program execution control discussion includes sequence, selection, and iteration. How these are implemented in C is demonstrated. The basic program structure required by C is discussed. Instructions are executed in sequence unless an **if, do, while,** or **for** instruction alters the execution flow.

2.4   Problem-solving considerations should be carefully considered. First you must understand the problem. Unless you have a very thorough understanding of precisely what is to be done, including the nature of the input data and the desired output, you will have a difficult time coding a problem solution for computer execution. You must understand the problem at the level required by the computer, that is, in terms of the five basic capabilities of the computer. Once you have expressed the solution in only the basic capabilities, you can begin coding in C, compile the program, and remove syntax errors identified by the compiler. Once you have a clean compile, execute the program and study the results to determine if the program presents the desired solution.

2.5   Program analysis, design, code, and test sequence is reinforced by multiple examples that you should follow as a model for your solutions.

► Programming Projects

2.1   Following the example given in Figure 2.4.6, analyze, design, code, and test a program that reads in three integer numbers representing the length, width, and depth of a box. Write a program that computes the volume of the box. Your program should report:

```
length = xx, width = xx, and depth = xx
The corresponding volume is xx
```

2.2   Using the software engineering process of analyze, design, code, and test, write a program to compute the circumference of a circle. Recall that the circumference is found by C = 2πr. You should enter π as a constant and read in the radius of the circle. The input to the program will be a floating-point number like 4.69. The output should appear as:

```
radius = xxx.x
The circumference is xxx.x
```

Formatting the floating-point number requires the use of %5.1f where the 5 is the print field width, f is for floating-point number, and 1 is one digit to the right of the decimal point. A format of 5.1 actually will print in 5 print positions or more depending on the number of significant digits.

2.3   Assume you are the accountant for a small business, a business that has five employees. You are to read in a time in hours worked for each employee and compute the wages for that person. You need not be concerned with taxes or other withholding, just compute wages per hour. Your program should read an integer number of hours and report a wage. All your employees earn $12.35 an hour. Your output should appear similar to:

```
Employee number 1 worked 35 hours and earns 432.25 dollars.
Employee number 2 worked 20 hours and earns 247.00 dollars.
Employee number 3 worked 44 hours and earns 543.40 dollars.
Employee number 4 worked 40 hours and earns 494.00 dollars.
Employee number 5 worked 10 hours and earns 123.50 dollars.
```

Use good programming principles of analyze, design, code, and test.

2.4   Extend problem 2.3 to allow any employee to earn time and a half for any hours worked over 40. For example, an employee who worked 44 hours would earn $12.35 for the first 40 hours and $18.525 for the remaining 4 hours. The output should appear as:

```
Employee xx worked 44 hours earning 543.40@12.35 and
74.10@18.525 totaling 617.50
```

2.5   Assume you are working for an engineering firm that is monitoring a sensor which reports temperatures of an integrated circuit. Your task is to write a program that reads in all the floating-point temperatures and reports the highest temperature and which one it was. For example, if the following data were given:

```
32.4 56.5 22.89 17.56 21.35
```

Your program should report:

```
Temperature number 2 was greatest at 56.5 degrees.
```

Again, be sure to

1.   understand the problem
2.   analyze the problem to develop a solution
3.   design the solution using only the five capabilities of a computer
4.   code the designed solution in C
5.   repeatedly compile the C program until the translator reports no syntax errors
6.   execute the program and determine if the results are appropriate

2.6   You are working for the same engineering firm that is again monitoring sensors. The president now wishes to know the average of all the temperatures reported by the sensors.

2.7   Write a program to calculate the sum 1+2+3+4+5+ ... +n where **n** is given as the first entry. That is, if the data is

6

it implies that 1+2+3+4+5+6 should be found. This arithmetic series is used in a variety of mathematical and engineering applications. Using appropriate design and analysis techniques you realize the sum can be found by

$$\Sigma \ = \ \frac{n(n \ + \ 1)}{2}$$

Your program should be able to calculate the sum for any reasonable *n* given.

CHAPTER 3

Storage Request Instructions

CHAPTER TOPICS

Data Types

Variables, Assignment, and Arithmetic

Input and Output Instructions

Arrays and Structures

INTRODUCTION

After reading this chapter, the student will

- be familiar with the concept of data types
- know the basic data types supported by C
- be able to discuss the concept of variables, and arithmetic instructions
- understand and be able to demonstrate the need for the C addressing operator and the C dereferencing operator
- be comfortable with arrays and subscripted variables
- understand what is meant by the scope of storage allocation requests
- understand user-defined data types

In Chapter 2 we looked at the computer execution of complete programs and at several models of this concept in the C programming language. In this chapter we will develop several important concepts associated with the programming process and provide some of the tools necessary for program implementation.

3.1 DATA TYPES

This section introduces the basic data types: integer, character, and float. We recall from the discussion in Chapter 1 that the computer's memory is composed of binary digits, making bytes and finally words. There are

8 bits to a byte and 4 bytes to a word. The byte is typically the smallest addressable unit of memory. Normally fullwords (32 binary digits) are used as the fundamental size to store information internally in the computer. This is the size expected by the central processing unit (CPU) as it performs its calculations. Moreover, as the CPU communicates with its peripheral devices and with main memory, it sends 32 bits at a time. (This is not true on some of the earlier personal computers). While this is overly simplified, let us say that many of the personal computers in use today (as well as many of the larger computers) use a 32-bit word and a 32-bit data path. Some older versions of the personal computer used an 8-bit data path. Let us emphasize, however, *that the amount of storage allotted to each of the fundamental data types is implementation-dependent.* This means that on one type of computer with a specific C compiler the amount of storage allocated for an **int** may be different than that available on another personal computer with a different C compiler. We shall adhere to the ANSI standard for the size of each fundamental data type. Let us now consider each of the basic data types in turn.

The Data Type int

A typical C program that would use an integer is shown in the following example.

```
main()
{
    int
        x;      /* x is the variable which will hold an integer */
        x = 5;  /* place the integer 5 in storage location x */
        printf("In my version of C, the size of an integer is
            %d\n",sizeof(x));
}
```

The actions caused by the program are shown in Figure 3.1.1. This figure shows the storage represented by **x.** Memory location **x** is 16 bits (2 bytes), which is the size of an ordinary **int** storage location in some implementations of C (**int**s are 4 bytes in many UNIX implementations). The value contained in that storage location is the binary integer repre-

Figure 3.1.1 Storage Contents

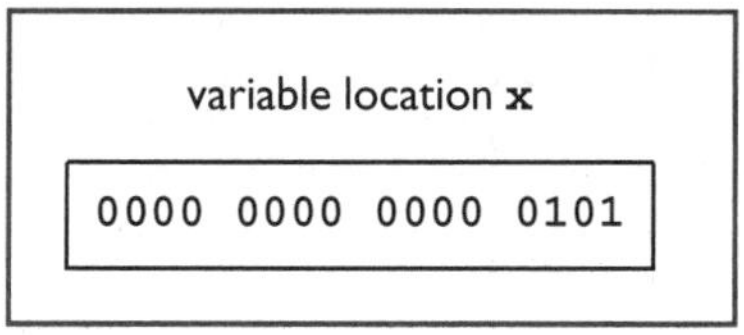

variable location **x**

0000 0000 0000 0101

sentation of 5 (with spaces added for readability). The largest positive integer that can be stored using 16 bits is 32767, since the leading bit is reserved for the sign. This is not very large, so the programmer must be concerned about overflow. Yes, it is possible to add two sufficiently large positive integers, so that the result of the addition carries over to the sign bit, which makes the sum of two positive integers possibly negative, and certainly an incorrect result will be realized!

Analyzing the program, the instruction

```
int x;
```

asks the computer to set aside storage capable of holding an integer. Note that *the amount of storage set aside depends on the C installation. Different versions of C may use different storage sizes for the variable data types illustrated here.* The **sizeof** function present in all versions of C will determine the amount of storage actually used by the various data types. The next instruction,

```
x = 5;
```

places a 5 in that storage location. The reader should be aware that the assignment operation is destructive. Whatever was contained in storage location **x** is destroyed when **x = 5;** is executed, and the content stored at that location is replaced with 5.

Consider the problem of storing a negative integer in memory. From earlier discussions we know that integers are stored in a two's complemented binary representation. If we request storage for a negative integer as in the program

```
main()
{
    int
        neg_x;
    neg_x = -5;
}
```

then what is stored in memory at memory location **neg_x** is the two's complement of the binary representation of the number 5 *in two bytes of storage.* See Figure 3.1.2.

Figure 3.1.2 Storage Contents — Negative Five

variable location **x**

| 1111 1111 1111 1011 |

The preceding discussion concerns itself with the actual contents of memory. We turn our attention now to the problem of actually writing computer code to store quantities in memory, and provide the reader with a gentle discussion of arrays.

What would you do if you wanted to store four distinct integers? For example, suppose we wanted to place 3, 66, 121, and 45 in the computer's memory. These numbers might be required to solve some later problem. Figure 3.1.3 suggests a solution.

Each number represented by **x, xx, y,** or **z** is placed in 2 bytes of storage in binary, just as 5 was in the preceding example. Thus, when necessary for processing, several numbers can be placed in the computer's storage at a time. Typical personal computers now have from one million to eight million or more bytes of storage, with larger computers having several million bytes of storage. Thus, there is room for thousands of integers to be stored. However, memory is not used solely for the purpose of storing integers. There must be room for storing the program that is to be executed and room for the operating system that controls the computer's operation. The operating system is responsible for determining which program to execute next and allocating resources to that program so that it can execute correctly. Entire classes are devoted to the design and analysis of operating system construction. Even with the operating system, a million bytes of storage can contain more than enough integers for most problems.

There are better ways of constructing the program than that given by Figure 3.1.3. Figure 3.1.4 suggests an alternative.

Figure 3.1.3   Program to Store Four Integers

```
main()
{
    int x;      /* request storage for x               */
    int xx;     /* request storage for xx, which is
                   different than x                     */
    int y;      /* request storage for y               */
    int z;      /* request storage for z               */

    x  = 3;     /* store the 3    */
    xx = 66;    /* store the 66   */
    y  = 121;   /* store the 121  */
    z  = 45;    /* store the 45   */
}
```

contents	3	66	121	45
variable name (address)	x	xx	y	z

Figure 3.1.4 Program to Store Four Integers

```
main()
{
    int
        x[4];          /* request storage for four x's   */
    x[0] = 3;          /* store the 3                    */
    x[1] = 66;         /* store the 66                   */
    x[2] = 121;        /* store the 121                  */
    x[3] = 45;         /* store the 45                   */

}
```

Figure 3.1.5 shows the representation for the four integers stored in the program illustrated in Figure 3.1.4.

Notice that each indexed variable represents a unique storage location just as z and x represented different storage locations in the example shown in Figure 3.1.3. You might ask, why bother with the subscripting? There are several reasons for using this, as you will see when you begin to write more complicated programs. One simple reason is that it saves trying to create several unique names for storage locations. Of course, when **x[1]** is used, it is different from **x[2]**, which is different from **x[3]**, which is different from **x[0]**.

```
#include <stdio.h>


main()
{
    int
        x[50];

    printf ("the number of bytes allocated is %d\n",
            sizeof(x));
}
```

Figure 3.1.5 Array Variable in Memory

Contents	3	66	121	45
Address (variable name)	x[0]	x[1]	x[2]	x[3]

This program responds

`the number of bytes allocated is 100`

which shows that fifty distinct two-byte integers have been allocated in memory. Figure 3.1.6 shows another reason for using indexed names.

The storage created by the program in Figure 3.1.6 is exactly the same as the storage of Figure 3.1.4. What is actually gained by using the array variable is illustrated in Figure 3.1.7. The ability to loop and refer-

Figure 3.1.6 Program to Store Four Integers

```
main()
{
   int
      x[4];              /* request storage for four x's          */
   int
      cntr;             /* create a counter, which is an integer */
   cntr = 0;            /* start the cntr at 0                    */
   x[cntr] = 3;         /* store 3 in the 0th position            */
   cntr = cntr + 1;     /* makes cntr 1                           */
   x[cntr] = 66;        /* store 66 in the 1st position           */
   cntr = cntr + 1;     /* makes cntr 2                           */
   x[cntr] = 121;       /* store 121 in the 2nd position          */
   cntr = cntr + 1;     /* makes cntr 3                           */
   x[cntr] = 45;        /* store 45 in the 3rd position           */
}
```

Figure 3.1.7 Program to Store Four Integers

```
main()
{
   int
      x[4],cntr;
   cntr = 0;                        /* start the cntr off at 0      */
   while (cntr < 4)                 /* the looping structure        */
   {
      scanf("%d",&x[cntr]);         /* get a value from the input stream  */
      cntr = cntr + 1;              /* increase the counter by 1    */
   }
}
```

ence successive members of our array variable is the main advantage of using indexed variables.

Figure 3.1.7 assumes the four numbers are given as data for the input function **scanf**. The numbers are read in one at a time and stored in the successive locations as indicated by the indexed variable **x** with index **cntr**. You should refer to the brief introduction to loops in Chapter 2 in order to understand this example. The program continues to loop as long as the value of the counter is less than 4. When the value of the counter becomes greater than or equal to 4, the loop terminates and continues processing with the statement immediately following the loop's last statement (there is none in this example).

The examples in Figures 3.1.3 through 3.1.7 develop a program from the first simplistic solution to the typical, more sophisticated method of storing the four numbers. Figure 3.1.7 is almost a different program though, since the numbers are assumed to be "read" into the program rather than "hard coded" into the program as was done in the previous examples. All of the figures demonstrate the usefulness of using indexed variables and that each indexed variable represents storage as any non-indexed variable might. Also, the last example would require little modification to store 40 integers instead of 4, another advantage of using subscripted variables.

The Data Type char

A character is any letter or symbol: a, b, $, *, and ! are examples of characters. The table in Appendix B shows the American Standard Code for Information Interchange (ASCII) character set. Notice from this table that each character is associated with a numeric code. For example, an 'a' has a decimal value of 97, which is 01100001 in base 2. An 'a' can be represented in the computer in one byte. We may think "one character, one byte."

Figure 3.1.8 demonstrates the method a programmer could use to store the character **a** in a variable location. Notice the need for the quotes. If the instruction were written as **x = a**; the compiler would interpret **a** as

Figure 3.1.8 Example of Character Storage

```
main()
{
   char
        x;       /* char is the C way of asking for character storage   */
      x = 'a';   /* makes x represent storage containing 01100001        */
}
```

Figure 3.1.9 A Character in Memory

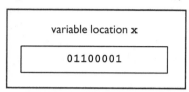

a variable name and attempt to assign the value stored in memory represented by **a** to the location in the computer's memory represented by **x**. Most compilers would indicate an error since most likely the variable **a** would be undeclared. Figure 3.1.9 depicts the storage represented by the storage request **char x;** and the assignment statement **x = 'a';** of Figure 3.1.8.

In C, a character string is an array of characters. To request storage for a string, we must indicate to the C compiler that an array of characters is required. Consider the example in Figure 3.1.10. This example will print

The last name of the authors of this text is Eggen

when executed. (Usage note: the UNIX C compiler cc will not automatically initialize the array **x[20]** in the example, whereas the UNIX C compiler gcc will!)

The example in Figure 3.1.10 sets aside an array of characters of size 20 and stores the string "Eggen" in the first five character positions of the array. Moreover, C also stores an end-of-string marker **'\0'** at the end of the string. We may think of strings as being of variable length, up to the maximum declared size of the array, with a marker at the end of each string. Let us emphasize that a character is enclosed in *single quotes,* such as the character **'a'** or the end-of-string character **'\0'**. A string, on the other hand, is enclosed in *double quotes,* such as the string "Eggen" or the string "I love you!"

Many situations require string manipulation functions. In fact, most modern programming languages provide an entire collection of string

Figure 3.1.10 Example of String Storage

```
main()
{
    char
        x[20] = "Eggen";
    printf("The last name of the authors of this text is %s\n",x);
}
```

handling functions, and C is no exception. To gain access to the C library that contains the string handling functions, include the line

```
#include <string.h>
```

in your program. This will give you access to all of the functions commonly associated with strings and string handling. These functions will be discussed in detail in Section 3.4.

We have seen in this section how characters are represented and stored in the computer. You can (with the assistance of the string library) begin to write programs that will perform character and string manipulation.

The Data Type float

Numbers that can have a fractional portion are real numbers. The representation for a real number is discussed in this section. The data type float requests storage for a real number. Consider the example in Figure 3.1.11.

We recall from earlier discussions that the representation of integers is two's complemented binary. The representation for floating-point quantities is fundamentally different. This representation scheme is not a complement scheme, but rather a sign-and-magnitude representation on most computers. (We point out that the representation scheme presented here is not universal, but is representative of the methods used by many programming languages). Most use 32 bits for a floating-point quantity, with a portion of the 32 bits used to represent the exponent and a portion used to represent the fraction. The model used is ordinary scientific notation. If we write 0.6023×10^{24}, then we must be able to represent the fraction 0.6023 as well as the exponent 24. Most all use the form indicated by Figure 3.1.12.

The exponent resides in the first byte of the word and the fraction in the remaining 3 bytes. The exponent portion contains the sign of the number, the sign of the exponent, and the value of the exponent. The fraction contains the value of the fractional portion of the number. For example, a representation of 3.24 is 0.324×10^1. The fraction 0.324, called the mantissa, is .0101001 in binary. The conversion is not exact (just as 1/3 in decimal cannot be represented exactly in a finite number of decimal digits), which accounts for some errors encountered when using floating-point

Figure 3.1.11   Example Storing a Floating-Point Number

```
main()
{
    float
        x;
    x = 3.24;
}
```

Figure 3.1.12 Representation of Float Quantities

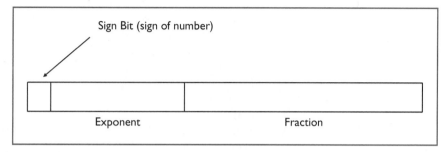

arithmetic. The value 1 in base 10 for the exponent is 1 in base 2. So we have a 0101001 mantissa and a 1 exponent that might be stored as

0000 0001 0101 0010 0000 0000 0000 0000

The spaces are included for readability. The first 8 bits (1 byte) represent the exponent, the remaining 24 bits represent the actual value of the fraction. Again, the variable **x** represents one full word of storage. The leftmost 0 represents a positive number, so if we wished to represent −3.24, we would simply indicate so by

1000 0001 0101 0010 0000 0000 0000 0000

The only difference between the two representations is the leading bit. The remainder of the representation of the floating-point quantity is identical. If the exponent were negative, we could represent it in two's complement form as was discussed in Chapter 1. As an example, consider Figure 3.1.13, which would be represented in the computer as

1111 1101 0101 0010 0000 0000 0000 0000

Since −0.000324 is $−0.324 \times 10^{-3}$ the mantissa remains the same, 1 in the leftmost bit for the negative number. We have already learned that 3 base 10 is 0000011 in base 2. We can use only 7 bits since the leftmost is taken up for the sign of the number being represented (not just the frac-

Figure 3.1.13 Example Storing a Negative Floating-Point Number

```
main()
{
    float
        x;
    x = -.000324;
}
```

tion). If we represent the negative exponent in two's complement form, it becomes 1111101, which is what was placed in the rightmost 7 bits of the leftmost byte. As was stated earlier, not all computer manufacturers use this method, but most use a system similar to what has been described. Some other representation schemes use an "excess 40 (hexadecimal)" method of representing the exponent of a floating-point quantity.

The importance of knowing the internal representations of quantities cannot be overstated. Knowing that certain fractions (like 1/3 in decimal) cannot be represented exactly in binary, and knowing that there are only 24 bits to represent the fractional portion of a number, leads to the conclusion that there will certainly be round-off errors when floating-point arithmetic is performed.

The Data Type double

What kinds of problems can occur from the representation shown in Figure 3.1.13? The most obvious one is that only 24 bits are available to represent the fractional portion of the number. The principle method of attempting to overcome this limitation is to provide more digits for the fraction. The data type double is provided by the C programming language and, while the amount of storage differs from installation to installation, it gives as many as 10 bytes of storage for a floating-point quantity. You can use the **sizeof** function on your system to find out how much storage is allocated for a double-precision floating-point quantity. Consider Figure 3.1.14.

The example in Figure 3.1.14 looks like Figure 3.1.13 except for **double** replacing **float**. **Double** also asks for floating-point storage, but requests more space than the data type **float**.

The program in Figure 3.1.15 examines the basic data types and indicates the amount of storage allocated for each type. The output from this program would appear as follows using Think C on the Macintosh:

```
int 2
char 1
float 4
double 10
```

Figure 3.1.14   Example Storing a Negative Double Floating-Point Number

```
main()
{
    double
        x;

    x = -.000324;
}
```

Figure 3.1.15 Storage Allocated by the Basic Data Types

```
#include <stdio.h>

main()
{
    /*     integer data type      */
    int
        a;
    /*     character data type      */

    char
        g;

    /*     real (floating point) data types      */

    float
        x;
    double
        y;

    printf ("int %d\n",sizeof (a));
    printf ("char %d\n",sizeof (g));
    printf ("float %d\n",sizeof (x));
    printf ("double %d\n",sizeof (y));
}
```

whereas, using the UNIX compiler gcc, the output would look like the following:

```
int 4
char 1
float 4
double 8
```

▶ Exercises 3.1

3.1.1 Tell the exact contents of the variable locations in binary upon execution of the following code segment:

```
int x,y;
x = 23;
y = -46;
```

3.1.2   Assume that the data type is **float** rather than **int** in problem 3.1.1. Determine the exact contents of memory in binary upon execution of the code segment.

3.1.3   Write a program similar to that illustrated in Figure 3.1.15 to determine the amount of storage allocation for the basic data types on your system.

3.1.4   Tell the exact contents of memory in binary upon execution of the following code segment:

```
char n[5] = "what";
```

Make sure you describe all variable locations effected by the instruction.

3.1.5   Tell the exact contents of memory in binary upon execution of the following code segment:

```
int numbers[5] = {45,33,11,6,18};
```

Make sure you describe all variable locations effected by the instruction.

3.2   VARIABLES, ASSIGNMENT, AND ARITHMETIC

SECTION TOPICS

Assignment

Addressing and Dereferencing Operators

We learned in Chapter 1 that a variable is merely a symbolic reference to a location in memory. A reference such as

```
x = 5;
```

places 5 in the memory location symbolically addressed by **x**. We also learned what makes an effective and useful variable name, and what variable names should be avoided. In effect, we should remember that we want to use variables and variable names that make our programs easy to read and follow. Even if these variable names are a bit harder to enter from the keyboard, they may save us hours of debugging and update time if we ever have to go back and figure out what a particular program does. We should therefore attempt to write "self documenting code" as much as possible—code that is easy to understand and follow because of the choices we make in naming variables. That is not to say that we won't enter volumes of internal documentation in our programs as well—we will do both in order to write code that is easy to read. In fact, it has been suggested by several authors that one should (in some situations) sacrifice just a bit of efficiency for readability. The only time this wouldn't be acceptable is if the program were "CPU bound," which means that it spends all of its time in the central processing unit, without additional input from the user.

Assignment

The first major concept we approach is assignment. Assignment is that operation which stores some value in a memory location. The value could be an integer, a character or string of characters, or a floating-point value (real number). The assignment statement takes the form

```
variable = expression;
```

When the assignment statement is executed, the expression is evaluated, and its value placed in the memory location referred to by the variable name. In any programming language there are rules governing the formation of the expression, as well as rules governing the actual assignment operation. Moreover, the actual symbol for the assignment operation varies from language to language. In C and Basic, for example, the assignment operator is the equal sign (=). In Pascal, assignment is colon-equal (:=). In other languages, the assignment operator might be <– or something similar. What represents the assignment operation is not important from a philosophical point of view—that there *is* an assignment operation is the important thing. From a practical programmatic standpoint, however, the symbol for assignment is important, since we don't want the persons who read our computer code to be confused by what is meant by a certain expression. Specifically, when we write

```
a = b;
```

do we want to assign the value of **b** to the variable **a,** or do we want to ask the question, "is **a** the same as **b**?" The difference between the assignment operation and the relational operation "is equal to" must be clearly understood. Each programming language must address this conceptual question. In C, we use = for assignment and == for relational comparison. In Pascal, := is the assignment operator and = is the comparison operator. In Basic, however, the programmer is expected to determine from the context of the expression whether = represents assignment or comparison, which may result in some confusion.

In Chapter 1 we learned about the various ways information can be represented internally in the computer's memory. In order for the assignment operation to store the correct representation of the quantity in memory, it must know what is to be represented. Ordinarily, every variable, memory location, construct, or data type must be declared so that the computing environment is able to set aside the correct amount of computer memory, correctly represent the quantities, and make the appropriate conversions.

Consider the following declarations and assignments:

```
int
    hours;
float
    payrate, GrossSalary;

hours = 40;
payrate = 4.25;
GrossSalary = hours*payrate;
```

The value assigned to a variable should agree with the type of variable—integers assigned to **int**s, floating-point quantities assigned to **float**, etc. However, modern programming languages will perform certain type conversions. Studying the code above, we see that **hours** is an integer variable, **payrate** is a real (floating-point) variable, and that **GrossSalary**, a floating-point variable, is the product of these two. Thus, some type conversion must take place for the computation to occur. It is important to realize that some of these expected type conversions can take place more or less automatically (transparent to the user) and that special functions have to be supplied for others.

On an even more fundamental level, the expression

```
GrossSalary = hours*payrate;
```

requires the following operations:

- Find the variable location **hours**
- Retrieve the value stored there
- Find the variable location **payrate**
- Retrieve the value stored there
- Perform type conversions if required (and if we are able to do so)
- Multiply the values together
- Find the memory location **GrossSalary**
- Store the product in that variable location

Figure 3.2.1 summarizes the fundamental arithmetic operations. The order in which operations are performed and the hierarchy of the operations themselves is important in determining the value of the expression. For example, if we attempted to execute the following sequence, what would be the value assigned to the variable result?

```
int
    result,first,second,third;

first = 5;
second = 6;
third = 7;
result = first+second*third;
```

The value stored in result could be 77, or it could be 47, depending upon whether we perform the addition first or the multiplication first. Writing

```
result = (first+second)*third;
```

yields 77 in the variable **result**, while

```
result = first + (second * third);
```

yields 47 in **result**. The programming language must know which operation is to be performed first. In Figure 3.2.1, the operations are listed in order of precedence, from lowest priority at the top to highest priority at the bottom. In other words, the multiplication must be performed before the addition in the expression to calculate the value of **result**.

Many programming languages supply other functions which may be added to the above list. In fact, C itself provides special operators not included in the above list. The important thing here is that we understand the concept associated with the formation of arithmetic expressions.

From the table above we see that the unary operators have a higher precedence than the binary operators. For example,

```
result = -first + second * third;
```

causes the value stored in the variable **first** to be negated before either

Figure 3.2.1   Operators and Precedence

+	binary addition	performed in order left to right
−	binary subtraction	performed in order left to right
*	binary multiplication	performed in order left to right
/	binary division	performed in order left to right
%	modulus	performed in order left to right
−	unary minus	performed in order right to left
+	unary plus	performed in order right to left
( )	parenthesis	performed in order left to right

the addition or the multiplication is performed, yielding a value of 37 stored in **result**. In any of these examples, we must realize that the order of the operations can be altered with the insertion of parentheses. For all practical purposes, parentheses can be nested as deeply as we wish, but again, there is no need to place parentheses in an expression unnecessarily. Consider the example

```
result = -((first+second) - third);
```

Here the addition of parentheses causes the leading unary minus to be performed last, even though it is the operator with the highest precedence. The value stored in **result** would be –4.

A bit of discussion concerning the modulus operator is in order. The modulus is an integer operator, which could be understood to be "find the remainder when integer division is performed." Consider the short programming example shown in Figure 3.2.2.

The program will display

```
6 mod 341 is 6.
341 mod 6 is 5.
```

because when 6 is divided by 341, the quotient is 0 and the remainder is 6, so the function **%** returns 6. On the other hand, when 341 is divided by 6 the quotient is 56 and the remainder is 5, which means the function **%** returns 5. You are encouraged to write test programs similar to the one in Figure 3.2.2 to test the behavior of the modulus function when one or both of its arguments are negative. What general rules can be stated? (Please see the exercises.)

Figure 3.2.2   The Modulus Operator

```
#include <stdio.h>

main()
{
    int
        a,b;

    a = 6;
    b = 341;
    printf("%d mod %d is %d.\n",a,b,a%b);
    printf("%d mod %d is %d.\n",b,a,b%a);
}
```

Addressing and Dereferencing Operators

Consider very carefully the programming example in Figure 3.2.3. Three very important concepts are addressed: the addressing operator, the dereferencing operator, and storage declaration for an address.

This program might respond

```
the address of x is 1040732
the value of x is 5
```

The first storage declaration,

```
int x;
```

requests storage for an integer. The next storage request,

```
int *y;
```

requests a variable **y**, *which is to contain the address of an integer.* We do not know where exactly in memory this address is. At this point, no address has been placed in **y**. Some compilers will allow four bytes of storage for this address. The next statement places the integer value 5 in the storage location referred to by **x**. The next instruction,

```
y = &x;
```

places *the actual address of the variable* **x** *in the storage represented by variable* **y**. We then print each of these locations using a **printf** state-

Figure 3.2.3 Addressing and Dereferencing

```
#include <stdio.h>

main()
{
    int x;        /* storage for x                               */
    int *y;       /* storage for the address of x                */

    x = 5;
    y = &x;       /* & is the address operator                   */
                  /* y = &x stores the address of x in y         */

    printf("the address of x is %ld\n",y);
                  /* *y dereferences y. It goes to the location  */
                  /* in memory whose address is stored in y      */
    printf("the value of x is %d\n",*y);
}
```

ment. Note also that the value of **x** was obtained by using the *dereferencing operator.* The symbol ***y** directs us to the storage location *whose address is stored in* **y**. Of course, the address of **x** is stored in **y**, so the ***y** directive is another way of referencing the storage location **x**. As we will see, being able to manipulate addresses in this way and being able to (indirectly) reference the contents of memory knowing the addresses will be an extremely powerful tool. In Figure 3.2.4 we have added two lines to the above code to learn how much storage is actually allocated by the compiler for a variable designed to hold the address of an integer.

The output from this program might appear similar to the following:

```
the address of x is 2296726
the value of x is 5

size of x is 4
size of the address of x (y) is 4
```

Please note also that in the short program in Figure 3.2.4, the * symbol is used in two different contexts. First, the request

```
int *
```

uses the symbol to request storage for *the address of an integer.* Essentially, in C, `int *` is to be considered as one symbol.On the other hand, the **printf** statement

```
printf("the value of x is %d\n",*y);
```

uses the symbol * with the variable **y** to request the *contents* of the mem-

Figure 3.2.4   Size of an Address

```
#include <stdio.h>

main()
{
  int
      x, *y;

  x = 5;
  y = &x;
  printf("the address of x is %ld\n",y);
  printf("the value of x is %d\n",*y);

  printf("\nsize of x is %d\n",sizeof(x));
  printf("size of the address of x (y) is %d\n",sizeof(y));
}
```

Figure 3.2.5 Address Variable in Memory

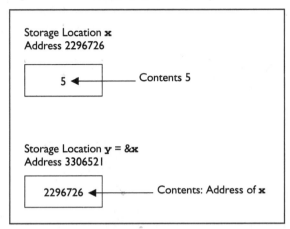

Storage Location **x**
Address 2296726

5 ◀———— Contents 5

Storage Location **y** = &**x**
Address 3306521

2296726 ◀———— Contents: Address of **x**

ory location whose *address* is stored in **y**. Of course, in Figure 3.2.5, the address of **x** is stored in **y**. Requesting the contents of the memory location whose address is stored in **y** is the same as requesting the contents of the memory location **x**.

When you become more comfortable with the concept of addresses and contents stored at those addresses, this distinction will become quite obvious. Consider the example in Figure 3.2.6, which illustrates that we can assign the addresses in much the same way as we assign other values of variables. Here we access the values of variables **x** and **y** and then interchange their addresses, and access the same locations using different address variables.

The output from this program might appear similar to the following:

```
x (*a) is 5
y (*b) is 67
a now points to 67
b now points to 5
```

Note the use of the phrase "points to" for the dereference. The variables that hold the addresses of the integers are called "pointers." There is nothing special about this terminology—these are merely variables declared in such a way that they hold the addresses of integers. In the same way, we may request storage for variables designed to hold the addresses of characters, floating-point quantities, or any of the other data types we wish to use.

Make sure that you use an address variable (pointer) only with the data type it was designed to hold. You must not, for example, use an integer address with a floating-point variable. Note also the multiple role played by the symbol *. As a binary operator, as in **a*b**, it means multi-

Figure 3.2.6 Address Manipulation

```
#include <stdio.h>
main()
{
   int
      x, y, *a, *b, *c;

   x = 5;
   y = 67;
   a = &x;
   b = &y;
   printf("x (*a) is %d\n",*a);
   printf("y (*b) is %d\n",*b);


   c = a;
   a = b;        /* address manipulation */
   b = c;

   printf("a now points to %d\n",*a);
   printf("b now points to %d\n",*b);
}
```

plication, but as a unary operator, as in **y = *x** or **y = z + *x**, it is the dereferencing operator.

► Exercises 3.2

3.2.1 In each of the following, assume **x = 3, y = 6, z = -2,** and **w = 5.** Evaluate each expression.

    1. x*y+3*w

    2. -x+3*y*(2-z)

    3. -z+3%y

    4. x+y*z+w

    5. 2%y%66

3.2.2 Execute the following code segment, and write the value stored in each variable location.

```
int x,y,z;
int *a,*b;
```

```
x = 5;                        _____
y = 67;                       _____
a = &x;                       _____
b = &y;                       _____
z = (*a) + (*b)               _____
```

3.3 INPUT AND OUTPUT INSTRUCTIONS

SECTION TOPICS

Input

Output

All programming languages must provide some facility for communication with peripheral devices, including the computer keyboard, output screen, auxiliary memory, disk drives, printers, and the like. In this section we shall examine the fundamental capabilities of a programming language for input and output.

Input

The input and output routines provided by programming languages should be able to read and process data in many forms efficiently. Additionally, these languages should be able to successfully interact with a host of available input devices, such as the workstation keyboard, data files on auxiliary storage devices, tape drives, and the like. We learned that several data types are of interest to programmers. Integers, characters, strings, and floating-point quantities must be read and printed. Since we know that each of these data types are converted and stored internally as a sequence of 0s and 1s, the input facility must perform a certain amount of conversion of the information in the input stream before it can be processed. For example, if the input stream appeared as

    23 45

we have (at least) two options. Shall we consider the input information as two integer numbers, or should we consider it as six consecutive characters (a two, a three, a space, a four, and a five, followed by a carriage return character)? Certain programming languages are designed to better handle numbers (FORTRAN), other programming languages are designed for character and string processing (COBOL), while other programming languages may be designed for some other special purpose. Modern programming languages such as C provide functions that will successfully input and convert data to various forms with almost equal capability. We first consider the **scanf** function.

The input function **scanf** is similar in its operation to the **printf** function. Its syntax is

```
return_code = scanf("control string", variable list);
```

When the keyboard is used to enter values into a program, a sequence of characters is typed, and these characters are converted to the appropriate format by the **scanf** function. When the **scanf** function executes, the input stream is examined and then converted (if possible) to the format indicated in the control string. Upon completion, the return code, **return_code**, indicates the number of successful reads. The return code, **return_code**, can be examined if **scanf** was unsuccessful, for then the value stored in **return_code** will be −1 (on most systems).

As an example, consider the sequence

```
int
    x;
scanf("%d",&x);
```

In this simple example, we are not concerned about the value returned by **scanf**. We simply wish to read an integer from the input stream. Note also that the function **scanf** requires the *address* of the location where it is to store the information read. The persons who designed the C programming language designed the **scanf** function to perform this way. Remember in the future that the argument list for the function **scanf** requires an address.

A table of conversion characters for the **scanf** function is presented in Figure 3.3.1.

If we wish to enter float quantities into our program we may use the following sequence:

```
float
    q;
scanf("%f",&q);
```

Figure 3.3.1 scanf Conversion Characters

CONTROL CHARACTER	CONVERTS CHARACTER IN INPUT STREAM
c	to a character
d	to an integer
f	to a floating-point (real) number (float)
lf	to a long floating-point number (double)
s	to a string

The **scanf** function can be used to read several values at once. Moreover, we do not need to be concerned about the appearance of the input stream, since the **scanf** function will read past the "white-space" characters. For example, consider Figure 3.3.2. This program would work equally as well if the input stream were

```
23      45      67
```

or if it appeared as

```
23
45
67
```

or as any combination of the above. The function **scanf** will read past spaces, carriage returns, or tab characters, or any other white-space character that is present in the input stream *provided that the specification is* **int** *or* **float**. The output from the program in Figure 3.3.2 would be

```
x is 23
y is 45
z is 67
```

On the other hand, consider the slightly revised version of the program in Figure 3.3.3. Since the input control sequence requests that characters be read from the input stream, and since we understand that a blank, tab, or other character is perfectly acceptable, the **scanf** function will read these (including white-space) characters from the input stream and assign them to the variables indicated. For example, if upon execution of this program we input the sequence "abc" from the keyboard, the output would appear precisely as follows. Why?

Figure 3.3.2   Input Using scanf

```
#include <stdio.h>

main()
{
    int
        x,y,z;
    scanf("%d%d%d",&x,&y,&z);
    printf("x is %d\n",x);
    printf("y is %d\n",y);
    printf("z is %d\n",z);
}
```

Figure 3.3.3   Character Input Using scanf

```
#include <stdio.h>

main()
{
   char
      x,y,z;
   scanf("%c%c%c",&x,&y,&z);
   printf("x is %d\n",x);
   printf("y is %d\n",y);
   printf("z is %d\n",z);
}
```

```
x is 97
y is 98
z is 99
```

The **%d** in the **printf** caused the values in **x, y,** and **z** to be *interpreted as integers* rather than characters.

C provides alternative methods for reading characters from the input stream. The function **getc()** exists specifically for character input. Consider the example in Figure 3.3.4. If the user follows the directions and enters exactly three characters for initials, then this program will execute as expected. Execute the program and enter exactly three characters and press the return key. The output should appear similar to the following:

Figure 3.3.4   Character Input Using getc()

```
#include <stdio.h>
main()
{
   int
      a,b,c;

   printf("Please enter your initials in the form xyz: ");
   a = getc(stdin);
   b = getc(stdin);
   c = getc(stdin);

   printf("you entered %c%c%c.\n",a,b,c);
}
```

```
Please enter your initials in the form xyz: mle
you entered mle.
```

However, if the user wishes to enter a character, followed by the return key, followed by another character, followed by another return key, etc., the program will not execute as expected. The **getc** function reads exactly one character from the input stream. If that character happens to be the character transmitted by pressing the return key, **getc()** will capture and store the newline character as well. Consider the slight modification of substituting **%d** for **%c** in the **printf** function, which transmits the output to the screen.

```c
#include <stdio.h>
main()
{
    int
      a,b,c;

    printf("Please enter your initials in the form xyz: ");
    a = getc(stdin);
    b = getc(stdin);
    c = getc(stdin);

    printf("you entered %d %d %d.\n",a,b,c);
}
```

Now upon entering the sequence character, return, character, the **printf** function will convert the output stream to integers and transmit these integers to the screen. Suppose we execute the program and enter a lowercase 'a' followed by a return, followed by a lowercase 'b' followed by a final return. The program output would appear similar to

```
Please enter your initials in the form xyz: a
b
you entered 97 10 98.
```

The values 97 and 98 are the correct decimal representations of 'a' and 'b' in ASCII, while the 10 is the decimal value of a newline character. With this example in mind, we must be very careful when using this function, the **scanf** function, or some other input function to be sure we are aware of its characteristics and its conversion properties. Students will save themselves hours of grief in debugging time if they carefully research their input function needs.

For entering a string, C provides the **gets()** function. The example in Figure 3.3.5 reads a string of characters from the keyboard and echoes that input back to the terminal screen. Possible output from the program in Figure 3.3.5 might be

Figure 3.3.5   String Input Using gets()

```
#include <stdio.h>
main()
{
    char
        a[40];

    printf("Please enter a sentence:\n");
    gets(a);
    printf("\nYou entered\n%s\n",a);
}
```

```
Please enter a sentence:
Oh, what a tangled web we weave . . .
You entered
Oh, what a tangled web we weave . . .
```

Certain problems exist with the function **gets()**. You should notice that the character array **a[40]** provided to hold the input string was fixed at 40 characters. If the user should enter more than 40 characters the behavior of this program can be quite unexpected. The function **gets()** does no checking on the number of characters actually entered, and overwriting the extent of an array in C can have disastrous consequences.

We have discussed what input capabilities a programming language must have: the ability to read a string of characters from the input device and convert the characters to an appropriate form, whether integer, float, character, or string. Additionally, we discussed the C functions **scanf**, **getc**, and **gets**.

Output

In general, the output facility must be able to print the values of variables and expressions independent of the data type represented by the variable. In addition, the output facility must be able to print the values of literal expressions that will describe for the user what is being printed. It also makes sense for us to expect that our output facility will deliver the values of our literals, variables, and expressions to the output screen, to the printer, or to external storage devices.

In some sense, we can think of the value to be presented by the output facility as the right side of an assignment statement. The literals, variables, and expressions are evaluated, converted to the appropriate format as directed by the output statement, and then presented in this form on the terminal screen or other output device, rather than being stored as would be the case with an assignment statement. The biggest job that the output facility must perform is the conversion of the output to the appropriate format. Internally, of course, all information is stored as a sequence of 0s and 1s. To have the output facility simply print these would be almost useless to the average computer user. Thus, whatever our output function is, it must perform a certain amount of conversion to be useful. We say that the output has been "formatted" if it is converted to a form usable for the programmer.

The fundamental output function provided by the C programming language is the **printf** function. The basic form of the **printf** function is

```
printf("control string", variable list);
```

The control string contains the formatting and conversion instructions (the f in **printf** stands for "formatted") to be carried out on the variable list. Additionally, the control string can contain literal strings to be used by the programmer to describe the output. For example, if we wrote

```
printf("Eggen");
```

we would receive the same output as if we had written

```
char x[] = "Eggen";
printf("%s",x);
```

since the **%s** control string indicates that the variable **x** in the variable list is to be converted to string form and then printed. The table in Figure 3.3.6 gives the fundamental conversion control characters used by the **printf** function in determining how the output is to appear.

Figure 3.3.6 printf Control String Conversion Characters

CONVERSION CHARACTER	HOW THE ARGUMENT IS PRINTED
c	as a character
d	as a decimal integer
e	as a floating point number in scientific notation
f	as a floating point number in ordinary decimal notation
g	in either e format or f format, whichever is shorter
s	as a string

As an additional example, consider the following program segment:

```
int
    x;
x = 345;
printf ("The integer is %5d \n",x);
```

Of course, we have an integer with the value 345 stored in it. The **printf** statement causes the output

```
The integer is 345
```

followed by a newline character.

Several control characters may be included in the control string. These characters control the position and, to some extent, the appearance of the output. The characters and their integer values are summarized in the table in Figure 3.3.7.

Consider again the sequence

```
char
    c;
c = 'a';
printf("%c\n",c);
printf("%d\n",c);
```

The output from the segment would appear on the screen as

```
a
97
```

since the first **printf** converts the memory location **c** to character format and displays it on the screen, while the second **printf** converts the memory location **c** to integer format and displays its value on

Figure 3.3.7 Control Characters

CHARACTER	ESCAPE SEQUENCE	INTEGER VALUE
alert	\a	7
carriage return	\r	13
form feed	\f	12
horizontal tab	\t	9
newline	\n	10
null character	\0	0

the screen. Internally the representation for both the 'a' and the 97 is the same; it is the **printf** function that causes the output to appear differently.

▶ Exercises 3.3

3.3.1 Investigate your installation and your particular version of C and determine how much space is allocated for each of the following data types.

    1. float
    2. int
    3. long
    4. double
    5. unsigned
    6. short

3.3.2 Write a program to input and print your name.

3.3.3 Write a program that will prompt the user to enter (**scanf**) the radius of a circle. The program should then print (**printf**) the area and circumference of the circle. Use $\pi = 3.14159$.

3.3.4 Write a program that will prompt the user to enter a character string. The program should then print the string in reverse order on the screen.

3.3.5 What does the following program print and why?

```
#include <stdio.h>
main()
{
    char
        x,y,z;
    scanf("%c%c%c",&x,&y,&z);
    printf("x is %d\n",x);
    printf("y is %d\n",y);
    printf("z is %d\n",z);
}
```

3.4 ARRAYS AND STRUCTURES

Earlier in the discussion we began to illustrate the advantage of using *data aggregates* when we began to discuss arrays. An aggregate is a word used to describe the fact that several items, things, related entities, or just stuff are stored together. A *data structure* is a presumably complex entity designed to hold these somehow related pieces of information. If the data to be held is all of the same type, such as `int` or `float`, then a *homogeneous* data structure can be used (array), whereas if the data to be stored as a unit is of varying types, then a *heterogeneous* data structure must be used (structure). One of the most important concepts addressed by computer scientists is how to *package* data and programs in such a way that they can be easily accessed and manipulated.

Arrays

An array is an example of a *homogeneous random-access data structure.* Terminology aside, the fundamental concept behind an array is not complex. An array is merely a collection of similar data elements (such as integers, floating-point quantities, characters, etc.) stored together with a common name, and addressed by means of an index that tells the location of the particular data entity in the array. The *homogeneous* aspect of the definition says that each of the cells in the array contains the same data type. The *random-access* aspect of the definition says that we may access any of the cells in the array directly, simply by using its index. For example, if we specified

```
int arr[50]
```

we would be asking for storage for 50 integers, accessed with indices 0 through 49. In particular, it would make perfectly good sense to ask for `arr[35]`, `arr[0]`, or `arr[22]` as memory locations. Any valid integer could be stored in any of the 50 available storage locations. The program in Figure 3.4.1 stores the squares of the first 50 integers (0 through 49) in the 50 storage locations and displays the results on the terminal screen.

Figure 3.4.1 Program for the First 50 Squares

```
#include <stdio.h>

main()
{
    int arr[50];
    int i;
    for (i = 0; i < 50; i=i+1)
    {
        arr[i] = i*i;
        printf("%d   ",arr[i]);
    }
}
```

The relevant line in Figure 3.4.1 is highlighted for you to study. A complete discussion of looping and all aspects of the **for** loop will be discussed in Chapter 4. For the time being, realize that the execution of the **for** loop proceeds by setting the index variable **i** to 0 initially, and then continues to increment **i** by 1 (**i = i+1**) as long as **i** remains less than 50. When **i** becomes 50, the execution of the loop terminates. As **i** begins at 0 and increments through the first 50 nonnegative integers, the value assigned to the storage location **arr[i]** is **i*i**. You are encouraged to enter this program and study its output.

▶ **PROBLEM** Consider the problem of finding the largest element stored in a linear (one-dimensional) array.

ANALYSIS There are many instances where arrays are very handy data structures to use. Because an array is a random-access data structure, we may directly access any of its cells. However, the fact that we can access an array *randomly* does not prohibit us from examining the elements of the array *sequentially*. In particular, the problem of finding the largest element stored in an array requires us to search through the array *sequentially* to find this largest element.

DESIGN The program in Figure 3.4.2 contains three routines: one to fill the array with values, another to print the values entered, and another to find and print the largest element stored in the array. Our design consists of three steps:

1. Fill the array with values.
2. Print the array values on the screen.
3. Find and print the maximum integer.

Figure 3.4.2   Finding the Maximum Element of an Array

```c
#include <stdio.h>
#define MAXARR 50

main()
{
    int
        arr[MAXARR], i, counter, value, no_of_elements, max;
    /*-----------------------------------------------------------------*/
    /* Input routine. The user is requested to enter values from       */
    /* the keyboard until the value -1 is encountered.                 */
    /*-----------------------------------------------------------------*/

    printf("\f");
    counter = 0;
    printf("Do not enter more than %d values please\n\n",MAXARR);
    printf("Please enter value (-1 to quit):  ");
    scanf("%d",&value);
    while (value != -1)
    {
        arr[counter] = value;
        printf("Please enter value (-1 to quit):  ");
        scanf("%d",&value);
        counter = counter + 1;
    }

    /*-----------------------------------------------------------------*/
    /* output routine. The number of elements entered is displayed     */
    /* along with the elements of the array.                           */
    /*-----------------------------------------------------------------*/

    no_of_elements = counter;
    printf("%d values were entered\n",no_of_elements);
    printf("these values are: \n");
    for(i=0;i<no_of_elements;i=i+1)
        printf("%d  ",arr[i]);

    /*-----------------------------------------------------------------*/
    /* Findmax routine. The maximum array element is found and         */
    /* displayed on the terminal screen.                               */
    /*-----------------------------------------------------------------*/
    max = arr[0];
    for(i=1;i<no_of_elements;i=i+1)
        if (arr[i]>max)
        max = arr[i];

    printf("\n\nThe largest element stored in the array is: %d\n",max);
}
```

To refine step 3 of the process, we place the value in the first cell of the array in the variable **max**, which will hold the maximum. After all, it could be the maximum. Then we compare the remaining cells of the array, one by one, with the maximum, and replace the maximum if necessary with the larger value. In this way, when each cell of the array has been examined, the appropriate value will be contained in **max**.

CODE   In the program in Figure 3.4.2 there is nothing magic about the value (–1) used to determine the end of the input stream. In fact, any value could be used, and probably would have to be considered if –1 were a valid input value. Usually high-level languages use a control character to specify the end of the input stream. If the input may come from some external file (the keyboard may be considered an external file), then the language must be able to detect the end of the file when it is reached.

Two-Dimensional Arrays

The arrays used to this point have been *linear* or *one-dimensional* arrays, sometimes called *vectors*. The array homogeneous data structure can conceivably have as many dimensions as the user wishes, but practically speaking, the programmer will have trouble if there are too many dimensions. To request storage for a two-dimensional array **tda** of integers the programmer will enter

```
int tda[20][10];
```

In this case, an array is a table of integers. It has a specified number of rows and columns. In the example, **tda** is an array name that will have storage for 20 rows and 10 columns. Each of the 200 storage locations so specified will be designed to contain an integer. To access each individual storage location, the user must specify the row index first, followed by the column index. To place the value 345 into the cell in the array that is in row 13 and column 7, we would write

```
tda[13][7] = 345;
```

Again, conceptually, a two-dimensional array is not difficult. Manipulating an array with a computer programming language might seem a bit cumbersome at first, but once you get used to it, you will be able to use multidimensional arrays with ease.

► **PROBLEM**   We wish to write a program that will create a two-dimensional array and fill each of the cells of the array with the product of its row index and its column index.

ANALYSIS   The element that appears in row 3 and column 4, for example, should be 12. In general, the element that appears in row i and column j should be **i * j**.

DESIGN   We can create such a product if we nest two loops, one inside the other, and form the desired product from the loop indices. We perform the work in two steps: first fill the array, and then print the array on the terminal screen in an appropriate format. See Figure 3.4.3.

CODE   The exact C code that implements the design is given in Figure 3.4.3.

TEST   The output from the program in Figure 3.4.3 appears as follows:

```
0    0    0    0    0    0
0    1    2    3    4    5
0    2    4    6    8   10
0    3    6    9   12   15
0    4    8   12   16   20
```

Figure 3.4.3   Filling and Printing a Two-Dimensional Array

```c
#include <stdio.h>
main()
{
    int
        tda[5][6], i, j;

    for (i=0;i<5;i=i+1)
    {
        for (j=0; j<6;j=j+1)
        {
            tda[i][j] = i*j;
        }
    }

    for (i=0; i<5; i=i+1)
    {
        for (j=0; j<6; j=j+1)
        {
            printf("%5d",tda[i][j]);
        }
        printf("\n");   /* this throws the carriage after a
                           row has been printed */

    }
}
```

Here again we wish you to enter the program into your system and check that the results appear as indicated. Envision the output placed one at a time into the cells indicated in Figure 3.4.4. Each of the cell addresses is indicated just below the cells. Notice that the initial row of the table is row 0; the initial column is column 0 as well. This array has five rows numbered 0 through 4 and six columns numbered 0 through 5. This explains why the first row and the first column of the output table are zeros.

Figure 3.4.4 shows a two-dimensional array with the cell address (variable name) directly below each cell. To find the element in the third row and column 0, we proceed to row 3, counting 0,1,2,3, and then to the initial column, which is column 0. You must get used to counting beginning with the integer 0, since many results depend on being able to index beginning with 0.

The computer code presented in Figure 3.4.3 prints the array in *row major order,* which is terminology used to explain that the first row is printed first, the second row next, and so on. In reality, the computer does not take a block of memory shaped like a table and store the array in it. In fact, the elements of the array are stored in a long string of consecutive memory locations internally in the random-access memory of the computer. We could print the array as it is stored in one long string:

```
for (i=0; i<5; i=i+1)
{
    for (j=0; j<6; j=j+1)
    {
        printf("%5d",tda[i][j]);
    }
}
```
```
0   0  0  0  0  0   0   1   2   3   4    5    0    2   4   6
8  10  0  3  6  9  12  15   0   4   8   12   16   20
```

or we could print the array in *column major order,* which means that column 0 would appear first, column 1 second, and so on.

```
for (j=0; j<6; j=j+1)
{
    for (i=0; i<5; i=i+1)
    {
        printf("%5d",tda[i][j]);
    }
    printf("\n");
}
```

The output from the above program segment would appear as follows:

Figure 3.4.4 Two-Dimensional Array

		Columns					
		0	**1**	**2**	**3**	**4**	**5**
Rows	Content	0	0	0	0	0	0
	Address	tda[0][0]	tda[0][1]	tda[0][2]	tda[0][3]	tda[0][4]	tda[0][5]
	Content	0	1	2	3	4	5
	Address	tda[1][0]	tda[1][1]	tda[1][2]	tda[1][3]	tda[1][4]	tda[1][5]
	Content	0	2	4	6	8	10
	Address	tda[2][0]	tda[2][1]	tda[2][2]	tda[2][3]	tda[2][4]	tda[2][5]
	Content	0	3	6	9	12	15
	Address	tda[3][0]	tda[3][1]	tda[3][2]	tda[3][3]	tda[3][4]	tda[3][5]
	Content	0	4	8	12	16	20
	Address	tda[4][0]	tda[4][1]	tda[4][2]	tda[4][3]	tda[4][4]	tda[4][5]

```
0   0    0    0    0
0   1    2    3    4
0   2    4    6    8
0   3    6    9   12
0   4    8   12   16
0   5   10   15   20
```

We should observe that there are now six rows and five columns, and that the columns and rows are reversed. This is *column major* order. The nesting of the loops and the arrangement of the row index and the column index is what determines the order in which the elements appear. Before the outer index can be incremented the inner index has to complete its cycle. That is, in the segment presented immediately above, before **j** can be incremented, **i** must increment from 0 through 4, then **j** is increased by 1, and **i** starts over again.

Arrays will be discussed again from a different point of view when pointers are discussed in Chapter 5.

Strings

Conceptually, a string is merely a collection of characters, like a sentence or a paragraph. In C, a string is an array, which must be terminated by the null character '\0'. This termination is necessary since without it C would not be able to find the end of the string.

Computers in general and personal computers in particular have widespread application as text processors (manipulating large bodies of text, such as the daily newspaper or this textbook) and as such, handling characters and strings of characters is an extremely important application of computing technology. As a result, we must study strings and string manipulation.

Since a string is an array, we have all the array manipulation tools to use as well as the special functions that have been developed specifically for string manipulation. The operations we wish to perform include finding the length of a string, extracting portions of a string, changing part of the contents of a string, copying strings from one location to another, hooking strings together, and various other tasks. To request storage for a string we will request storage for an array of characters in the C programming language. As an array, a string is a homogeneous data structure that contains a collection of characters. That is, each of the cells in the array will contain a character. As a result, the declaration

```
char name[20];
```

sets aside storage for up to 20 characters (one of which must be the null character). We may store as many as 19 characters in the array in positions available to us. The program in Figure 3.4.5 stores a person's name and prints it character by character on the terminal screen.

Figure 3.4.5   String Length

```
#include <stdio.h>
#include <string.h>
main()
{
   char
      name[20] = "Maurice Eggen";
   int
      length,index;
   length = strlen(name);
   printf("the length of the string is %d\n",length);
   for (index = 0;index < length;index=index+1)
   {
      printf("%c\n",name[index]);
   }
   printf("%s\n",name);
}
```

Observe that if we wish to use the string handling functions in C we must include the C library that contains them. The first line of the program sets aside enough room for a character string of up to 20 characters and initializes the string with "Maurice Eggen." The next line uses a library function to find out how many characters are contained in the string just defined. The **printf** displays the length of the string on the terminal screen. The loop displays the characters from the string one at a time. The output from the program would appear precisely as follows (using Think C on the Macintosh):

```
the length of the string is 13
M
a
u
r
i
c
e

E
g
g
e
n
Maurice Eggen
```

As previously discussed, if we wish to use the string handling functions we must include the library that contains these functions. The reference to **strlen** is a call to one of these library functions. To provide a complete discussion of strings, we must determine the characteristics of a string and provide a method of manipulating an entity that has these characteristics.

A string is a fixed-length character array that may contain a variable number of characters (up to the maximum length). To process and manipulate strings, we must be able to:

- Perform tasks such as initialization, input, output
- Find the length of the string
- Insert strings within strings
- Delete portions of a string
- Copy strings from one location in memory to another
- Determine whether strings are the same
- Extract a substring from a given string

C provides standard functions that accomplish these tasks.

Initialization of strings in C may be accomplished at the time space is reserved for the string. As we did earlier, we may reserve space for a string up to 20 characters long and initialize it with a value by writing

```
char name[21] = "Maurice Eggen";
```

Observe that the double quotes are necessary. To enter a string from the keyboard under control of a program, we may use code similar to the input routine shown in Figure 3.4.6.

It is important to remember that a string must be terminated by the null character in order for many of the string handling functions to operate properly. When using the **gets(name)** function, you must make sure the declared length of the string is long enough to hold all the characters entered; if not, the function will not receive the null character, thus leaving the end of the string unmarked. You will have a perfectly good array of characters, but it simply will not be a string using C's definition of a string, and therefore the string handling functions will not perform correctly.

To output a string we may use the **printf** function as we did in Figure 3.4.6. We may also use the **puts** function. To print the name in the above example we may simply enter

```
puts(name);
```

to display the name on the terminal screen.

Figure 3.4.7 illustrates the use of the string function for copying strings from one memory location to another. The output from the program would appear as follows:

```
length of 'this is my string' is 17
```

The name of the function is **strcpy**. It takes two arguments and copies the source string to the destination string.

```
strcpy(destination_string, source_string);
```

Figure 3.4.6 Enter a String from the Keyboard

```
#include <stdio.h>
#include <string.h>
main()
{
    char
        name[20];
    int
        length;

    printf("Please enter a sentence. Press the \n");
    printf("return key when finished.\n");
    gets(name);
    printf("%s\n",name);
    length = strlen(name);
    printf("The length of the string is %d\n",length);

}
```

Figure 3.4.7 Use of the strcpy() Function

```
#include <stdio.h>
#include <string.h>
main()
{
    char
        name[20];
    int
        length;
    strcpy(name,"this is my string");
    length = strlen(name);
    printf("length of '%s' is %d\n",name,length);
}
```

A more general version of the string copy function is available for extracting a substring of a given string. The **strncpy** function takes three arguments:

```
strncpy(destination_string, source_string,
    number_of_characters);
```

and can thus extract any substring of a given string by specifying where in the source string we wish to start. Figure 3.4.8 illustrates the use of **strncpy**.

If we entered the string "this is a string," the program would extract two characters beginning at location **source+5**, which means it would skip over the first five characters and take the next two. The output from the program is

```
Please enter the source string:
this is a string
length of 'is' is 2
```

The **strcat** function is available to perform concatenation of strings. There are many instances where it is necessary to "hook strings together" to form a longer string. The program in Figure 3.4.9 illustrates the use of **strcat**.

The function concatenates the strings first and second, and replaces the string first with the result. The program execution is

Figure 3.4.8   Use of the strncpy() Function

```c
#include <stdio.h>
#include <string.h>
main()
{
    char
        source[20], dest[20];
    int
        length;
    printf("Please enter the source string:\n");
    gets(source);
    strncpy(dest,source+5,2);
    length = strlen(dest);
    printf("length of '%s' is %d\n",dest,length);
}
```

```
Please enter the first string:
Kirsten
Please enter the second string:
Eggen
the resulting string is KirstenEggen
```

When prompted, we entered **Kirsten** as the first string and **Eggen** as the second string. Since no spaces were added to either of these strings, no space between the names would be provided in the result. If you wish to place a space in the result, you must provide code to do so.

To determine whether strings are equal, we must again call upon the functions in the string library. Given the general nature of strings, it must be clear that they cannot be compared as though they were integers, characters, or float quantities. A string is a homogeneous data structure, and as such, has the concepts and properties we have been discussing associated with it. Calling upon the string function **strcmp** will allow us to determine whether two strings are the same. A typical call to the function **strcmp** appears as follows:

```
int strcmp(first_string, second_string);
```

where the integer value returned by the function is 0 if the strings are the same, is positive if the first string is greater than the second string, and is negative if the first string is less than the second string. To determine whether the first string is greater than the second string, the function compares characters until it finds the first occurrence where the strings do not match. If the character in that position is greater then the string is

Figure 3.4.9   Use of the strcat() Function

```c
#include <stdio.h>
#include <string.h>
main()
{
    char
        first[20], second[20];
    printf("Please enter the first string:\n");
    gets(first);
    printf("Please enter the second string:\n");
    gets(second);
    strcat(first,second);
    printf("the resulting string is %s \n",first);
}
```

greater. For example, the string "abce" is greater than the string "abcd" since the character 'e' follows the character 'd' in the ordinary ASCII sequence. To illustrate the use of this function, consider the programming example in Figure 3.4.10.

To insert a string within a string, one must first extract the first portion of the string, put it aside, extract the last portion of the string, put it aside, concatenate the first with the desired insertion, and then concatenate this result with the last portion of the string. Figure 3.4.11 illustrates this concept.

The programming example copies the first 16 characters from the given string, yielding "Are you feeling "; next it copies 19 characters, skipping the first 15 characters, which is the end of the string " better, Dr. Eggen?" The next two lines concatenate the three pieces together, yielding the result, "Are you feeling much better, Dr. Eggen?" Figure 3.4.11 demonstrates the general technique used when inserting strings into strings.

Figure 3.4.10 String Comparison

```
#include <stdio.h>
#include <string.h>
main()
{
   char
      first[20], second[20];
   int
      result;
   printf("Please enter the first string:\n");
   gets(first);
   printf("Please enter the second string:\n");
   gets(second);
   result = strcmp(first,second);
   if (result == 0)
      printf("strings are equal\n");
   else
      if (result > 0)
         printf("first string is greater than second string\n");
      else
         printf("second string is greater than first string\n");
}
```

Figure 3.4.11 Inserting a String Within a String

```
#include <stdio.h>
#include <string.h>
main()
{
   char
      first[40] = "Are you feeling better, Dr. Eggen?";
   char
      second[40] = " ";
   char
      third[40] = " ";

   printf("%s\n",first);
   strncpy(second, first, 16);
   strncpy(third, first+15, 19);
   strcat(second, "much");
   strcat(second, third);
   printf("%s\n",second);
}
```

Structures

A *structure,* sometimes called a *record,* is a heterogeneous data structure. Simply, this means that a structure is an aggregate that may contain data elements of different types. There is nothing magic or difficult about a structure—it is merely a way to collect together possibly unlike data items. Sometimes it is convenient to store related integers, floating-point quantities, characters, and strings as one entity. For example, we may wish to store information about an individual: name (string), age (numeric), address (string), social security number (string). It is worthwhile to group these together since we are discussing a single individual. Our data entity should have the following information:

person
    name
    age
    address
    ssn

Moreover, it may be desirable to further refine some of the data elements so that we can more easily work with them. For example, we may wish to describe the person's address as

```
address
    street
    city
    state
    zip
```

Thus, our record will have the following appearance:

```
person
    name       string[20];
    age        int;
    address
       street  string[20];
       city    string[20];
       state   string[2];
       zip     int;
    ssn        string[9];
```

A typical record might be

```
Dr. Roger Eggen
39
    1234 His Street
    Jacksonville
    FL
    32216
123456789
```

All of the information presented is related since it is about Dr. Eggen. It is convenient to store all of the information as one entity, since it is related, and extract portions of the record when needed.

In C, we would ask for a structure as shown in Figure 3.4.12. The structure request in this figure does not actually set aside any storage, nor does it provide for any variables with the given structure. Moreover, this structure definition is perhaps more complex than it needs to be for our illustration, since it contains a structure within a structure. To begin with, we shall set our sights a bit lower, and consider a much simpler structure definition. Assume for the sake of illustration that we would like to define a structure that contains a person's name and age.

```
struct NameAndAge
{
    char
        name[20];
    int
        age;
};
```

Figure 3.4.12 Complex Structure Definition

```
struct person
{
    char        name[20];
    int         age;
    struct      address
    {
        char        street[20];
        char        city[20];
        char        state[2];
        long        zip;
    };
    char        ssn[9];
};
```

This structure definition establishes what might be called a *template* for variables of this type. We have not actually asked for any storage, nor have we defined any variables. Records using this template will have two fields—a **name** field that is a string of length 20 and an **age** field that is an integer. To actually ask for storage for a variable of this type, we will enter

```
    struct NameAndAge Joe;
```

Then **Joe** becomes a record of the type **struct NameAndAge**. We still have not entered any actual data into the record structure **Joe** established. Before we do so, we must learn how to access each of the fields in the record. To access the name field of the record **Joe**, we will write **Joe.name**, while to access the age field of the record **Joe**, we will write **Joe.age**. In this way, these two items, **Joe.name** and **Joe.age** become ordinary variable names with all the rights and privileges that variable names have. Executing the program as shown in Figure 3.4.13 yields the following output:

```
    Joe, Please enter your name
    Joe Smith
    What is your age, Joe?
    39
    Your name is Joe Smith, and your age is 39
```

The greatest benefit of using structures is that diverse and dissimilar information may be grouped together under a common name. Said another way, a structure is a compound data type (heterogeneous data

Figure 3.4.13 Using a Structure

```
#include <stdio.h>
#include <string.h>

main()
{
    struct NameAndAge
    {
        char
            name[20];
        int
            age;
    };

    struct
        NameAndAge Joe;

    printf("Joe, Please enter your name\n");
    gets (Joe.name);
    printf("What is your age, Joe?\n");
    scanf("%d",&Joe.age);
    printf("Your name is %s, and your age is
            %d\n",Joe.name,Joe.age);
}
```

structure) that may be referenced under a single name. A structure provides a convenient way of grouping related information of (possibly) dif-
fering data types. In C, the record structure definition can be combined
with the request for storage for the variable.

```
struct NameAndAge
{
    char
        name[20];
    int
        age;
} Joe;
```

Here we simply place the variable name we wish to define before the
terminating semicolon. Moreover, also specific to C, if we needed only
one variable of the given type, the structure name could be eliminated.

```
struct
{
    char
        name[20];
    int
        age;
} Joe;
```

At this point in the discussion, let us say that the data structures already discussed may be combined. Our first example (which we did not develop) indicated that structures may be contained in other structures. Additionally, structures may contain arrays (but then we already knew that since our structure definition contained a string and a string is an array) and we may use arrays of structures. We shall delay discussions of these more complex data structures until later in the text.

▶ **PROBLEM** We wish to develop a collection of routines that will perform rational number arithmetic. In other words, we wish to develop a computer program that will add rational numbers (fractions) just as we learned in elementary school. Specifically, adding the fractions 1/2 and 1/3 should yield the fraction 5/6.

ANALYSIS Almost everyone understands the arithmetic necessary to perform addition, multiplication, and division of fractions. In particular, to add the fractions a/b and c/d where a,b,c, and d are integers involves calculating $(ad + bc)/bd$. It would also be nice to reduce the resulting fraction to lowest terms.

DESIGN In this case, since a fraction consists of a numerator and a denominator, it would be convenient to group these entities together. The numerator and denominator are the same data type, but some advantage may be gained by using a structure to organize our arithmetic. The structure

```
struct fraction
{
        int num;
        int den;
};
```

provides a template for the fractions under consideration, while the statement

```
struct fraction x,y,z,w;
```

allocates space for four such fractions.

CODE The code shown in Figure 3.4.14 illustrates how to access each of the elements of the fraction and performs addition of fractions. However, the results of the addition will not be reduced to lowest terms. Moreover, this

Figure 3.4.14 Fraction Arithmetic Using a Structure

```c
#include <stdio.h>

main()
{
    struct fraction
    {
        int num;
        int den;
    };
    struct fraction x,y,z;

    printf("Enter the numerator of the first fraction: ");
    scanf("%d",&x.num);
    printf("Enter the denominator of the second fraction: ");
    scanf("%d",&x.den);
    printf("Enter the numerator of the second fraction: ");
    scanf("%d",&y.num);
    printf("Enter the denominator of the second fraction: ");
    scanf("%d",&y.den);
    z.num = x.num * y.den + y.num * x.den;
    z.den = x.den * y.den;
    printf("The sum of %2d/%2d and %2d/%2d is
        %2d/%2d\n\n",x.num,x.den,y.num,y.den,z.num,z.den);
}
```

code only performs the most elementary arithmetic. Additional properties of fractions are left to the exercises.

TEST The UNIX environment using the gcc compiler produced the following output:

```
Enter the numerator of the first fraction: 1
Enter the denominator of the second fraction: 2
Enter the numerator of the second fraction: 1
Enter the denominator of the second fraction: 3
The sum of 1/2 and 1/3 is 5/6
```

We have discussed how structures are allocated, learned how structure elements may be referenced, and discussed how to get data into and out of a structure.

User-defined Data Types

Conceptually, there is nothing magical about arrays, strings, or structures. These are just some of the data types the designers of programming languages thought were used enough that they are included in the fundamental structure of the language. However, a programmer might need many other data types for special-purpose computing applications. The computing language must not be so restrictive as to confine the programmer within the provided data types. Modern programming languages should provide the programmer the capability to define data types for specific needs, based on the existing data types. If the programmer discovers that these new defined data types are useful, perhaps they might be included in future generations of programming languages. This is precisely how arrays and structures became part of programming languages to start with.

The capability for user-defined data types relies on the standard data types. Providing this capability for the programmer allows, first of all, the creation of names that are (possibly) more descriptive of the quantities being defined. Second, this capability provides for considerable flexibility in the "packaging" of the data types a programmer wishes to use.

The C key word that allows the user to define a data type is **typedef**. For example, if we wrote

```
typedef  MONEY     int;
```

then any request for a variable of type **MONEY** would be a variable request for an **int**. This may not seem like much of an advantage, but perhaps in the context of the programming application, the variable type **MONEY** is much more descriptive than the variable type **int**. While it is not strictly necessary to do so, C programmers commonly present their user-defined data types in uppercase.

Commonly, complicated structure definitions are **typedef**'d by the user. Defining data types in this way allows for easy recognition of complex heterogeneous data types. For example,

```
typedef struct PERSON
{
    char
        name[20];
    int
        age;
};
```

defines a variable of type **PERSON**. Then, having this variable type,

```
PERSON    BaseballTeam[18];
```

defines an array of structures that might contain the names and ages of all of the persons on your baseball team. Each cell in the array contains a structure, and each of these structures is a variable of type **PERSON**. The name of the first baseman on the baseball team might be referred to by **BaseballTeam[2].name**. The variable name is **BaseballTeam**, the index is 2 (the third entry), and the desired field within the third structure is the **name** field.

Notice the use of the period (.) to separate the name of the structure with the specific field of the structure referenced. As an additional example, consider Figure 3.4.15, which shows a complete example of a **typedef** and an array of structures that contain an array.

The program in Figure 3.4.15 is rather complicated at first glance, but after you have some experience, it becomes much more palatable. It creates an array of size 5 of the structure. That is, effectively 5 structures accessed by **author[0]...author[4]**. Within each of these structures is an array of **name**. The **name** field is capable of holding three characters and the end of string symbol '\0'. The initials of the authors are placed in the first two instances of **author**, in the **name** field. The **age** field of the structure can hold an integer. The **printf** statements display the contents of the **name** field one character at a time and later as a string. Also, the **age** field is printed. How would the second set of initials be displayed?

Much more discussion on structures and **typedef**s will be provided later in this text. The **typedef**s allow association of names with data types, which makes source code easier to read and can make programs simpler to modify and update.

▶ **Exercises 3.4**

3.4.1   Write a program that will prompt the user to enter an array of 10 characters. The program should then print the array, and then print the array in reverse order.

3.4.2   Write a program that will prompt the user to enter an array of 15 characters. The program should then print the array, and then print the array again, but this time as a 3-by-5 array in row-major order.

3.4.3   Write the code for a structure consisting of a student record containing the student's name, address, phone number, age, year in school, and number of credit hours currently enrolled. Try to decide what appropriate storage requests would be.

Figure 3.4.15   Array of Structures with Array

```c
#include <stdio.h>
main()
{
    typedef struct
        {
        char name[4];
        int age;    .
        } PERSON;
    PERSON
        author[5];
    int
        i;
    /* the following statements assign values to the structures         */
    /* in a simplistic fashion                                          */
    author[0].name[0] = 'R';
    author[0].name[1] = 'E';
    author[0].name[2] = 'E';
    author[0].name[3] = '\0';
    author[0].age = 39; /* and holding */

    author[1].name[0] = 'M';
    author[1].name[1] = 'L';
    author[1].name[2] = 'E';
    author[1].name[3] = '\0';
    author[1].age = 40;

    /* we will show two ways of printing the contents of the structure */

    printf("One character at a time!\n");
    printf("\tThe initials of the name author are: ");
    for (i = 0; i<3; i=i+1)
        printf("%c",author[0].name[i]);
    printf(" and his age: %d\n\n",author[0].age);

    printf("The name initials as a string!\n");
    printf("\tThe initials of the name author are:");
    printf(" %s ",author[0].name);
    printf("and his age: %d\n\n",author[0].age);
}
```

3.4.4 Please study the following code and explain exactly what it does:

```c
#include <stdio.h>
#include <string.h>
main()
{
    char
        a[21];
    int
        i;
    printf ("Please enter exactly 20 characters \n");
    gets(a);
    for(i=0;i<20;i=i+1)
    {
        printf("%c",a[i]);
        if (((i+1)%5) == 0) printf("\n");
    }
}
```

▶ Key Words

address	pointer
array	precedence
ASCII	printf
assignment	random-access data structure
char	scanf
data types	sign and magnitude
dereference	storage request
double	strcat
expression	strcmp
float	strcpy
getc	string
gets	string length
heterogeneous data structure	strncpy
homogeneous data structure	structure
index	two-dimensional array
int	typedef
operator	

▶ Chapter Concepts

3.1   Data types must be supplied to the programming environment so that the computer and programmer know the kinds of data that are to be manipulated.

3.2   Floating point representation is a sign and magnitude representation, whereas integers are stored and manipulated using a complemented arithmetic.

3.3   The programming environment provides functions for input and output of data to the programming project. C provides `scanf`, `getc`, `gets` for input, and provides `printf` as well as several others for output.

3.4   The ability to manipulate the address of a variable, whether a single variable or an aggregate, is an important capability of a programming language. C provides the addressing operator and the dereferencing operator.

3.5   The array is a random-access homogeneous data structure that may be used to store a collection of similar data.

3.6   A string is an array of characters. Certain functions for manipulating strings are provided in the string library.

3.7   An array may be a multidimensional entity. One- and two-dimensional arrays are commonly manipulated by programming languages.

3.8   The assignment operator is fundamental to programming languages. This operator allows certain manipulations and calculations to be performed and the results placed in a variable memory location.

3.9   Programming languages provide a collection of primitive (built-in) operators that allow the programmer to perform the fundamental arithmetic operations as well as operations on nonnumeric data types.

3.10   In addition to the data types integer, real, and character and the aggregate data types array and structure, user-defined data types are possible with the `typedef` instruction.

▶ Programming Projects

3.1   Write a C program that will provide the user with a complete rational number arithmetic package. Use a structure similar to Figure 3.4.14 to data-type your rational numbers. Your program should perform addition, subtraction, multiplication, and division of rational numbers. Each of the resulting fractions should be reduced to lowest terms by dividing both the numerator and denominator of the fractions by the greatest common divisor. Make sure you do not allow the denominator of any fraction to be zero.

3.2 Write a program that will prompt the user to enter a string from the keyboard. The program should then count and report the number of characters in the string. The program should also count and report the number of times each letter of the alphabet occurs in the string, and print the percentage of the total represented. Using the principles discussed in finding the maximum element of an array, find the letter of the alphabet that occurs most frequently in the sentence. Find the letter of the alphabet that occurs secondmost frequently.

3.3 The greatest common divisor of two positive integers is the largest positive integer which will evenly divide the two integers. Euclid showed that the GCD of x and y, GCD(x,y), is the same as the GCD of y and the remainder of x divided by y, assuming x is the larger of the two positive integers. Exploit this fact to write a program which will calculate the GCD of any two positive integers. What is the appropriate termination criterion for this algorithm?

3.4 Write a program that will print the prime factorization of any positive integer N.

3.5 An uppercase character is a character whose ASCII value is between 65 (A) and 90 (Z). Write a program that will prompt the user to enter a string from the keyboard and count the number of uppercase characters in the string.

3.6 Write a program that will determine whether a given positive integer is prime (divisible by only 1 and itself).

3.7 Use the algorithm of problem 3.6 to determine a list of all of the prime numbers less than 32767.

3.8 Assume that an input string consists of a string of 32 0s and 1s representing a binary integer. Write a program which will find the two's complement of this string. (Remember from Chapter 1 that you have to change the 0s to 1s and the 1s to 0s—and add 1 to the result.)

3.9 Assume that an input string consists of a string of 32 0s and 1s representing a binary integer. Convert this binary integer to its base 10 representation.

3.10 Given a string representing a base 10 integer, convert this integer to its two's complement binary integer representation. Your output should consist of a string of 32 0s and 1s.

CHAPTER 4

Fundamental Control Structures

CHAPTER TOPICS

Selection

Repetition

Complex Decision Making

Sorting and Searching

INTRODUCTION

This chapter explains the construction and use of conditionals and loops. Conditionals allow the computer to make decisions, such as determining if one integer is larger than another or if one character precedes another in the alphabet. If the variable **x** contains an integer 2 and a variable **y** contains an integer 3, the following conditional will print **y is greater**.

```
if (y > x)
    printf("y is greater");
else
    printf("y is not greater");
```

The **if** and **else** are key words used to construct the decision statement. The conditional following the **if** indicates what is to be compared. The statement following the **if (x > y)** is executed when the comparison is found true; the statement following the **else** is executed when the comparison is found false. So, if the value stored in **y** was not greater than the value stored in **x** the statement **y is not greater** would appear on the computer screen. The **else** portion is optional; it does not have to be included.

Iteration allows a group of statements, called a loop, to be executed several times. Loops come in three forms: **for**, **while**, or **do**. The following code prints **1 2 3 4 5** using a **for** loop.

```
for(i = 1; i < 6; i=i+1)
    printf("%d",i);
```

Section 4.1 discusses the selection (conditional) statement, which uses the **if** construct. The second concept we consider in Section 4.2 is looping. Each loop is entered through the key words **while**, **for**, or, **do**. These key words mark the beginning of the loop. **While**, **for**, **do**, and nested loops are discussed in Section 4.2. Logical *and* and *or* will be presented in Section 4.3. *And* and *or* allow the construction of more complex decisions. For example,

```
if ((x > y) && (z < w)) . . .
```

Examples of the iteration and conditional concepts are demonstrated in Section 4.4 through searching and sorting. When you finish studying this chapter you should be comfortable with indexing and using arrays, with **if** statements, and with the three forms of iteration. Computer science concepts presented in this chapter beyond those of selection, iteration, and looping, are ordering data (sorting) and searching for a specified data item. Much computer time is spent putting data in order and retrieving a particular data item (sorting and searching). These are real-world computer applications used in many scientific and business communities.

4.1 SELECTION

SECTION TOPICS

If Construction

Formation of Conditionals

Simple **if** statements are discussed in this section. The selection concept is demonstrated with many practical examples. The representation of values, testing those values, both in character and integer format, is demonstrated in this section.

If Construction

Some texts and computer users call the selection process a conditional. When constructing a selection statement, you are making a statement that will evaluate to true or false. For example, the statement **if (x > y)** causes the computer to compare the values stored at **x** and **y**. The result of the comparison is 0 for false or 1 for true. Note that any value other than 0 is considered true in C. We observed in Chapter 1 that one of the fundamental capabilities of the computer is to make decisions. The computer can compare like quantities and react to the results of the comparison. The basic concept of selection was presented in Chapter 2 and is repeated here. The basic control structure for **if** statements is shown in Figure 4.1.1.

A complete program example illustrating the decision structure is contained in Figure 4.1.2. The goal of the program is to read an integer into the program. The computer can only work on numbers that are resident in main memory; thus, the integer is read in from the keyboard. Then a question is asked to determine whether the number is greater than or equal to 0. The appropriate message is displayed on the computer

Figure 4.1.1   If-then-else Construct

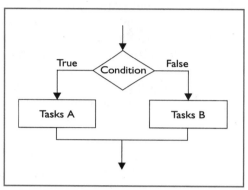

screen depending upon the result of the comparison. If the number is greater or equal to zero the first message is displayed; otherwise the second message is displayed.

Figure 4.1.2 demonstrates the flow of control shown in Figure 4.1.1. The *task A* as shown in Figure 4.1.1 is the

```
printf("the number %d is greater than or equal to
        0\n",num);
```

of Figure 4.1.2 and *task B* is the

```
printf("the number %d is less than 0\n",num);
```

Figure 4.1.2   Selection Program

```c
#include <stdio.h>

main()
{
    int
        num;

    printf("input a number\n");
    scanf("%d",&num);

    if  (num >= 0)          /* task A */
        printf("the number %d is greater than or equal to 0\n",num);
    else                    /* task B */
        printf("the number %d is less than 0\n",num);
}
```

Note that task A and/or task B could consist of several instructions if enclosed in braces { }. Also, the **else** portion of the **if** statement is optional; not every **if** needs a corresponding **else**. The statements are written exactly like Figure 4.1.2 with the **else** portion omitted when desired. Program flow either executes the true (then) portion and continues with the remainder of the program, or executes the **else** portion, and continues with the program. If no **else** block is present and the condition is false, execution continues with the remainder of the program, skipping the true (then) portion of the construct entirely.

The following shows the **if** without a corresponding **else**.

```
      .
      .
      .
if (num >= 1000)
    printf("the number is big!!!\n");
      .
      .
      .
```

Formation of Conditionals

Formation of conditionals may be quite complex, involving *and's* and *or's* and other relational operations. The *and's* and *or's* are discussed in Section 4.3, but we will consider other relations here. The conditional expression may involve *relational operations* such as those shown in Figure 4.1.3.

Note the use of the symbol == for the relational operator *is equal to*. The = operator is the assignment operator. C uses different operators for equality (==) and assignment (=). Many other programming languages use different operators to distinguish between these two concepts as well. Pascal, for example, uses := for assignment, and = for the relational equality operator. Some languages, such as BASIC and PL/1, use the same operator, =, for both concepts, and determine the meaning of = by its context. It could mean comparison or assignment depending on its usage in an expression. This is not the case in C. The relational operator,

Figure 4.1.3 Relational Operators

==	equal
!=	not equal
>	greater than
<	less than
>=	greater than or equal to
<=	less than or equal to

==, and the assignment operator, =, are clearly distinguished. Note, also, that the >= and <= are order dependent, that is, >= is correct, but => is not correct. The compiler used to translate C is written to accept only <= and >=. The following paragraphs present some examples to show how the computer can be used to make selections.

Suppose we need to determine if a person's age qualifies them for the American Association of Retired People (AARP). To qualify, a person must be 55 or older. We need to write the decision statement that will be true if the variable, **age**, contains at least 55. The following statement will do the job:

```
if (age >= 55)
    printf("yes, this qualifies\n");
```

As a second example, suppose we wish the computer to determine if the roots of a quadratic equation, $ax^2 + bx + c = 0$, are real or imaginary. Recall that the discriminant of the quadratic, b^2-4ac, determines whether the roots will be real or imaginary. The following decision statement does the job:

```
if (b*b-4*a*c >= 0)
    printf("the roots are real");
else
    printf("the roots are imaginary");
```

Notice that the first example shows the **else** is optional and that the second example demonstrates the complete **if** construct. The second example also shows that certain operators take precedence over others. In the example, multiplication, subtraction, and the relational >= will be done in the order multiplication first, subtraction second, and the comparison last. Conceptually, this observation is important, since without such knowledge, it is possible that the computer would compare **c** to 0, and attempt to multiply that result (a 0 or a 1) into the remainder of the expression.

As a final example, suppose we needed to determine if a color was green (g), blue (b), or red (r). Upon deciding, we needed to count the fact it was green, blue, or red and count the total number of colors. The following sequence of decisions could be used:

```
if (color == 'g')
{
    color_green = color_green + 1;
    total_colors = total_colors + 1;
}
else
{
    if (color == 'b')
    {
```

```
        color_blue = color_blue + 1;
        total_colors = total_colors + 1;
    }
    else
    {
        color_red = color_red + 1;
        total_colors = total_colors + 1;
    }
}
```

The above example shows that multiple statements can be executed when the **if** is true. It also shows how a simple character is compared. For the example, we assume there are only three choices and if the color is not green or blue, then it has to be red.

▶ Exercises 4.1

4.1.1 What errors will occur in the following program segment?

```
if (ht > 72)
    printf("too tall\n")
printf("ok\n");
```

4.1.2 Will the following statement compile correctly? What is the effect of the statement?

```
if (sum < 100);
else
        printf("error, sum too large\n");
```

4.1.3 If **ht** is 90, what will the program conditional in problem 4.1.1 print, after the syntax is corrected?

4.1.4 Which of the following statements are not relational operators?

1. !=
2. >
3. <=
4. =>
5. =
6. >
7. !
8. ==
9. |
10. ||

      11. &

      12. &&

      13. !&&

      14. !<

4.1.5 List the precedence, from lowest to highest, of the following operators:

      1. +

      2. −

      3. *

      4. !

      5. /

4.1.6 Write a decision statement that will print the absolute value of a positive or negative number.

4.1.7 Explain the difference between the following two sets of instructions:

```
1.   if (x > 10)              2.  if (x > 10)
     {                                y = x + 1;
         y = x + 1;           else
         z = 5;                       z = 5;
     }
```

4.1.8 What is the output of the following program?

```
#include <stdio.h>
main()
{
    int
        i, j = 5;
    for (i = 9; (i > 0) && (j > 3); i=i-1)
    {
        j=j-1;
        printf("%d ",i);
    }
}
```

4.1.9 What will be printed by the following statements?

```
wt = 180;
if (wt > 100)
    printf("heavy enough!\n");
printf("weight has been tested");
```

4.1.10 What will be printed by the following statements?

```
wt = 180;
if (wt > 200)
    printf("heavy enough!\n");
printf("weight has been tested");
```

4.1.11 What will be printed by the following statements?

```
wt = 100;
if (wt > 200)
    printf("too heavy\n");
else
    printf("just right\n");
printf("weight tested\n");
```

4.2 REPETITION

SECTION TOPICS

For Construction

While Construction

Do Construction

This section discusses how loops are formed and controlled. The key words **do**, **while**, and **for** are explained. The concept of iteration is shown and used in many practical examples.

We learned from a brief discussion in Chapter 1 that a loop must consist of four parts, an initialization, data modification, the body of the loop, and a check for termination. We also learned in Chapter 2 that loops are either pretest loops or posttest loops. We will examine the loop structure in detail in these sections.

For Construction

A special case of the pretest loop, whose structure is shown in Figure 4.2.1, is that of a **for** loop, or a *counter* loop.

Computer code for a simple example of a counter loop is shown in Figure 4.2.2. The output of this program is:

```
EGGEN
EGGEN
EGGEN
EGGEN
```

Figure 4.2.1 Looping Construct

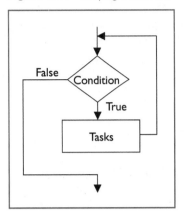

Now consider each part of the **for** statement. In C, the **for** construction contains three of the four parts of the loop construct in the **for** statement itself. The initialization, **index = 1;** is contained in the first part of the statement, the check for termination or continuation, **index < 5;** is next, and finally, the data modification, **index = index + 1** is contained in the last part of the **for** statement. In this example, the fourth part of the loop construct, the body of the loop, consists of the single **printf** statement. If there were to be many statements making up the body of the loop, they must be enclosed by braces { }. The variable **index** is called the *control variable* for the loop. Every loop must have one or more control variables. The conditional is tested the first time the loop is entered (which makes it a pretest loop), but the increment is done only after the loop has executed the first time. You can think of the conditional test being executed at the beginning of the loop and the increment being executed at the end of the loop. If the conditional never becomes false, an infinite loop occurs.

Figure 4.2.2 Iteration — for

```
#include <stdio.h>

main()
{
    int
        index;
    for (index = 1; index < 5; index = index + 1)
        printf("EGGEN \n");
}
```

From this example, we see that all loops must contain

```
loop initialization
data modification
body of loop
test for completion
```

If any of these four components does not exist, the loop will fail. Note that the termination condition is indeed a conditional and all of the comments in the preceding section discussing conditionals apply to this statement. The third statement, `index=index+1`, can be any statement that brings the loop control variable, `index`, closer to the termination condition, that is, the condition that makes the condition statement *false.* Consider Figure 4.2.3 as another example. The output produced by the program in this figure is:

```
count = 5
count = 4
count = 3
count = 2
count = 1
```

Notice that the index variable can be used within the loop body, but should not be modified by statements in the loop body. Some unusual effects can be obtained if we inadvertently change our `index` control variable. Also, the loop control `index` can count up, count down, or be modified in any manner consistent with the terminating condition and the desire of the programmer. What is wrong with the loop in Figure 4.2.4?

If you answered that the loop would take a long time to finish, you are correct. The `index` variable starts at 0, which is less than 5, and

Figure 4.2.3   Pretest Loop — for Construction

```
#include <stdio.h>
main()
{
    int
        index;

    for (index = 5; index > 0; index = index - 1)
    {
        printf("count = %d\n",index);
    }
}
```

Figure 4.2.4   Loop Never Ending

```c
#include <stdio.h>

main()
{
    int
        index;
    for (index = 0; index < 5; index = index - 1)
        printf("count = %d\n",index);
}
```

counts backwards. The terminating condition is never satisfied since the **index** is always less than 5. The computer does not realize there is a problem—it just continues to execute the program until the user enters a ^**c** (control-c) to kill the execution of the program. What is wrong with the loop in Figure 4.2.5?

Recognizing that the loop is a pretest loop, the test for termination is checked and satisfied at the outset, and the loop is never entered. The statements that make up the body of the loop are skipped in Figure 4.2.5.

Any variable can be used as loop control—**index** was chosen here—but often **i** or **j** is used depending on the data being represented by the variable. Remember, we always try to use names reflecting the purpose of the variable. The initialization, termination, and modification statements are just C statements. You can use any valid C statements provided they meet the conditions of the loop. That is, initialization and modification toward the terminating condition. The body of the loop can contain many instructions when enclosed in braces { }.

Also be aware that any statements can make up the body of the loop. In fact, **if** statements, other looping statements, or any valid statement

Figure 4.2.5   Loop Never Entered

```c
#include <stdio.h>

main()
{
    int
        index;

    for (index = 0; index > 5; index = index - 1)
        printf("count = %d\n",index);
}
```

from our programming language can make up the body of the loop. Study the example in Figure 4.2.6 carefully and see if you can determine the output of the program.

For each choice of **i** in the outer loop, the inner loop with **j** as index must execute to completion. When the variable **i** is modified and the program enters its body, the **j** loop must start over from the beginning and execute to completion again. The data modification, the third part of the **for** statement, may contain any suitable data modification statement. If you guessed that the output would be

```
i=   1        j=   2
i=   1        j=   5
i=   1        j=   8
i=   3        j=   2
i=   3        j=   5
i=   3        j=   8
i=   5        j=   2
i=   5        j=   5
i=   5        j=   8
i=   7        j=   2
i=   7        j=   5
i=   7        j=   8
i=   9        j=   2
i=   9        j=   5
i=   9        j=   8
```

you are right. Congratulations. Notice also that when we increment the variable **j** by three each time, we may jump past the termination value. It

Figure 4.2.6   Nested Loops

```
#include <stdio.h>

main()
{
    int
        i,j;
    for (i=1;i<10;i=i+2)
    {
        for (j=2;j<9;j=j+3)
        {
            printf("i=%3d j=%3d\n",i,j);
        }
    }
}
```

is not necessary to match this value exactly. In the example, 8 is still less than 9, but $11 = 8 + 3$ is not less than 9, so the inner loop terminates.

While Construction

The flow diagram for a **while** loop looks exactly like Figure 4.2.1. (It should—both are pretest loops!) The key word is different and how it is written changes compared to the **for** loop, but flow control remains the same. Consider the program shown in Figure 4.2.7.

To identify this as a pretest loop, we must be able to identify the various parts of the loop structure. The statement **cntrl = 1** is the initialization statement. The phrase **(cntrl < 5)** in the **while** statement itself is the check for termination, and the statement **cntrl = cntrl + 1;** in the body of the loop is the increment or data modification statement. When the loop is entered, the termination criterion is checked; the loop may not execute even once if the condition is false. The loop continues to execute provided the condition remains true. If the termination condition is not reached, the loop will execute forever. Infinite loops are more common with **while** than any other loop construct, so be careful. The output of the above program is:

```
count = 1
count = 2
count = 3
count = 4
```

The **while** loops are more common than **for** loops since a **while** condition can be used for a variety of applications beyond counting. Typically, a **for** loop is used when you know exactly the number of times a loop is to execute, such as stepping through each element of an array. All

Figure 4.2.7 Pretest Loop — While Construction

```c
#include <stdio.h>

main()
{
    int
        cntrl;

    cntrl = 1;
    while (cntrl < 5)
    {
        printf("count = %d\n",cntrl);
        cntrl = cntrl + 1;
    }
}
```

looping constructs can be substituted for one another, but each offers some convenience over the other, depending on the application.

Do Construction

The **do** loop works very much like the **while** except the check for termination is placed at the end of the loop rather than the beginning. Figure 4.2.8 shows the change in the flow diagram.

Figure 4.2.9 shows a program example using the **do** construct. The output of this program is:

```
count = 1
count = 2
count = 3
count = 4
```

The fundamental difference between the **for/while** loop construct and the **do while** loop construct is the placement of the check for termination of the loop. In the latter case, the loop will always execute at least once, since the check for termination is not performed until the end of the loop. Whereas the **while** loop described above may never execute, depending on the initial values of its variables, the **do** loop presented will execute at least once. Otherwise, the loops execute in very much the same way. As long as the conditional in the **while** statement remains true, the loop continues to execute. The **while** loop checks the conditional at the beginning of the loop whereas the **do** loop checks the condition at the end of the loop. Both loops execute as long as the condition in the **while** statement remains true.

Figure 4.2.8   Posttest Loop — Do Construction

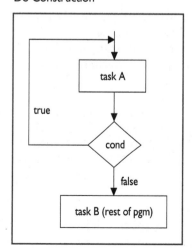

Figure 4.2.9   Do Loop

```
#include <stdio.h>

main()
{
    int
        cntrl;

    cntrl = 1;
    do
    {
        printf("count = %d\n",cntrl);
        cntrl=cntrl+1;
    }    while (cntrl < 5);
}
```

▶ **PROBLEM**   Consider the problem of presenting a table of driving times for individuals traveling at various speeds for various distances.

ANALYSIS   It is nice to know, when considering a trip, how long it will take to arrive at your destination. We wish to solve this problem by presenting a table of driving times for individuals traveling at speeds ranging from 50 to 75 miles per hour at increments of 5 miles per hour, for distances from 10 to 100 miles at increments of 10 miles. We know distance = rate × time, so if distance is given in miles, and rate is given in miles per hour, then time in hours will be given by dividing the appropriate distance by the rate of travel.

DESIGN   To solve this problem, we shall simply set up two appropriately structured nested loops, allow the loop indices to proceed over the desired ranges, and structure the output into an appropriate table of values. The tool to use is the **for** loop, since in each case we know exactly how many times the loops are to execute.

CODE   Consider the C code shown in Figure 4.2.10.

TEST   We tested the program by entering it in the UNIX environment, compiling it with the gcc compiler, and executing it. It produced the following output:

Rate --->	50	55	60	65	70	75
10 miles:	12.0	10.9	10.0	9.2	8.6	8.0
20 miles:	24.0	21.8	20.0	18.5	17.1	16.0
30 miles:	36.0	32.7	30.0	27.7	25.7	24.0
40 miles:	48.0	43.6	40.0	36.9	34.3	32.0

50 miles:	60.0	54.5	50.0	46.2	42.9	40.0
60 miles:	72.0	65.5	60.0	55.4	51.4	48.0
70 miles:	84.0	76.4	70.0	64.6	60.0	56.0
80 miles:	96.0	87.3	80.0	73.8	68.6	64.0
90 miles:	108.0	98.2	90.0	83.1	77.1	72.0
100 miles:	120.0	109.1	100.0	92.3	85.7	80.0

Notice that the **printf** in the inner loop has no newline character in its formatting string

```
for (rate = 50; rate <= 75; rate = rate + 5)
{
    printf (" %8.1f",distance/rate*60.0);
}
printf("\n");
```

Figure 4.2.10   Nested Loops

```
#include <stdio.h>

main()
{
    float
        distance,
        rate;
    printf("\n\n");
/* print the headers */
    printf(" Rate ---> ");
    for (rate = 50; rate <= 75; rate = rate + 5)
    {
        printf("%9.0f",rate);
    }
/* print a newline character and print the body of the table */
    printf("\n");
    for (distance = 10; distance <= 100; distance = distance + 10)
    {
        printf("%3.0f miles: ",distance);
        for (rate = 50; rate <= 75; rate = rate + 5)
        {
            printf(" %8.1f",distance/rate*60.0);
        }
        printf("\n");
    }
}
```

since we wish the elements of the table printed across the screen in rows. We finally print a newline character when the loop has completed. Then the outer loop index is incremented, and the inner loop begins its execution all over again. Since the calculation is presented as distance/rate*60.0, the driving times in the table are in minutes.

Note also that, as an advertisement for safe driving, the time saved by traveling a dangerous 75 miles per hour over a safer 60 miles per hour for a 20 mile commute to work or school is only 4 minutes! A 100-mile trip takes two hours at 50 miles per hour, but still takes an hour and 20 minutes at 75 miles per hour. Very little is gained by driving at high speeds.

This is a nice example of nested loops, since it shows that a considerable amount of calculation can be imposed on the computer using a minimum of computer code. Note that 60 values must be printed in order for the computer to complete the nested loops.

```
for (distance=10; distance <=100; distance=distance + 10)
{
    printf("%3.0f miles: ",distance);
    for (rate = 50; rate <= 75; rate = rate + 5)
    {
        printf(" %8.1f",distance/rate*60.0);
    }
    printf("\n");
}
```

Note also that nothing stops the programmer from nesting loops inside loops inside loops inside loops. Keep in mind, however, that the number of calculations that would have to be performed is the product of the number of times each loop executes.

► **PROBLEM**   Consider the problem of printing all of the permutations of four elements on the workstation screen.

ANALYSIS   A permutation of the elements will be a list of the numbers from 1 to 4 in some order with no repeats. The arrangement 4132 is one of the possible permutations of the numbers 1234. With a bit of thought, we can verify that there are four factorial possible permutations of these numbers, since four digits can be written in the first position, three digits can then occur in the second position, two digits in the third position, and finally one digit for the fourth position. Thus the total possible permutations are $4*3*2*1 = 4!$ choices.

DESIGN   To construct the permutations we shall use a nest of four **for** loops, each with indices running from 1 to 4. The only thing we must do is to make sure there are no repeats in the list, which prompts us to construct a complex decision statement—and leads us to the next section of this book where such things are discussed in detail.

CODE Figure 4.2.11 illustrates the permutations using four nested **for** loops.

TEST Entering and executing the program in Figure 4.2.11 in the C programming environment produces the following output:

```
1234
1243
1324
1342
1423
1432
2134
2143
2314
2341
2413
2431
3124
3142
3214
3241
3412
3421
```

Figure 4.2.11 Permutations

```c
#include <stdio.h>

main()
{
  int
    i,j,k,l;
  for (i=1;i<=4;i=i+1)
    for (j=1;j<=4;j=j+1)
      for (k=1;k<=4;k=k+1)
        for (l=1;l<=4;l=l+1)
          if (i != j && i != k && i != l && j != k && j != l && k != l)
            printf("%d%d%d%d\n",i,j,k,l);
}
```

```
4123
4132
4213
4231
4312
4321
```

Be aware that the **if** statement

```
if (i != j && i != k && i != 1 && j != k && j != 1 && k != 1)
```

was encountered 4*4*4 = 256 times in the execution of the program, but that the **print** statement was only executed 24 times, since in each of the other cases one or more of the indices had the same value, and hence was not one of the desired permutations causing the **if** to be false. To get an idea of the amount of work that would have to be done if loops were nested deeper, consider the problem of writing the permutation of ten numbers rather than four. The same technique could be used as that above, but don't do this unless you are mad at your computer. A nest of ten loops with indices running from one to ten would involve 10^{10} = 10,000,000,000 examinations of the **if** statement, assuming the program was constructed similarly to that presented in Figure 4.2.11.

Count the number of semicolons presented in the code of Figure 4.2.11.

```
for (i=1;i<=4;i=i+1)
  for (j=1;j<=4;j=j+1)
    for (k=1;k<=4;k=k+1)
      for (l=1;l<=4;l=l+1)
        if (i != j && i != k && i != l && j != k && j
            != l && k != l)
          printf("%d%d%d%d\n",i,j,k,l);
```

The only semicolon presented is at the very end of the loop structures, after the **printf** statement. In each case, only one entity is contained in each of the loops, and only one entity is contained in the **if** statement. In the case where only one thing is contained in a block no braces are needed to enclose the body of the loop or the body of the **if** statement. The sentence begins with the first **for** statement and ends with the final **printf** statement.

► Exercises 4.2

4.2.1　Given the following **for** loop, rewrite the code so that it executes exactly the same, but use a **while** loop.

```
for (i = 5; i > -5; i=i-1)
    x[i + 5] = i;
```

4.2.2 Rewrite the following code so that it contains a **do** loop rather than the **while** for loop control.

```
x = 4;
while (x > 0)
{
    some C instructions
    x=x-1;
}
```

4.2.3 Write the **for** loop that will compute the sum of an array of 10 elements.

4.2.4 Write the **while** loop that will compute the sum of an array of 10 elements.

4.2.5 Write the **do** loop that will compute the sum of an array of 10 elements.

4.2.6 How many times will the following **while** loop execute?

```
x = 0;
while (x < 5)
{
    x=x+1;
    printf("x = %d\n",x);
}
```

4.2.7 How many times will the following **do** loop execute?

```
x = 5;
do
{
    x=x+1;
    printf("x = %d\n",x);
} while(x < 0);
```

4.2.8 How many times will the following **do** loop execute?

```
x = 5;
do
{
    x=x+1;
    printf("x = %d\n",x);
} while(x > 0);
```

4.2.9 How many times will the following **do** loop execute?

```
x = 5;
do
```

```
    {
       x=x+1;
       printf("x = %d\n",x);

    } while(x < 10);
```

4.2.10 How many total times will the following **for** loops execute? What is the output?

```
for (i=1;i<10;i=i+2)
   for (j=13;j>0;j=j-3)
       printf("%d    %d\n",i,j);
```

4.2.11 Study the following program. What is the output? How many times will the loops execute?

```
#include <stdio.h>

main()
{
   int
      i,j;
   for (i=5;i<11;i=i+1)
   {
      j=1;
      while (j<i)
      {
          printf("i=%d j=%d\n",i,j);
          j=j+2;
      }
   }
}
```

4.3 COMPLEX DECISION MAKING

SECTION TOPICS

Compound if Using *and* and *or*

Multiway Selection

Nested Selection

This section includes concepts that allow multiple conditions to be tested in one or more decision statements. The use of logical *and, or,* and *not,* as well as nested **if**, **else if**, and **else** structures are shown.

Compound if Using *and* and *or*

What do **if**, **for**, **while**, and **do** statements all have in common? They all use a conditional to determine when and for how long instructions are executed. The **if** statement is effectively a two-way branch, executing certain instructions when the condition is true and other instructions when the condition is false. The looping instructions execute the body of the loop as long as the condition is true.

In addition to the relational operators previously shown, certain logical operations may be used to form more complex conditional expressions. Commonly referred to as *and* (whose symbol in C is **&&**), *or* (whose symbol in C is **||**), and *not* (whose symbol in C is **!**), these logical operators perform as they would in logical spoken English. That is, **if (x > 2)** asks if **x** is greater than 2, **if (!(x > 2))** asks if **x** is not greater than 2, which is the same as asking if **x** is less than or equal to 2. However, we must be very precise in describing their effect in a computing language. Specifically, if A and B are conditional expressions (like **x < 2**) whose value can only be true (1) or false (0), then the conditional expression **A && B** has value true or false depending on the components A and B, as illustrated in Figure 4.3.1.

The figure illustrates the fact that the only way the conditional expression **A && B** can be true is if both A and B are true. If someone said "Dr. Eggen is tall and handsome," and, in fact, Dr. Eggen is only 4 feet 8 inches tall, the statement would be false no matter how good looking Dr. Eggen is, because he is not tall!

Computing languages use the **&&** to determine values in an interval or group. For example, we might determine the age by writing

```
if ((age > 20) && (age < 40))
```

which will be true only when the **age** is a value between 21 and 39, inclusive.

To illustrate the conditional expression A *or* B, written **A || B** in the C programming language, consider Figure 4.3.2. This figure illustrates that if either one of A or B is true, the conditional expression **A || B** is true. Think about what this means in English. If a person said, "I am going dancing or I am going to the movies," and the person was seen at

Figure 4.3.1 Truth Table for Logical Operator *and*

A	B	A && B
T	T	T
T	F	F
F	T	F
F	F	F

Figure 4.3.2   Truth Table for Logical Operator *or*

A	B	A || B
T	T	T
T	F	T
F	T	T
F	F	F

the movies, you wouldn't call that person a liar. The statement is true, because one of the component parts was true. In this case A represents "I am going dancing" and B represents "I am going to the movies." Here B is true since the person was seen at the movies. On the other hand, if the person was seen at the basketball game, then the person could be considered a liar, because neither of the things the person promised—dancing or movies—was done. If neither of the parts of a compound *or* statement is true, the statement is false; if any component part is true, the statement is true.

You will use this logical operator to determine if one of a collection of conditions occurs—for example,

```
if ((color == 'g') || (color == 'r') || (color == 'b') . . .)
```

determines if the value of the variable color contains **g**, **r**, or **b**, which presumably might represent colors.

Figure 4.3.3 illustrates the unary logical operator *not* (**!** in the C programming language). As the figure shows, if the logical expression A is true then !A is false, and similarly if A is false then !A is true. We might use this to determine if **x** contains a value other than 5.

```
if (!(x == 5))   . . .
```

determines if **x** has some other value than 5. It is easier than asking

```
if ((x < 5) || (x > 5))   . . .
```

which has the same effect. Formation of conditional expressions using these relational and logical operators forms the basis of the decisions commonly made in programming languages. If, for example, we agree

Figure 4.3.3   Logical Operator *not*

A	!A
T	F
F	T

Figure 4.3.4   Formation of Conditionals in C

```
if (age > 20 && age < 70)
        printf("*** prime of life ***");
```

that less than 20 years old is too young, older than 70 is too old, and that between 20 and 70 is the prime of life, we might test for "prime of life" by the expression given in Figure 4.3.4.

Suppose `age` is 35; then `age > 20` is true and `age < 70` is also true. Thus, the *and* conditional is true and ***** prime of life ***** is displayed on the screen. Consider the operation of the conditional when age is 72. `Age > 20` is true, but `age < 70` is false so the conditional is false. Remember, the *and* conditional requires all components of the conditional to be true before the conditional is true. In this case, the `if` fails and the `printf` statement is not executed.

The astute reader might suggest that there is a possible difficulty with the above conditional expression. Specifically, since three operators are present (`>`, `&&`, `<`) in the expression, which operator is to be executed first? Are we to make the comparisons greater than and less than first, or are we to attempt to execute the *and* first? Or, should we execute them in order from left to right? Or perhaps right to left? Apparently it is necessary to make some decisions concerning precedence of operations. Before we are specific about this, the reader should be aware that the order of operations can always be modified by the inclusion of parentheses in the conditional expressions. If we wish to be sure, the inclusion of parentheses for readability and clarity is always advised. The above expression could be written

```
if ((age > 20) && (age < 70))
```

allowing no confusion related to the order in which the operations will be executed. Study Figure 4.3.5 and refer to it often when a potential difficulty with order of operations arises. Operators are listed in order of execution, with highest order expressions listed at the top of the figure.

There are additional C operators that have not been discussed which could be added to this figure. For the time being, however, these operators are the ones necessary for most programming needs. So, parentheses have the highest priority, with unary +, -, and ! executed first. The left to right or right to left in the Figure 4.3.5 determines the direction from which the expression will be evaluated. For example,

```
x = y + z - w
```

causes the operations + done first, then - second. This is left-to-right

Figure 4.3.5 Precedence Classes, Order of Operations

OPERATION	SYMBOL			ORDER
Parenthesis	(	)		Left to right
Unary +, −, !	+x,	−x,	! x	Right to left
Multiplication, division, modulus	*	/	%	Left to right
Addition, subtraction	+	−		Left to right
Less, greater, less or equal, greater or equal	< >=	>	<=	Left to right
Equal, not equal	==	!=		Left to right
And	&&			Left to right
Or	| |			Left to right
Assignment	=			Right to left

evaluation. Followed by the assignment, =, which is done right to left. Consider also the following statement, which assigns 2 to all of **x**, **y** and **z**:

```
x = y = z = 2;
```

The statement is executed by first assigning **2** to **z**, then to **y**, then to **x**; a right to left order. As a last example, consider Figure 4.3.6.

What will be printed? The value of **y** is initially **2**. The statement **x = !-y** assigns a value to **x**. The unary operators are evaluated right to left, so **y** is first negated, then the logical *not* operator is applied and the result assigned to **x**. Since nonzero integers are true in C, a negative 2 is considered true, so to negate this value means assign false to **x**. We know that false is represented as 0, so 0 is assigned to **x** and also printed.

Suppose we need to recognize ages between 25 and 30 and names that start with "A." The decision might be useful in a program written to

Figure 4.3.6 Precedence Example

```
#include <stdio.h>

main()
{
    int
        y = 2;
    int
        x;
    x = !-y;
    printf("x = %d\n",x);
}
```

recognize young people whose names occur early in the alphabet. These names might be needed for computing a density distribution of the population. The following `if` statement will test for the condition.

```
if ((age >=25) && (age <=30) && (name[0] == 'A'))
    printf("YES !!!\n");
```

We recall that Chapter 3 discussed the storage of strings as members of an array. We can access the individual members in an array of characters in the same way we access integer array elements. Thus, to see if a name starts with an "A" we need look in the first position, in this case `name[0]`, remember arrays in C start at 0. When age contains a 28, for example, and name contains "ALLEN," the `if` statement will succeed and the `printf` will execute. Therefore, `age >=25` is true, `age <=30` is true, and `name[0] = 'A'` is also true; true and true and true is true so the `if` succeeds. On the other hand, consider what the case will be if age is 24 and name is "ALLEN." Then `age >=25` is false, so the compound statement is false and the `printf` will not execute; false and true and true is false. For that matter, all components must be true in an *and* statement for the complete statement to be true.

Now, suppose we want ages between 25 and 30 or people whose name begins with "A"—one or the other. The following statement will provide the desired result.

```
if ((age >=25) && (age <=30) || (name[0] == 'A'))
    printf("YES !!!\n");
```

Which statements get executed first, those connected by *and*, `&&`, or those connected by *or*, `||`? Recall that the precedence indicates that *and* is done before *or*. Thus, the statement will be evaluated as

```
if (((age >=25) && (age <=30)) || (name[0] == 'A'))
```

The `&&` will then be evaluated yielding true or false, which will then be considered with the `||`. Suppose `age` was 28. Both comparisons with `age` will be true so the *and* is true. If `name` holds "Bagnoli," `name[0] == 'A'` will be false. True or false yields true so the `if` succeeds and the `printf` will execute.

Multiway Selection

Suppose we needed to group ages, that is, an age between 0 and 20 should be counted in group one, between 21 and 40 as group two, between 41 and 60 in group three, and between 61 and 80 as group four, etc. The goal is to read a set of integers representing ages and count the number of ages that fall in each group. A compound conditional clearly will not do the job since it will not differentiate between that portion which succeeds. For example, the statement

Figure 4.3.7   Multiway Selection

```
if ((age > 0) && (age <= 20))
    group1=group1+1;
else if ((age > 20) && (age <= 40))
    group2=group2+1;
else if ((age > 40) && (age <= 60))
    group3=group3+1;
else if ((age > 60) && (age <= 80))
    group4=group4+1;
else if ((age > 80) && (age <= 100))
    group5=group5+1;
else
    group6=group6+1;
/*if an age isn't in any other group, it is in group six */
```

```
if ((age>0) && (age<=20)) || ((age>20) && (age <=40))...
```

asks the right question but does not allow the computer to know in which group the age actually belongs. Figure 4.3.7 contains a series of nested **if**s that will provide the correct solution. In this figure, only one of the **if** or **else if**s will succeed, thereby counting a particular age in only one group. The **if** statement with its corresponding **else** can be "strung out" in this manner as long as necessary. There is really nothing magic about this **else if** construction. It merely allows the programmer to perform a multiway selection. Note that if the variable age does in fact contain a value between 0 and 20, then the first **if** is true, and none of the other **if** statements are seen.

Nested Selection

Suppose we want to determine if a name is in the first half of the alphabet or the second half in each age group of the example in Figure 4.3.7. The data now consists of an age and a corresponding name. For each age we are interested in determining if the name is in the first half of the alphabet or the second. So **25 Bagnoli** will count in the group between 21 and 40 and also in the first half of the alphabet for the name. Figure 4.3.8 shows the C instructions to count the number in each category.

The example in Figure 4.3.8 shows that **if** statements can exist inside other **if** statements. This nesting process can be used whenever there is a desire to answer a question after a previous question has been

Figure 4.3.8 Nested if and Corresponding else if

```
/* counts number of names in first half of the alphabet in each age group */
   if ((age > 0) && (age <= 20))
   {
      if (name[0] < 'm')
         first_half_name_grp1=first_half_name_grp1+1;
      else
         second_half_name_grp1=second_half_name_grp1+1;
      age_group1=age_group1+1;
   }
   else if ((age > 20) && (age <= 40))
   {
      if (name[0] < 'm')
         first_half_name_grp2=first_half_name_grp2+1;
      else
         second_half_name_grp2=second_half_name_grp2+1;
      age_group2=age_group2+1;
   }
   else if ((age > 40) && (age <= 60))
   {
      if (name[0] < 'm')
         first_half_name_grp3=first_half_name_grp3+1;
      else
         second_half_name_grp3=second_half_name_grp3+1;
      age_group3=age_group3+1;
   }
   else if ((age > 60) && (age <= 80))
   {
      if (name[0] < 'm')
         first_half_name_grp4=first_half_name_grp4+1;
      else
         second_half_name_grp4=second_half_name_grp4+1;
      age_group4=age_group4+1;
   }
   else if ((age > 80) && (age <= 100))
   {
      if (name[0] < 'm')
         first_half_name_grp5=first_half_name_grp5+1;
      else
```

(continued)

Figure 4.3.8   Nested if and Corresponding else if *(continued)*

```
        second_half_name_grp5=second_half_name_grp5+1;
    age_group5=age_group5+1;
}
else
{
    if (name[0] < 'm')
        first_half_name_grp6=first_half_name_grp6+1;
    else
        second_half_name_grp6=second_half_name_grp6+1;
    age_group6=age_group6+1;
    /*if an age isn't in any other group, it is in group six*/
}
```

asked. The process of continuing to refine and make more precise decisions can be carried out indefinitely—`if` statements can be nested virtually as deeply as desired, but this is dependent on the computer system used.

When using the `if . . . else . . .` statements, what `if` does the `else` belong to? Consider Figure 4.3.9. Does the else statement belong to the first `if`, `if (one)`, or the second `if, if (two)`? Remember since the indentation is used only for our readability, the computer is not influenced by the location of instructions. The rule to follow in these cases is that the `else` is paired with the closest `if`. So, the `else` statement will be executed when the `if (two)` is false and `if (one)` is true. Whenever the `if (one)` is false, the `if (two)` and its associated `else` will all be skipped since they are executed only when the initial `if, if (one)`, is true. We recommend that the programmer not only indent appropriately,

Figure 4.3.9   Nested if with else

```
if (one)
    if (two)
    {
        do some stuff
    }
    else
    {
        do some other stuff
    }
```

but also include braces { } to delimit blocks even when such are not necessary. Whatever we can do to make the code understandable to the programmer is good programming practice. We must learn to make our lives as programmers as easy as we can.

Suppose we wanted the **else { do some other stuff }** to be associated with the first **if**. How would it be written? Figure 4.3.10 shows us. The first **else** is associated with the **if (two)** and does nothing, allowing the last **else** to be associated with the first **if** as desired. Note that the indentation of the instructions assists in reading the program, and the addition of the braces enhances our understanding. The computer (C compiler) does not understand nor care about indentation or additional braces. These are added strictly for us, the programmers, who must understand such things.

Consider the program in Figure 4.3.11 as an additional example. Which statement will print? If you answered **yippee**, you are correct. The value of **one** is 1, which is true. The first **if** succeeds. The value of **two** is 0, which is false so the **else** is executed testing the **if (three)**. **Three** is 0, which is false, so its corresponding **else** is executed, causing **yippee** to display. Figure 4.3.11 shows the nesting of **if**s is allowed in essentially any manner desired. Remember, the **else** is always associated with the closest **if**. In Figure 4.3.12 we present again the code for the decision problem of Figure 4.3.11, but with added braces and exaggerated indentation. While all of this may not be necessary, we recommend doing whatever it takes to enhance understanding the decision structure.

Examining the structure in Figure 4.3.12 makes it easier for us to decide why **yippee** is displayed. Clearly **this is tough!** is not printed

Figure 4.3.10 Nested if with Multiple else

```
if (one)
{
    if (two)
    {
      do some stuff
    }
    else;
}
else
{
    do some other stuff
}
```

Figure 4.3.11   Nested if Check

```c
#include <stdio.h>

main()
{
    int
            one = 1,
            two = 0,
            three = 0;
    if (one)
        if (two)
        {
            printf("yes");
        }
        else if (three)
        {
            printf("yipe");
        }
        else
        {
            printf("yippee");
        }
    else
    {
        printf("this is tough!");
    }
}
```

since **(one)** is true. Since **(two)** is false, **yes** is not displayed. Since **(three)** is also false, **yipe** is not printed. The alternative is **yippee**, which is displayed.

▶ Exercises 4.3

4.3.1   What is the output of the following program segment?

```c
ht = 72;
low_ceiling = 0;
if ((ht > 65) && (!low_ceiling))
    printf("head ok!\n");
else
    printf("head might get bumped\n");
```

Figure 4.3.12   Fully Structured Nested if

```c
#include <stdio.h>
main()
{
   int
      one = 1,
      two = 0,
      three = 0;
   if (one)
   {
      if (two)
      {
         printf("yes\n");
      }
      else
      {
         if (three)
         {
            printf("yipe\n");
         }
         else
         {
            printf("yippee\n");
         }
      }
   }
   else
   {
      printf("this is tough!\n");
   }
}
```

4.3.2   What is the output of the following program segment?

```c
temp = 0;
snow = 10;
if ((temp < 0) && (snow > 9))
   printf("it is cold and lots of snow!\n");
else if (temp < 0)
   printf("it is cold!\n");
else if (snow > 9)
   printf("lots of snow\n");
else
   printf("not cold or snowy\n");
```

4.3.3   What is the output of the following program segment?

```
age = 55;
if (age < 20)
    printf("young");
else if (age < 40)
    printf("prime");
else if (age < 60)
    printf("middle age");
else
    printf("old");
```

4.3.4   Determine the value of the following conditional expressions. Write your results as true or false. Remember that 0 is false and any other number is considered true.

```
size = 10;
sum = 150;
value = 'G';
cont = 0;
flag = 1;
halt = 0;
test = 1;
```

1. `(size <= 12)`
2. `((size > 10) || (sum >= 150))`
3. `((size > 10) && (sum >= 150))`
4. `((size > 5) || (sum >= 150))`
5. `((size > 5) && (sum >= 150))`
6. `((cont) && (value > 'A'))`
7. `((flag) && (value > 'A'))`
8. `(flag || test)`
9. `(sum - size)`
10. `(!halt && sum < 100 || test)`
11. `((!halt && sum < 100) || test)`
12. `(!halt && (sum < 100 || test))`

4.3.5   What is the error in the following statement?

```
if (age > 80 | < 90)
    printf("not old, but getting there\n");
```

4.3.6   Write a conditional statement that will assign to the character variable **grade** a `'B'` if the **average** is between **79.5** and **89.5**.

4.3.7 Transform the following if . . . else . . . construct to a fully braced and nested if construct similar to that presented in Figure 4.3.12. (The authors realize this question will soon be dated!)

```
if (cpu == 8088)
    printf("you have a pc with an 8 bit bus and 16 bit
            registers\n");
else if (cpu == 80286)
    printf("you have an AT with a 16 bit bus and 16 bit
            registers\n");
else if (cpu == 80386 || cpu == 80486)
    printf("you have a ps2 model 170 or 190 with a 32 bit
            bus and 32 bit registers\n");
else if (cpu == 68000)
    printf("you have a MacClassic with a 16 bit bus and
            32 bit registers\n");
else if (cpu == 68020)
    printf("you have a MacLc with a 32 bit bus and 32 bit
            registers\n");
else if (cpu == 68030)
    printf("you have a MacSE30 with a 32 bit bus and 32
            bit registers\n");
else printf("you have garbage :-) \n");
```

4.3.8 Write a compound decision statement that will determine the validity of "exclusive or." That is, a body of code is to be executed if one or the other expression is true, but not both.

4.3.9 Explain the difference in the following two sets of instructions:

```
1. if ((x > 10) && (y < 20))        2. if (x > 10)
        z = z * m;                          if (y < 20)
    else                                        z = z * m;
        y = y + m;                      else
                                            y = y + m;
```

4.3.10 Explain the difference in the following two sets of instructions:

```
1. if (x > 10)                      2. if (x > 10)
        z = z * m;                          z = z * m;
    if (y < 0)                      else if (y < 0)
        p = p * 5;                          p = p * 5;
```

4.3.11 When will the following decision statement be true?

```
if ((age < 20) && (age > 40))  . . .
```

4.4 SORTING AND SEARCHING

SECTION TOPICS

Sorting

Searching

Programming Tips

Indenting

Consider the work involved in looking up a phone number if the names were entered in random order. You would have to start at the beginning and look at each name to determine the number desired. A *sequential search* through the phone book would have to be performed. At times sequential search is the only technique available for the computer to retrieve data. However, if the data can be placed in a known order, searching can proceed much faster. The names in the phone book are alphabetized. Thus, when seeking "Anderson" you look near the beginning, "Neuman" near the middle, and "Wallace" near the end of the book. The search proceeds much faster since many data (names) can be eliminated from consideration by one search query. Placing names in a particular order is called *sorting*. Seeking information, like a particular name in a phone book, is called *searching*. These are the subjects of this section. Computer science professionals have spent considerable time and effort studying sorting and searching algorithms. Sorting and searching problems provide practical examples of array usage, loops, and selection statements — the computing concepts presented in this and preceding chapters.

Sorting

Suppose we have a list of integers that are to be ordered. These integers might represent weights or heights of people and we might be interested in computing the smallest, the largest, and the height in the middle. There are sophisticated algorithms to efficiently solve these problems, but ordering the data allows the computer to answer these questions rather easily. The meaning of the data is really unimportant to us; we are interested in demonstrating the concept of sorting. For the purpose of demonstrating the concept, we will use a pseudorandom-number generator to create the data. The computer is not capable of generating pure random numbers, but can generate numbers that appear to be in random order, thus the name pseudorandom-number generator. In C this number

Figure 4.4.1 Rand

```
/* this program will demonstrate the use of the built
        in function rand for generating pseudo random
        numbers    */

#include <stdio.h>
main()
{
   int
      i;
   for (i = 0; i < 5; i=i+1)     /* random numbers are
         generated by rand */
      printf("number %d = %d\n",i,rand());
   return(0);
}
```

generator is called the by the **rand** function as demonstrated in Figure 4.4.1. Possible output from this program is

```
number 0 = 346
number 1 = 130
number 2 = 10982
number 3 = 1090
number 4 = 11656
```

This output was generated on a personal computer running Borland's Turbo C++. You will get similar results if you run on another type of computer, including UNIX-based machines.

▶ **PROBLEM** Sort a collection of integers into descending order using the bubble sort algorithm.

ANALYSIS The bubble sort algorithm works by successively comparing adjacent elements in an array of data items, interchanging the items that are not in order. We continue to compare adjacent items on successive passes through the array until no data movements are made, in which case the data items are all pairwise in order, which implies the entire data set is in order.

DESIGN For our implementation of the algorithm, we shall force the computer to do some (possibly) unnecessary comparisons. Forcing the computer to perform as many comparisons as are contained in the program in Figure 4.4.2 will ensure that the data are in order when the algorithm is com-

Figure 4.4.2 Bubble Sort

```c
#include <stdio.h>
main()
{
    int
        numbers[10], /* remember -- indices 0 through 9 */
        i,j,k,tmp;

    printf("\nthe original numbers are:\n");
    for (i = 0; i < 10; i=i+1)
    {
        /*generate random numbers to sort*/
        numbers[i] = rand();
        printf(" %d ",numbers[i]);
    }
    printf("\n\n");

    /* the numbers now reside in the numbers array */
    /* lets begin the sort */

    for (i = 0; i < 10; i=i+1)
    {
        for (j = 0; j < 9; j=j+1)
        {
            if (numbers[j] < numbers[j+1])
            {
                tmp = numbers[j];
                numbers[j] = numbers[j+1];
                numbers[j+1] = tmp;
            }
        }
    }
    /* the numbers are now sorted, let's see them */
    printf("the sorted numbers are:\n");
    for (i = 0; i < 10; i=i+1)
    {
        printf(" %d ",numbers[i]);
    }
    printf("\n\n");
}
```

plete. Since each pass through the array forces at least one data item into its correct position (verify!), the program is making unnecessary comparisons. Enhancements and refinements to this algorithm are suggested in the exercises.

CODE   The complete C code for the bubble sort algorithm is found in Figure 4.4.2.

TEST   The output of Figure 4.4.2 is (the actual numbers you have will vary depending on the computer you use):

```
the original numbers are:
 16838 5758 10113 17515 31051 5627 23010 7419 16212 4086
the sorted numbers are:
 31051 23010 17515 16838 16212 10113 7419 5758 5627 4086
```

Figure 4.4.3 shows the first pass through the data. Notice how the smaller numbers are "bubbling" to the right of the array as the program works through the set of numbers. The data presented in Figure 4.4.3 represent only one execution of the inner loop. Of course, since the outer loop has only executed once, the array is not (necessarily) sorted.

To thoroughly understand the operation of the program, you should sit down with pencil and paper, pretend you are the computer, and execute the program. Write down the value of each variable and show yourself how the array changes as a result of exchanges. When you can accomplish this task, you will thoroughly understand how arrays work, how indexing works, how loops work, and consequently how sorting is accomplished.

Figure 4.4.4 shows each completed successive pass. If you compare Figure 4.4.3 with Figure 4.4.4, each line of Figure 4.4.4 represents a complete Figure 4.4.3. We would need nine Figure 4.4.3's to show results similar to those in Figure 4.4.4.

Figure 4.4.3   First Pass of Bubble Sort

16838	5758	10113	17515	31051	5627	23010	7419	16212	4086
16838	5758	10113	17515	31051	5627	23010	7419	16212	4086
16838	10113	5758	17515	31051	5627	23010	7419	16212	4086
16838	10113	17515	5758	31051	5627	23010	7419	16212	4086
16838	10113	17515	31051	5758	5627	23010	7419	16212	4086
16838	10113	17515	31051	5758	5627	23010	7419	16212	4086
16838	10113	17515	31051	5758	23010	5627	7419	16212	4086
16838	10113	17515	31051	5758	23010	7419	5627	16212	4086
16838	10113	17515	31051	5758	23010	7419	16212	5627	4086

Figure 4.4.4 Successive Passes of Bubble Sort

```
the original numbers are:
 16838 5758 10113 17515 31051 5627 23010 7419 16212 4086

pass 0
 16838 10113 17515 31051 5758 23010 7419 16212 5627 4086
(smallest guaranteed correctly positioned)
pass 1
 16838 17515 31051 10113 23010 7419 16212 5758 5627 4086
(next smallest guaranteed correctly positioned)
pass 2
 17515 31051 16838 23010 10113 16212 7419 5758 5627 4086
(next smallest guaranteed correctly positioned)
pass 3
 31051 17515 23010 16838 16212 10113 7419 5758 5627 4086
(next smallest guaranteed correctly positioned)
pass 4
 31051 23010 17515 16838 16212 10113 7419 5758 5627 4086
(next smallest guaranteed correctly positioned)
pass 5
 31051 23010 17515 16838 16212 10113 7419 5758 5627 4086
(next smallest guaranteed correctly positioned)
pass 6
 31051 23010 17515 16838 16212 10113 7419 5758 5627 4086
(next smallest guaranteed correctly positioned)
pass 7
 31051 23010 17515 16838 16212 10113 7419 5758 5627 4086
(next smallest guaranteed correctly positioned)
pass 8
 31051 23010 17515 16838 16212 10113 7419 5758 5627 4086
(next smallest guaranteed correctly positioned)
pass 9
 31051 23010 17515 16838 16212 10113 7419 5758 5627 4086
(next smallest guaranteed correctly positioned)
the sorted numbers are:
 31051 23010 17515 16838 16212 10113 7419 5758 5627 4086
```

This particular implementation of the bubble sort required nine passes through ten numbers to complete the sort. Nine passes is almost the number of numbers to be sorted; bubble sort will make **n-1** passes for **n** numbers. Thus, it is said that bubble sort is an **n**^{2} sort where **n** is the number of numbers. That is, the amount of work the computer must do to sort **n** numbers is approximately **n²**. So, if there are ten numbers, it takes bubble sort about 100 comparisons to complete the sort (ten passes through ten numbers). If we use a comparison as a measure of work, it takes bubble sort **n²** amount of work to sort the numbers. We will see that there are more efficient sorting algorithms.

▶ **PROBLEM** Sort an array of **n** numbers using an exchange sort.

ANALYSIS The exchange sort examines the array to find the smallest number, moves it into the correct position, then examines the remainder of the list, finding the second-smallest number, moves it into position, and so on. In each case, the smallest number found "so far" is moved into position. Like the bubble sort, this algorithm may involve a considerable amount of data movement.

DESIGN The process described may be accomplished with two nested loops. The outer loop will examine each of the positions, and the inner loop will correctly position the element. We note that the exchange sort does about the same amount of work as bubble sort in a worst case. Each algorithm will have to perform **n** passes through **n** data items, indicating that both algorithms are order **n**-squared algorithms.

CODE The complete C code for the exchange sort is in Figure 4.4.5.

TEST The output of Figure 4.4.5 is shown below.

```
the original numbers are:
 16838 5758 10113 17515 31051 5627 23010 7419 16212 4086

the sorted numbers are:
 31051 23010 17515 16838 16212 10113 7419 5758 5627 4086
```

We see that the results of the program in Figure 4.4.5 are the same as for the bubble sort. This, of course, should cause us no surprise since the goal of all sorting techniques is to put the data in order. You might ask then, "Why do we bother with different sorts?" The answer to the question is that some sorts run faster than others (do less work), and other sorts are easier to program. Also, the examples provided in this text allow you to see that there is more than just one way to solve a problem. There are several sorting routines—each has certain advantages over the other. For example, you will study a sort called quicksort, which in general performs very well. That is, it is easy to program and does only $n \log_2 n$ amount of work. But, if the data is already sorted, quicksort requires **n²** amount of work. If the possibility exists of quicksort receiving sorted data, one might choose heapsort, which is slightly less efficient, but always does $n \log_2 n$ amount of work.

Figure 4.4.5 Exchange Sort

```c
/* this program will demonstrate the exchange sort using
   rand for generating pseudo random numbers   */
#include <stdio.h>
main()
{
   int
      numbers[10],
      i,j,tmp;

   printf("\nthe original numbers are:\n");
   for (i = 0; i < 10; i=i+1)
   {
      numbers[i] = rand();
      printf(" %d ",numbers[i]);
   }
   printf("\n\n");

   /* the numbers now reside in the numbers array */

   for (i = 0; i < 9; i=i+1)
   {
      for (j = i+1; j < 10; j=j+1)
      {
         if (numbers[i] < numbers[j])
         {
            tmp = numbers[j];
            numbers[j] = numbers[i];
            numbers[i] = tmp;
         }
      }
   }
   /* the numbers are now sorted, let's see them */
   printf("the sorted numbers are:\n");
   for (i = 0; i < 10; i=i+1)
      printf(" %d ",numbers[i]);
   printf("\n\n");

   return(0); /* some compilers request a return statement in
                 all functions, even main */
}
```

Figure 4.4.6 First Pass of Exchange Sort

```
the original numbers are:
  16838    5758    10113    17515    31051    5627    23010    7419    16212    4086

  16838    5758    10113    17515    31051    5627    23010    7419    16212    4086
  16838    5758    10113    17515    31051    5627    23010    7419    16212    4086
  16838    5758    10113    17515    31051    5627    23010    7419    16212    4086
  17515    5758    10113    16838    31051    5627    23010    7419    16212    4086
  31051    5758    10113    16838    17515    5627    23010    7419    16212    4086
  31051    5758    10113    16838    17515    5627    23010    7419    16212    4086
  31051    5758    10113    16838    17515    5627    23010    7419    16212    4086
  31051    5758    10113    16838    17515    5627    23010    7419    16212    4086
  31051    5758    10113    16838    17515    5627    23010    7419    16212    4086
```

Let us get back to exchange sort. Figure 4.4.6 shows the workings of the first pass. The goal of pass one is to correctly place the first number. To do this the program compares the number in position 0 with that in position 1 and exchanges if necessary. Then, numbers in positions 0 and 2 are compared, numbers in positions 0 and 3, 0 and 4, etc.; each time exchanging if necessary. When the first pass is complete we have the largest number in position 0. In pass two the number in position 1 will be compared to each successive position, thus placing the second largest number in its correct position, position 1. After nine passes the data will be sorted. This is different than the bubble sort, where exchange sort compares numbers in positions 0 and 1, 0 and 2, 0 and 3, etc. The bubble sort compared numbers in positions 0 and 1, 1 and 2, 2 and 3, etc. Figure 4.4.7 shows the state of the data array after each successive pass using exchange sort.

These examples demonstrate two of the simpler sorts to program. Both require about n^2 amount of work—they are not the most efficient sorts around. However, they are easy to program and if there is not much data or if execution time is not a factor, they may be the sorts of choice.

Searching

This section addresses the problem of finding a particular number from a list of numbers. Two searches will be demonstrated: sequential search and binary search.

▶ **PROBLEM**   Perform a sequential search on an array of data to determine the position of a specified data item.

Figure 4.4.7   Successive Passes of Exchange Sort

```
the original numbers are:
  16838     5758    10113    17515    31051     5627    23010     7419    16212     4086


pass 0
  31051     5758    10113    16838    17515     5627    23010     7419    16212     4086
pass 1
  31051    23010     5758    10113    16838     5627    17515     7419    16212     4086
pass 2
  31051    23010    17515     5758    10113     5627    16838     7419    16212     4086
pass 3
  31051    23010    17515    16838     5758     5627    10113     7419    16212     4086
pass 4
  31051    23010    17515    16838    16212     5627     5758     7419    10113     4086
pass 5
  31051    23010    17515    16838    16212    10113     5627     5758     7419     4086
pass 6
  31051    23010    17515    16838    16212    10113     7419     5627     5758     4086
pass 7
  31051    23010    17515    16838    16212    10113     7419     5758     5627     4086
pass 8
  31051    23010    17515    16838    16212    10113     7419     5758     5627     4086

the sorted numbers are:
  31051    23010    17515    16838    16212    10113     7419     5758     5627     4086
```

ANALYSIS   The word "sequential" implies that the searching activity will be performed in sequence. Searching sequentially implies looking at the first
data item, then the second, then the third, and so on until either the data
item is found, or we have looked at the entire list.

DESIGN   For our particular demonstration of the sequential search algorithm, we
shall

1. Fill an array with random integers.

2. Prompt the user to enter an integer.

3. Execute a loop to examine each of the elements of the array.

4. Report to the user whether the number was found in the
array.

CODE   The program that performs a sequential search is found in Figure 4.4.8.

Figure 4.4.8 Sequential Search

```c
#include <stdio.h>
main()
{
  int
    numbers[10],i,numb,found;

  printf("\nthe original numbers are:\n");
  for (i = 0; i < 10; i=i+1)
  {
    numbers[i] = rand();
    printf(" %d ",numbers[i]);
  }
  printf("\n\n");

   /*the numbers now reside in the number array */
   /*the search begins here */

  printf("Please enter desired number: ");
  scanf("%d",&numb);

  found = 0;
  i = 0;
  while ((i < 10) && (found != 1))
  {
    if (numbers[i] == numb) /* look at numbers[i] */
    {
      printf("the number has been found in position %d\n",i);
      found = 1;
    }
    i=i+1;
  }
  if (found != 1) printf("number not found\n");
}
```

TEST Repeated executions of the program code in Figure 4.4.8 will produce output similar to the following:

```
the original numbers are:
16838 5758 10113 17515 31051 5627 23010 7419 16212 4086

Please enter desired number: 5758
the number has been found in position 1
```

A second execution is

```
the original numbers are:
16838 5758 10113 17515 31051 5627 23010 7419 16212 4086

Please enter desired number: 5759
number not found
```

An additional execution yields

```
the original numbers are:
16838 5758 10113 17515 31051 5627 23010 7419 16212 4086

Please enter desired number: 4086
the number has been found in position 9
```

The advantage of sequential search is that it is easy to program. Moreover, the sequential search algorithm does not require a sorted list. On the other hand, the number of numbers to be examined is about **n/2** (on the average, half the array will need to be checked) and in the worst case, **n** numbers (the complete array) will have to be examined. When the number desired is not in the array or is in the last position of the array, the program must look in every array position, thus comparing **n** numbers.

Note the use of the compound conditional in the **while** loop.

```
while ((i < 10) && (found != 1))
```

This statement allows us to exit the loop when we find the number, or when we have exhausted the list.

▶ **PROBLEM** Use a binary search algorithm to report the position of a desired data item.

ANALYSIS The binary search algorithm requires a sorted list. The object is to minimize the number of times we have to look into the array to find the given data item—this algorithm takes advantage of the fact that the list is sorted to minimize the number of looks into the array to find the number, or to determine that the number is not present in the array. Since the array is sorted, we may examine an element in the middle of the remaining array (initially the entire array). If the sought-for item is less than the middle item, the entire top half of the array may be discarded, since the desired element cannot lie in this region. If the sought-for item is greater than the middle item, the entire bottom half of the array may be discarded, since the desired element cannot lie in this region. Of course, if the middle item is the sought-for item, then the search stops.

DESIGN The idea is to use the fact the data is sorted to help locate the desired item. By looking at the middle number first, we divide the data into halves, one containing the number desired and the other not containing the number. Thus, with one comparison, we can eliminate half the numbers. With a straight sequential search, after one comparison we have eliminated only one number rather than half. A binary search will locate the desired number or determine if the number does not exist in at most $\log_2$ **n** number of comparisons, where **n** is the number of numbers. When compared to the straight sequential search of n comparisons, binary search offers a major improvement. Recall that sequential search required, in the worst case, the complete array "looked at" in order to determine a number is not present. Of course, nothing is free, and there is a price to pay for this increased retrieval efficiency realized by binary search. The array must first be sorted. Depending on the application, either sequential search or binary search might be best. If the data is to be searched only once, a sequential search might be just fine. However, if there will be several searches performed, the cost of first sorting the data and doing a binary search may be justified.

CODE   The binary search program is found in Figure 4.4.9.

TEST   The output from the program is:

```
looking in position 24
looking in position 11
looking in position 5
looking in position 8
looking in position 6
desired value 14 found in position 7
```

The goal of binary search is to report just the position of the desired number, but Figure 4.4.9 shows the positions inspected to help you understand its execution. Essentially, the program looks at the middle point of the array. If the desired element is smaller, it looks in the first half; if larger, it looks in the second half, assuming, of course, that the array is sorted in ascending order. This process of dividing the search space in two over and over again until the item is found allows the search to proceed very efficiently. In fact, when searching by doing comparisons, binary search is the best that can be done. It has been proven that no other search technique, when comparing keys, can do better than binary search.

The general technique represented by binary search is called "Divide and Conquer." The concept is one where the computer program accomplishes the job by dividing the primary task into smaller tasks until the solution is ultimately found. Not all problems can be solved by a divide-and-conquer technique, but the solution method is used in a variety of applications. This solution technique is studied in the computer science curriculum in courses such as analysis of algorithms and artificial intelligence.

Figure 4.4.9   Binary Search

```c
/* this program demonstrates the binary search concept */
#include <stdio.h>
#define DESIRED_VAL 14    /* the value being sought                  */
#define ARR_SIZE 50       /* size of the search space                */

main()
{
   int
      arr[ARR_SIZE],   /* the array of numbers to search             */
      i,j,             /* loop control variables                     */
      lower,
      upper,
      middle;          /* the interval and mid point considered      */

   for (i = 0; i < ARR_SIZE; i=i+1) /* generate numbers for the array */
      arr[i] = 2*i;    /* the numbers must be ordered so put these in  */
   lower = 0;
   upper = ARR_SIZE - 1;
   middle = (upper - lower) / 2;

   while((arr[middle] != DESIRED_VAL) && (lower <= upper))
   {
      printf("looking in position %d\n",middle);
      if (arr[middle] < DESIRED_VAL)
      {
         lower = middle + 1;
         middle = (upper - lower) / 2 + lower;
      }
      else
      {
         upper = middle - 1;
         middle = (upper - lower) / 2 + lower;
      }
   }

   if (arr[middle] == DESIRED_VAL)
      printf("desired value %d found in position %d\n",
      DESIRED_VAL,middle);
   else
      printf("desired value %d not in array\n", DESIRED_VAL);
   return(0);
}
```

Sorting techniques are fundamental to many problems solved on the computer. Sorting has been studied in depth for years and a wide variety of sorting techniques exists. In future classes you will learn many of the popular sorting methods. The sorts we examined run in approximately n^2 time. The better sorts such as heap sort, quicksort, tree sort, and merge sort run in $n*\log_2(n)$. In fact, when sorting by comparison of keys, $n*\log_2(n)$ sorting time is the best that can be done. Radix sort, which does not compare keys, can surpass this time, but at another time radix sort might do poorly. Radix sort is very dependent on the nature of the data. These are just some of the topics studied by computer scientists and topics that you learn as you progress in your education.

Programming Tips

We can construct programs that look like a hodge-podge of statements and variable names. These programs will be difficult to understand and modify by you and people who have to deal with your code in the future. Instead, we strive for clearly written programs that use variable names reflecting their purpose, indentation reflecting the coded blocks, and appropriate use of white space (blank lines, spaces between words, etc.). So, like writing novels or computer books, we must strive to make our programs the most readable we can. We do this with white space, indentation, use of good names, use of modular construction, and structured programming style.

When solving a problem using the computer, you first strive for thorough understanding of the problem itself. Then formalize a solution of the problem using the features supported by computers as discussed in the earlier chapters of this book. After the solution is well designed, implement it in the language of choice and test the implementation on the computer. After all of these steps have been accomplished, the real work begins. Program maintenance and modification—adapting it to new demands—are where businesses and scientific application programmers spend most of their programming effort. Virtually everyone begins their career in computing by doing program maintenance—that is, taking someone else's program and changing it to meet new demands. Thus, when constructing a program you must try to make the code as clear as possible. "Clever" code that runs fast is generally less desirable than code that is easy to understand.

Indenting

When using conditionals, you should always indent the body of the conditional. Consider the following example, which records characteristics about races for a census bureau.

```
if (race == 'w')
{
    number_of_white=number_of_white+1;
    total_number_counted=total_number_counted+1;
    per_cent = number_of_white/total_number_counted*100;
}
else if (race == 'b')
{
    number_of_black=number_of_black+1;
    total_number_counted=total_number_counted+1;
    per_cent = number_of_black/total_number_counted*100;
}
else if (race == 'y')
{
    number_of_yellow=number_of_yellow+1;
    total_number_counted=total_number_counted+1;
    per_cent = number_of_yellow/total_number_counted*100;
}
else
{
    number_of_other=number_of_other+1;
    total_number_counted=total_number_counted+1;
    per_cent = number_of_other/total_number_counted*100;
}
```

This program segment counts and computes a percentage of a sample population. Even without documentation, the reader is able to follow the intent of the code. Now consider the following program segment, which accomplishes the same task.

```
if (x == 'w'){
y=y+1;
z=z+1;w = y/z*100;}
else if (x == 'b')
{q=q+1;z=z+1;w= q              /z*           100;
}
else if (x          == 'y'){r=r+1;z=z+1;w=r/z*100;}
else
{
u=u+1;
        z=z+1;w = u              /z*100;    }
```

Both program fragments accomplish exactly the same function and to the computer represent exactly the same program; both execute correctly. However, the second program segment is not as easy to read and understand as the first. The point is, use mnemonic variable names, that is, names that are an abbreviation of their function, and indent bodies of code so that their logical structure is represented by their physical structure. Exactly how you physically write your programs is to a certain extent a matter of personal choice, but you must always strive for code that is as readable and understandable as possible. Someday you may have to modify a program you wrote a year ago. You will have difficulty understanding your own program if it is not well constructed. A major portion of time spent is maintaining and modifying programs already written. You will be much more valuable to yourself and to your employer if you write readable programs that are easily understood.

▶ **Exercises 4.4**

4.4.1 Given the following program, pencil check (trace) the execution of the instructions, showing how each value in storage changes as the program executes.

```
#include <stdio.h>
main()
{
    int
        ages[10] = {8, 3, 22, 65, 13, 15, 55, 27, 33, 45};
    /* the above initialization is in the ansi standard but
    does not work on all compilers. You may have to code in-
    dividual assignment statements to fill the array */
    int
        i,
        temp;
    for(i = 0; i < 9; i=i+1)
        if (ages[i] > ages[i+1])
        {
            temp = ages[i];
            ages[i] = ages[i+1];
            ages[i+1] = temp;
        }
    for (i = 0; i < 10; i=i+1)
        printf("%d ",ages[i]);
    printf("\n");
}
```

4.4.2 Pencil trace the following set of instructions and describe what they accomplish.

```
#include <stdio.h>
main()
{
    int
        ages[10] = {8, 3, 22, 65, 13, 15, 55, 27, 33, 45};
    int
        i,
        temp = ages[0];

    for(i = 1; i < 9; i=i+1)
        if (temp < ages[i])
            temp = ages[i];
        printf("%d ",temp);
    printf("\n"):
}
```

4.4.3   Why are *comparisons* a good operation to measure the amount of work done by the computer when executing an algorithm?

► Key Words

and	loop
binary search	nested loops
body of loop	not
bubble sort	or
conditional	posttest
data modification	pretest
divide and conquer	rand (random-number generator)
do	relational operator
else	searching
else if	selection
exchange sort	sequential search
for	sorting
if	termination
initialization	truth table
logical operator	while

► Chapter Concepts

4.1   The **if . . . else . . .** construct is used by the programmer to allow the programming environment to make decisions concerning processing.

4.2   There are three looping constructs in the C programming language: counting loops (**for** loops), pretest loops (**while**), and posttest loops (**do**). Each of these looping constructs must contain an initialization, modification, termination, and a body.

4.3   To form the conditionals involved in decisions and loops, the programmer may use logical and relational operators to form compound conditionals.

4.4   The logical operators are *and, or,* and *not* (&&, | |, !).

4.5   The relational operators are <, <=, >, >=, = and !=.

4.6   To determine the value of a compound conditional, the programmer may wish to resort to a truth table to decide the value of the conditional statement.

4.7   Two common tasks performed by computers are sorting and searching.

4.8   Two sorting algorithms are the bubble sort and the exchange sort. Both do the same amount of work.

4.9   If a given array is unsorted, a sequential search must be employed to determine whether a particular data item is present in the array.

4.10   If a given array is in sorted order, a binary search may be employed to determine whether a particular data item is present in the array.

▶ Programming Projects

4.1   Write a program that reads in a set of ages and an additional integer. The integer determines which largest age to report. For example, if there were ten ages, and the integer were 3, the program should respond with the third largest age. Note that it is possible to solve this problem by sorting the ages, but a more efficient algorithm exists without sorting. An example of the input is:

    34 78 22 45 89 21 3

and corresponding output is:

    The 3 age is 22.

4.2   You are now working for the census bureau. This program is to count the number of people in each of the following age groups: 0–18 infant, 18–29 young, 29–50 middle aged, 50–69 old, 69 and older, really old. Report the number of people in each age group.

4.3   You are working for a software firm that is to develop a word processor. In order to create an efficient spell checker, you want to know the frequency of occurrence of vowels and consonants. You are to determine the frequency of symbols in four groups: consonants, vowels, punctuation, and spaces. Write a complete program that reads in a body of text, one character at a time, and counts the number of vowels, consonants, punctuation, and spaces. The program should report the occurrence of each group from highest to lowest.

4.4 Since grades are very important and students are always concerned about the grade they will receive, you are to write a grading program, one which receives a set of several scores of a student and the possible points for that question. Compute and print the letter grade as a straight percentage. That is, points earned divided by points possible times 100. The breakdown should be every 10 points. That is, 90 to 100 is A, 80 to 90 is B, etc. The printout should look something like:

> Student 1's scores are 70, 80, 90, 100; the average is 85 — B

4.5 You are now working for an accounting firm. Your employer is interested in determining the pay an individual is to receive. The number of hours and pay rate should be read in. If the hours are over 40 the pay rate is "time and a half" for those hours over 40. Report the total earned amount, the amount earned for regular hours, and the amount earned for overtime hours.

4.6 When working at the machine level, it is sometimes necessary to be able to read a memory image. The computer stores its data as 1s and 0s that are translated to base 16 on the printout. Since you might want to go to base 16 from base 10 or to base 10 from base 16, you need a translation program that can do either. As long as you are into it, write a program to read in a number and a base, and a new base. Convert the number to the new base. Bases greater than 16 or less than 0 may be given, but the program should catch them and report an error in base entry. Only integer numbers should be given within the representation capability of the computer. Your translation program should be able to go from any base between 2 and 16 inclusive to any other base between 2 and 16 inclusive. Remember, the valid digits in base 16 are 0, 1, 2, 3, 4, 5, 6, 7, 8, 9, A, B, C, D, E, F.

4.7 You are again working for the census bureau and they need some statistics regarding the distribution of ages. Write a program to read in a number of ages. Compute the average age and the age that occurs most frequently (some of the ages might be the same). Ages should be read in as integers, and the average should be a real number.

4.8 A palindrome is a word that reads the same forward and backward—for example, "A Toyota," "radar," "Was it a rat I saw." Write a program that will ignore spaces but read in strings of characters and determine if they are palindromes.

4.9 The solutions to a quadratic equation $ax^2 + bx + c = 0$ can be found by the following formula:

$$x = \frac{-b \pm \sqrt{b^2 - 4ac}}{2a}$$

Note that no real solutions exist if the b^2-$4ac$ is less than 0, and that only one solution exists if b^2-$4ac$ is 0. Write a program to implement this formula and solve for the solutions of a quadratic equation. Your program should report only the real solution(s).

4.10 Write a program that will read in an unknown number of temperatures and report the number of times the temperature has fallen below zero.

4.11 Write a program that computes the distance between two points in the **x**, **y** coordinate system. Recall that the points are labelled as **(x,y)** pairs and that the distance between **(a,b)** and **(c,d)** is given by the formula **d = sqrt((a-c)² + (b-d)²)**.

4.12 Write a program to iteratively compute Fibonacci numbers (named after an Italian mathematician). Some Fibonacci numbers are 1, 1, 2, 3, 5, 8 ... where the next number is found by summing the preceding two numbers. Your program will read in a number, like 7, and report the first 7 numbers —in this case 1,1,2,3,5,8,13. Your program is not assured of receiving good data. Thus if −2 is received as the number of numbers, an error should be reported.

4.13 Write a program that monitors a person's bank balance. The program reads in numbers in dollars and cents (34.22), each of which represents transactions on the person's account. Negative numbers are withdrawals and positive numbers are deposits. A warning message should be printed any time the account goes below zero. Also, a penalty for a negative balance, 10% of the amount of the negative balance, is assessed to the account for each transaction that leaves the account in the red. For example:

    10.00 —> deposit
    −15.00 —> withdraw, leaving a −5.00 balance; assess the penalty
    0.10*5 = 0.5 so the account now has −5.50 final balance

4.14 Write a text-modifying program that will read in characters of text and convert them to uppercase or lowercase dependent on a special character. The flag to begin conversion to uppercase is ! and the flag to convert to lowercase is @. All punctuation and other special symbols are to be left alone. For example:

    !The text @ Should, upon receipt, ! appear as @ follows!
    THE TEXT should, upon receipt, APPEAR AS follows!

4.15 Write a program that determines the position of the letter in the alphabet. For example, if an e has been read in, the program should respond with "e is in position 5 in the alphabet." Your program should be able to respond for both uppercase and lowercase. Punctuation marks should yield position 0 since they are not part of the alphabet.

4.16 Write a program that will search an ordered list, A, for an item **x** by checking every fifth element. If **x** is smaller than the item checked in A, it will be necessary to search sequentially backwards to locate the item **x**. How much better will this algorithm run than the traditional sequential search and how much poorer do you expect the algorithm to run than the binary search?

4.17 Improve the bubble sort algorithm presented in Figure 4.4.2 by replacing the outer loop with a loop that executes only while data movements have been made. If no data movements are made, then the list is sorted.

4.18 Improve the algorithm of problem 4.17 by keeping track of the last place where a data movement was made. If no data movements were made beyond a certain point in the array, then all elements beyond that point are in order and do not have to be checked. Note that we may always decrease the number of comparisons by one, since at least one data item will be bubbled into position with each execution of the inner loop.

CHAPTER
5

Arrays, Functions, and Pointers

INTRODUCTION

After reading this chapter you will understand the concepts of modular programming, software engineering, and top-down design. In addition, you will understand user-defined functions, parameter passing, call by reference, and call by value. You will also gain an understanding of arrays, character strings, and the relationship between pointers, functions, and arrays. You will understand the need for pointers and be able to manipulate arrays and character strings using pointer arithmetic.

In Chapter 1 we discussed how problem-solving strategies were important to program code development. In Chapter 2 we saw how these techniques could be used to develop complete programs in C. Fundamental programming tools and techniques were introduced in Chapter 2 as well. In Chapter 3, arrays and strings were discussed, as well as data types and addressing of operands. Chapter 4 saw a complete and thorough discussion of the fundamental control structures, the actual tools of program construction. Sequence, selection, and repetition have proven to be the only constructs necessary to solve any programming problem. Thus, the stage is set for the artistry and creativity associated with the programming process. In this chapter we will try to completely expose the modular programming process, discuss software engineering, and use functions and procedures to modularize our programming process.

5.1 POINTERS

SECTION TOPICS

Indirect Addressing

Pointer Arithmetic

In Section 3.2 the concept of knowing, using, and manipulating a variable's address was introduced. The addressing and dereferencing operator were discussed. In this section we will explore the usefulness of these ideas and extend the concept to arrays and structures.

The ability to access and manipulate a variable's address is an extremely powerful tool. A pointer is a variable that contains the address of another variable. Consider the possibility of working with a variable that contains the address of a variable that contains the address of a variable that contains the address of a variable, and so on. Complicated? Certainly, but by being able to reference a certain portion of memory that contains the addresses of other portions of memory, we say we can *indirectly* reference memory. We will learn that *indirect addressing* is a very powerful and desirable feature. Because pointers to pointers to pointers are a possibility, pointer variables and indirect addressing have been criticized as another way of writing computer code that is impossible to understand. However, if used correctly, the power of this tool far outweighs this criticism.

Keep in mind that the concept being exposed in this section is not the fact that C has powerful pointer capabilities, but that indirect addressing using pointers (or whatever the programming language might choose to call them) is the important idea. We recall for your examination Figure 3.2.3, where addressing and dereferencing were first discussed, and repeat it in Figure 5.1.1.

Here **x** is an ordinary integer variable, and **y** is a variable that holds the address of **x**. Please note that both the address of **x** and **x** itself were referenced using the variable **y**. Since **y** is a pointer, it is a variable in memory with special properties. Consider the simplified picture of memory in Figure 5.1.2, where each square might represent a byte of memory.

In order to retrieve the contents stored in the variable location **x**, we may use the variable **y** which contains the address of **x**. We say that **y** points to **x**, or that **y** is a pointer to **x**. The unary operator **&** gives the address of a variable so that assigning **y** = **&x** assigns **y** the address of **x**.

Figure 5.1.1 Addressing and Dereferencing

```
#include <stdio.h>

main()
{
   int
        x, *y;
        x = 5;
        y = &x;

        printf("the address of x is %ld\n",y);
        printf("the value of x is %d\n",*y);

}
```

Figure 5.1.2   Address in Memory

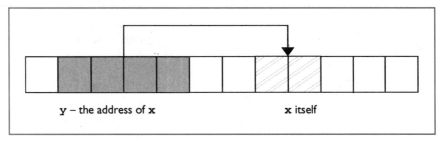

The operator **&** may be applied to find the address of any variable in memory. It may not be applied to expressions or constants.

The unary operation ***** is the indirection or dereferencing operator. As indicated in the statement

```
printf("the value of x is %d\n",*y);
```

the expression ***y** accesses the value the variable **y** points to. The student should be aware that pointers are specific in the sense that an integer pointer points to integers, whereas a **float** pointer points to floating-point variables. You should not use an integer pointer with a floating-point variable because pointer arithmetic is possible. Since integers, floating-point variables, and other objects in memory are different sizes, performing pointer arithmetic with objects that are the wrong sizes is sure to cause one to land in memory at the wrong position.

Specifically, suppose we wish to perform some arithmetic on an integer array named **linear**. If the address of the first element of the array is stored in the pointer variable **ptr**, then **ptr+1** is the address of the second element, **ptr+2** the third, and so on. To illustrate the concept, consider the programming example in Figure 5.1.3.

The output from this program might appear similar to the following:

```
Array element 0 is 9
Array element 1 is 8
Array element 2 is 7
Array element 3 is 6
Array element 4 is 5
Array element 5 is 4
Array element 6 is 3
Array element 7 is 2
Array element 8 is 1
Array element 9 is 0
```

If the pointer types do not match, as in Figure 5.1.4 (which is the same as

Figure 5.1.3 Pointer Arithmetic

```
#include <stdio.h>
main()
{
    int
        linear[10] = {9,8,7,6,5,4,3,2,1,0};
    int
        *ptr, i;
    ptr = &linear[0];

    for (i=0;i<10;i=i+1)
    {
        printf("Array element %d is %d\n",i,*ptr);
        ptr=ptr+1;
    }
}
```

Figure 5.1.3 except for the declaration of the array), then the behavior of the program is unpredictable.

Possible output from the program might be similar to the following:

```
Array element 0 is 16656
Array element 1 is 0
Array element 2 is 16640
```

Figure 5.1.4 Mixed Pointer Types

```
#include <stdio.h>
main()
{
    int
        linear[10] = {9,8,7,6,5,4,3,2,1,0};
    int
        *ptr, i;
    /* int pointer with float array */
    ptr = &linear[0];

    for (i=0;i<10;i=i+1)
    {
        printf("Array element %d is %d\n",i,*ptr);
        ptr=ptr+1;
    }
}
```

```
Array element 3 is 0
Array element 4 is 16608
Array element 5 is 0
Array element 6 is 16576
Array element 7 is 0
Array element 8 is 16544
Array element 9 is 0
```

The reason is that by using an integer pointer, we access memory locations that are not on the boundary of a **float** value. Moreover, the representation of floating-point values in memory is different from the representation of integer values, as we saw in Chapter 1. Output from programs similar to this one might be different on other C installations, since the size of an **int** and the size of a **float** value in memory could be different. Some C installations, such as Think C on the Macintosh, allow checking of pointer types. We recommend that you enable the compiler checking of pointer types since this will allow the compiler to catch errors similar to the error in the illustration.

A programming difficulty must be observed at this point. Note that the pointer variable **ptr** was assigned the address of the first element of the array **ptr = &linear[0];**. The fact that C considers array names to be constant pointers makes a statement like **ptr = &linear** incorrect. One might think that this statement assigns the address of the array to the pointer, which is precisely what we would like to do, but instead we must assign the address of the first element of the array to the pointer. The variable **ptr** is just that—a variable—its value may be changed. On the other hand, the name **linear** is an array name and hence not a variable, but a constant like the number 5 or the transcendental π—its value may not be changed.

It is important to realize that the assignment **ptr=ptr+1** causes the pointer to advance to the next integer. If the pointer were declared as a **float** pointer then the pointer would advance to the next **float** boundary. Thus this statement might cause an advance of **two** bytes for a short integer, **four** bytes for a long integer, or perhaps as many as **ten** bytes in memory for a double-precision floating-point variable. It all depends on how the pointer was declared. For this reason programmers must be careful not to mix pointer types.

▶ Exercises 5.1

5.1.1　Examine the following code segment. What will be printed? If there are errors, indicate the nature of the error.

```
int x,*y;
x = 3;
```

```
y = &x;
printf("%d %d %d %d\n",x,*y,*y+1,*(y+1));
```

5.1.2 Examine the following code segment. What will be printed? If there are errors, indicate the nature of the error.

```
int x[3] = {12,14,39};
int *y;
y = &x[0];
printf("%d %d %d %d\n",x[0], *y, (*y) + 1, *y+1);
```

5.1.3 Examine the following code segment. What will be printed? If there are errors, indicate the nature of the error.

```
float x[4] = {3.2, 4.1, 5.5, 2.23};
float *y;
y = &x[2];
printf("%f %f %f %f\n", x[0], x[1], *y, *(y+1));
```

5.1.4 Assume that **a** and **b** are **int**s, and **x** and **y** are pointers to **int**. Which of the following are legal statements?

```
x = &a;
b = *(&a);
y = &*x;
y = &x;
a = b;
```

5.1.5 Write a program to test whether floating-point numbers are stored in *consecutive* memory locations. Use the **sizeof** function to determine the size of a floating-point quantity, and determine what *consecutive* means.

5.2 FUNCTIONS

SECTION TOPICS

Functions and Function Arguments

Parameters and Arguments

Call by Value

Call by Reference

Automatic and Static Variables

Global Variables

In this section we introduce what many consider to be the most important concept in an introductory textbook on computer science. Functions, procedures, subroutines, modules, or routines by any other name allow the software developer to take a complex task and divide it into manageable pieces. The strategy advocated by this divide-and-conquer technique is especially important in real-world programming applications. In the university environment the approach allows the student to divide a homework programming project into pieces, each of which may be understood and coded in a reasonable amount of time. So much for the commercial. We all should understand that dividing a task into manageable pieces is a good idea.

Functions help the programmer when some task must be repeated in a process several times. Rather than including code for the task each time it is encountered, we include the code for the task once—as a function—and then *call* the function each time the task is to be performed. But functions can be used in other ways as well. Perhaps a complex function is carefully constructed and performs its complex task well. This complex function might be suitable for inclusion in several varied programming applications and, as such, should be included in a library of functions since its general nature gives it wide applicability. Such a function might perform some special conversion or might display values on the workstation screen—**printf** is an example of such a function.

Functions and Function Arguments

The simplest function has no *arguments* and returns no *value.* A prototype function call for such a function might be

```
(void) function_name (void);
```

Study the example in Figure 5.2.1 for such a function. Here the main

Figure 5.2.1 Simple Function

```
#include <stdio.h>

void simple_function (void);

main()
{
    printf("Hi there\n");
    simple_function();

}

void simple_function (void)
{
    printf("How are you\n");
}
```

Figure 5.2.2 Function Call

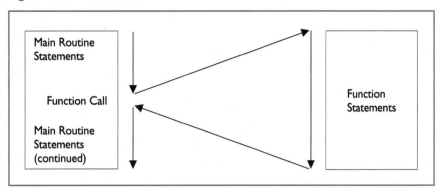

routine prints the message **Hi there** while the function called **simple_function** prints the message **How are you**. Note that in C a function is called by simply referencing its function name as we did in the main routine by writing **simple_function();**. Other programming languages have different conventions for invoking a subroutine or function but the effect is the same.

Figure 5.2.2 illustrates the order of execution of the statements of a main routine calling a single function. Following the arrows, we see that the statements of the main routine will be executed until the function call, then the statements of the function will be executed. When the function terminates, the statements of the main routine following the function call will be executed. The function may be called as many times as we wish—each time the function is called the effect will be the same as pictured in Figure 5.2.2. In this way the function may be written once, and if it is sufficiently general, it may be executed several times in a host of different situations.

Parameters and Arguments

We now explain *passing parameters* to a function. Figure 5.2.1 illustrated a function that received no arguments and returned no value to the calling function. All other combinations are possible. A function may receive no arguments and may return a value, a function may receive arguments and may return no value, or a function may receive arguments and may return a value. Note that a function (true to the mathematical definition of the word *function*) may return only one value to the function that invokes it. Fortunately, this value may be a pointer (address), which opens a world of possibilities to functions. Moreover, the arguments may also be pointers (addresses), which again adds considerable flexibility to the capabilities of a function.

In the example in Figure 5.2.3, the function **power** is to calculate and return the value of an integer base raised to an integer exponent. The function is to receive two integer arguments, the base and exponent, and is to return the appropriate integer power. The **main** function prompts the user to enter the desired base and exponent from the keyboard and displays the results on the terminal screen. As in the example in Figure 5.2.1, the function **power** is invoked from the **main** function by referencing its name. A possible execution of the function might appear similar to the following:

```
Raise what number to a power? 2
What is the integer exponent? 5
2 to the power 5 is 32.
```

The function call is contained in the statement **result = power(base,exponent)**. The variables **base** and **exponent** are the

Figure 5.2.3 Power Function

```c
#include <stdio.h>

int power (int,int);

main()
{
    int
        base, exponent, result;

    printf("Raise what number to a power? ");
    scanf("%d",&base);
    printf("What is the integer exponent? ");
    scanf("%d",&exponent);
    result = power(base,exponent);
    printf("%d to the power %d is %d.\n",base,exponent,
        result);

}

int power (int base,int exponent)
{
    int
        i, result=1;
    for (i=0;i<exponent;i=i+1)
        result = result*base;
    return(result);
}
```

arguments of the function, and **result** is the value returned. Control in the **main** function passes line by line until the function is invoked, then control passes to the function. When the **return** statement is encountered, control passes back to the main function. The **main** function then executes to completion. A function in C must have a **return** statement for the explicit value it returns (if any). If no value is to be returned, the **return** statement may be omitted.

Call by Value

The C programming language passes parameters to functions *by value,* which means that the language makes a *copy* of the parameters passed to the function, and the function uses the copies to perform its tasks. To illustrate, consider the program shown in Figure 5.2.4, which attempts to change the value of its input parameter in the subroutine.

```
in main, the value of x is 5
in sub, before the change the value of x is 5
in sub, after the change the value of x is 6
back in main, the value of x is 5
```

Figure 5.2.4   Call by Value

```
#include <stdio.h>

void sub (int);

main()
{
    int
        x=5;

    printf("in main, the value of x is %d\n",x);
    sub(x);
    printf("back in main, the value of x is %d\n",x);
}

void sub (int x)
{
    printf("in sub, before the change the value of x is
        %d\n",x);
    x = 6;
    printf("in sub, after the change the value of x is
        %d\n",x);
}
```

The important thing to realize is that in the function **sub**, only the *copy* of **x** was changed, not the original variable location. Despite the copy changing, the original remained unaltered. It makes no difference that the variable name used in **main** and in **sub** was the same—in fact, the name of the variable **x** in the function **sub** could have been different from the name used in **main**. In any case, the two **x**'s reference different storage locations.

We now illustrate how we can use pointers to change the values of the input parameters. An important task to be performed in many applications is the simple task of interchanging the values contained in two variable locations. Our first example, Figure 5.2.5, shows how *not* to perform the switch, while the second example, Figure 5.2.6, shows the correct way to accomplish this task using a function.

This program will respond

```
the values of x and y are 5 and 6
the values after the swap are 5 and 6
```

Figure 5.2.5   Incorrect Swap

```c
#include <stdio.h>

void swap (int,int);

main()
{
    int
        x,y;
    x = 5;
    y = 6;
    printf("the values of x and y are %d and %d\n",x,y);
    swap(x,y);
    printf("the values after the swap are %d and %d\n",x,y);

}

void swap (int x,int y)
{
    int
        temp;
    temp = x;
    x = y;
    y = temp;
}
```

Figure 5.2.6 Correct Swap — Call by Reference

```
#include <stdio.h>

void swap (int *,int *);

main()
{
    int
        x,y;
    x = 5;
    y = 6;
    printf("the values of x and y are %d and %d\n",x,y);
    swap(&x,&y);
    printf("the values after the swap are %d and %d\n",x,y);

}

void swap (int *x,int *y)
{
    int
        temp;
    temp = *x;
    *x = *y;
    *y = temp;
}
```

Call by Reference

An analysis of the function suggests that the values of **x** and **y** should be switched. What went wrong? The answer, of course, is that we were duped by *call by value.* The function **swap** successfully switches the *copies* of **x** and **y**, but the original **x** and **y** were left unchanged. To remedy this situation, we will use pointers—the addresses of the variables. Then, even if the function uses *copies of the addresses,* the copy of the address will reference the same location as the original address referenced. Study the program in Figure 5.2.6 to understand the process.

This program will respond

```
the values of x and y are 5 and 6
the values after the swap are 6 and 5
```

The important point is that when we dereference the address of **x**, we end up in memory in the same location as if we dereferenced a *copy* of the address of **x**. It does not matter that the variables were declared in the **main**

Figure 5.2.7   Addresses in Called Function

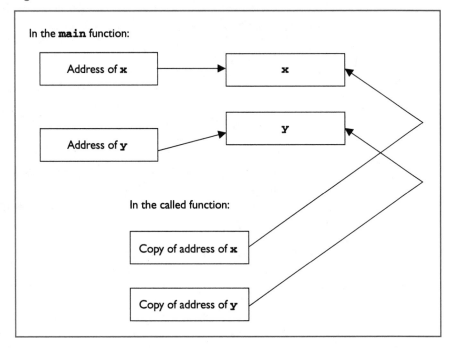

function, the called function, or any other function. As long as we have the address of the variable in question we can reach that variable. See Figure 5.2.7. Using the address of a variable to reach a variable is termed *call by reference*. Some programming languages pass the address of a variable to a function by default. In C, however, we must explicitly pass the address of the variable in question to a function using a pointer.

The term *call by value* suggests that the called function will be given the values of the arguments, rather than the arguments themselves. To accomplish this the values of the arguments are copied into new variable locations. *Call by reference* suggests that the called function can reference the original variable locations. To be able to reference the original variable locations the called function must have their addresses, either automatically or explicitly.

Functions may declare their own storage, functions may invoke other functions, and in fact, a function may invoke itself. However, the important theoretical consideration of *recursive* functions is delayed until the next chapter.

Automatic and Static Variables

When a function declares storage, the storage declared is known only in that particular function. These variables are said to be *local* to the function that declares them. When control passes to a function, storage for the declared variables is allocated, and when the function completes its execution, this storage is freed to be used for something else. This allocation and deallocation of memory for use by the variables in a function happens automatically; hence the name *automatic* is used to describe these variables. These variables live only as long as the function is active. If the function is called again at a later date, storage is reallocated for the variables declared within it.

A variable may also be declared **static** so that it retains its value from function call to function call. To declare a variable static, the word **static** is appended to the type in the declaration, as in

```
static int x;
```

Without this specification, the programmer must be aware that unless variables local to a function are properly initialized, their storage location may contain garbage.

Global Variables

In contrast to local variables, known only in the function that declares them, variables may also be declared *global,* which means the variable is known to all functions in that particular source file. To declare variables *global,* they must be declared outside the bounds of all functions. Then all functions have access to and may change the value of these global variables. In the straightforward example shown in Figure 5.2.8, the variables **length** and **width** are global. Analysis of the code indicates that all functions, **main()**, **perimeter()**, and **area()** have access to these variable locations.

Possible output from an execution of this program might appear similar to the following:

```
Please enter the length of the rectangle 5
Please enter the width of the rectangle 6
The perimeter is 22, while the area is 30
```

▶ Exercises 5.2

5.2.1 Write a function **add** that has prototype

```
int add(int, int);
```

which will add two integers and return as its value the integer sum of its arguments.

Figure 5.2.8   Global Variables

```
/*-------------------------------------*/
/* includes and defines come first     */
/*-------------------------------------*/
#include <stdio.h>

/*-------------------------------------*/
/* function prototypes                  */
/*-------------------------------------*/
int perimeter(void);
int area(void);

/*-------------------------------------*/
/* global variables                     */
/*-------------------------------------*/
int
    length, width;

main()
{
    printf("Please enter the length of the rectangle ");
    scanf("%d",&length);
    printf("Please enter the width of the rectangle ");
    scanf("%d",&width);
    printf("The perimeter is %d, while the area is %d\n",
        perimeter(),area());
}

int perimeter()
{
    return(2*length + 2*width);
}

int area()
{
    return(length*width);
}
```

5.2.2   Write a function that has prototype

```
void add (int, int, int *);
```

which adds its first two arguments and places the sum in the location pointed to by the third argument.

5.2.3 Write a function that will interchange its arguments if the first argument is smaller than its second argument, but will not interchange them if the first argument is greater than or equal to the first argument. The function should return 1 if an interchange was made, and 0 otherwise.

5.2.4 Write a program that inputs four integers representing the **x** and **y** coordinates of two points in a plane. The program should then invoke a function that will receive the points as call by value parameters and return the slope of the line connecting the points. Recall that the slope can be found by the equation

$$m = \frac{y_2 - y_1}{x_2 - x_1}$$

where the data is given as x_1, y_1, x_2, x_2. The function prototype should be

```
float slope(int, int, int, int);
```

5.2.5 Write a program that inputs an integer representing resistance and an integer representing current through a resistor. Compute the voltage realized as a result of the current and resistance in a function using the following equation where **i** is the current, **r** the resistance and **v** the voltage.

$$v = i*r$$

Use the function prototype

```
int volts(int, int);
```

The output should appear similar to

```
The current is xx amps, the resistance is xx ohms
and the corresponding voltage is xx volts.
```

5.2.6 Suppose you are working for an insurance firm that is tracking the highest amount paid for a claim. Your program is to read the claim paid and invoke a function to compare this new claim with the old maximum value paid. If the old value is larger, leave it alone, but if the old value is smaller, put the new value as the current maximum and return the maximum. That is, suppose the current largest value paid is $300 and the new value read in is $400. Both 300 and 400 would be passed to a function, and 400 would be returned as the old value. If $300 were the old value and $200 were read in as the new value, 300 would be returned as the old value. Use the function prototype

```
int max_claim(int, int);
```

5.3 FUNCTIONS, ARRAYS, AND CHARACTER STRINGS

SECTION TOPICS

One-Dimensional Arrays and Functions

Two-Dimensional Arrays and Functions

Strings and Functions

In this section we shall learn the relationship between functions and various entities that functions serve. Specifically, functions may take as arguments any of the data types already discussed. We shall be primarily concerned in this section with the relationship between arrays, character strings, and functions.

One-Dimensional Arrays and Functions

First let us consider the relationship between functions, pointers, and arrays. An array may be passed to a function as a pointer, which contains the address of the first element of the array as the example in Figure 5.3.1 illustrates.

In this example, the function **findsum** receives not only a pointer to the first element of the array, but also receives the number of elements in the array. With this specification, the function **findsum** will find the (integer) sum of any array with any number of elements. The output caused by the execution of the above program would appear similar to the following:

```
array element 0 is 5
array element 1 is 4
array element 2 is 3
array element 3 is 2
array element 4 is 1
the sum of the elements in the array is 15
```

Alternatively, the array may be explicitly passed as an argument. The only thing we must tell the function is that it is to be receiving an array in the first argument. It is not necessary to tell the function the size of the array, in the same way as it is unnecessary to tell the pointer in the previous example how many locations are available. The example in Figure 5.3.2 will produce exactly the same output as the previous example.

When addressing the elements of the array in the called function, a third alternative exists. Specifically, we may use pointer arithmetic to address the individual cells in the array. The effect is the same, and we soon realize there is an intimate relationship between pointers and ar-

Figure 5.3.1 Array Argument to a Function

```c
#include <stdio.h>

int findsum(int *, int);

main()
{
    int
        number = 5, *ptr, i, sum, array[5] = {5,4,3,2,1};
    for(i=0;i<number;i++)
        printf("array element %d is %d\n",i,array[i]);
    ptr = &array[0];
    sum = findsum(ptr,number);
    printf("the sum of the elements in the array is %d\n",sum);

}

int findsum(int *ptr,int number)
{
    int
        i, sum = 0;
    for (i=0;i<number;i=i+1)
        sum = sum + ptr[i];
    return sum;
}
```

rays. The example in Figure 5.3.3 will produce the same output as each of the previous two examples. Note the use of pointer arithmetic in the called function **findsum**.

Here the reference **ptr** is the address of the first element of the array, making the reference **ptr+i** the address of the *i*th element of the array. Dereferencing the address ***(ptr+i)** gives us the actual value of the *i*th element of the array, and this value is added to the sum in the statement

```c
sum = sum + *(ptr + i);
```

Perhaps this is a bit complicated, but as you become comfortable with pointers, this kind of addressing arithmetic will become easier. C is often used as a systems programming language; that is, programs reside in the system over extended periods of time. As such, efficiency of the system becomes very important. By using pointer arithmetic to address array elements, large programs can execute more quickly. The pointer arithmetic method is more efficient than traditional indexing methods.

Figure 5.3.2   Array Argument to a Function

```
#include <stdio.h>

int findsum(int p[], int number);

main()
{
    int
        array[5] = {5,4,3,2,1}, number = 5, i, sum;

    for(i=0;i<number;i=i+1)
        printf("array element %d is %d\n",i,array[i]);
    sum = findsum(array,number);
    printf("the sum of the elements in the array is %d\n",
            sum);

}

int findsum(int p[],int number)
{
    int
        i, sum=0;
    for (i=0;i<number;i=i+1)
        sum = sum + p[i];
    return sum;
}
```

Two-Dimensional Arrays and Functions

No discussion of arrays would be complete unless multidimensional arrays were considered. Arrays will be discussed again in Chapter 7 when we will introduce a theoretical consideration of dynamic memory allocation.

▶ PROBLEM   As an example of multidimensional array manipulation, consider the problem of entering, adding, and printing two-dimensional arrays.

ANALYSIS   Two-dimensional arrays are added *coordinatewise.* That means the element of the first array in position (i,j) is added to the corresponding element of the second array in position (i,j) for each i and j.

DESIGN   To solve this problem, we need three functions. Our design includes three steps:

1. Enter the arrays from the keyboard.
2. Add the arrays coordinatewise.
3. Display the resulting arrays on the screen.

Figure 5.3.3 Array Argument to a Function, Pointer Arithmetic

```
#include <stdio.h>

int findsum(int *,int);

main()
{
    int
        array[5] = {5,4,3,2,1}, number, *ptr, i, sum;
    number = 5;
    for(i=0;i<number;i=i+1)
        printf("array element %d is %d\n",i,array[i]);
    ptr = &array[0];
    sum = findsum(ptr,number);
    printf("the sum of the elements in the array is %d\n",
        sum);

}

int findsum(int *ptr,int number)
{
    int
        i, sum=0;
    for (i=0;i<number;i=i+1)
        sum = sum + *(ptr + i);
    return sum;
}
```

The first function will allow the user to enter a two-dimensional array from the keyboard. The function will prompt the user to enter the number of rows, the number of columns, and the elements of the array. The second function will display a given array on the screen in a format that is acceptable to the user. The third function will perform the array addition as suggested above.

Questions which must be answered include the critical question, "How are a two-dimensional array and its rows and columns passed to a function?" We will develop three functions: **getarray**, **printarray**, and **addarrays**. The C programming language requires that the second dimension be specified in a function call involving a two-dimensional array. (The alternative is to use pointers—to be discussed in Chapter 7.) To refine step 1 of the design, we may outline the steps as follows:

1. Get the number of rows.
2. Get the number of columns.

3. Use a pair of loops to get the elements of the array, one row at a time.

The code for **getarray** appears as follows:

```
void getarray(int mat[][10], int *rows, int *cols)
{
    int
        i,j;

    printf("How many rows ");
    scanf("%d",rows);
    printf("How many columns ");
    scanf("%d",cols);
    printf("Please enter the elements of the array, row by
            row\n");
    for (i=0;i<*rows;i=i+1)
        for (j=0;j<*cols;j=j+1)
            scanf("%d",&mat[i][j]);
}
```

This function prompts the user to enter the number of rows, followed by the number of columns, followed by the elements of the array, one at a time. Notice that pointers are used for the number of rows and the number of columns. Since C passes parameters by value, these pointers are necessary so that the calling function may know the number of rows and columns entered. Note that **mat** is already a constant pointer since it is an array name. The **scanf** function is used to enter the values from the keyboard.

The function to display the arrays on the screen is similar to the **getarray** function. The only difference is the arrangement of the values in the array in rows and columns.

```
void printarray(int mat[][10], int *rows, int *cols)
{
    int
        i,j;

    printf("\nHere is your array: \n\n");
    for (i=0;i<*rows;i=i+1)
    {
        for (j=0;j<*cols;j=j+1)
        {
            printf("%3d ",mat[i][j]);
        }
        printf("\n");
    }
}
```

Note again the use of pointers as function arguments for the number of rows and columns. While not strictly necessary in this function, these pointers are used for consistency with the previous function.

The **addarrays** function is more complex than the previous functions since it must receive as argument the addend arrays as well as a place to put the sum of these arrays. It must also receive the number of rows and columns of the component arrays.

```
void addarrays(int mata[][10],int matb[][10],int matc[][10],
               int *rows,int *cols)
{
    int
        i,j;
    for(i=0;i<*rows;i=i+1)
        for(j=0;j<*cols;j=j+1)
            matc[i][j] = mata[i][j] + matb[i][j];
}
```

Note that the body of this function is actually relatively simple. Of course, as noted previously, the function **addarrays** involves only the addition of the components of the arrays coordinatewise.

CODE   Figure 5.3.4 contains the entire problem solution along with a **main** function that will test for compatibility and call the component functions at the right times.

TEST   The output from the program will appear as follows:

```
How many rows 2
How many columns 3
Please enter the elements of the array, row by row
1
3
4
2
5
6
How many rows 2
How many columns 3
Please enter the elements of the array, row by row
6
7
2
4
8
```

```
1
Here is your array:
    1   3  4
    2   5  6
Here is your array:
    6   7  2
    4   8  1
Here is your array:
    7  10  6
    6  13  7
```

A significant difficulty with the example in Figure 5.3.4 is that the second dimension is fixed at 10 elements. (In fact, both dimensions are fixed at 10 elements). As a result, the user must be careful not to enter an array larger than 10 by 10. If a larger array is entered, the behavior of this program is unpredictable, since the bounds of the array will have been overwritten. Ordinarily, if the sizes of the arrays to be manipulated are known in advance, then this method of handling array passing can be used. However, if the dimensions of the arrays are not known in advance, the user should set aside enough space to hold the largest possible array that might be manipulated.

▶ **PROBLEM**　As an additional example of array manipulation, let us consider the problem of multiplying arrays. Here, when we say multiply, we mean array multiplication in the algebraic sense, as might be taught in an Algebra II class or a class in fundamentals of linear algebra.

ANALYSIS　Reviewing the definition of array multiplication, if **a** is an array with **m** rows and **n** columns, and **b** is an array with **n** rows and **p** columns, then **c**, the array product, will contain **m** rows and **p** columns. The (**i,j**) entry in the product is formed by multiplying the elements of the **i**th row of **a** by the elements of the **j**th column of **b**, and adding the products, as suggested by the following formula:

$$c_{ij} = \Sigma \ a_{ik} * b_{kj}$$

Here the index **k** runs to **n**, the number of columns in the first array (which is the same as the number of rows in the second array).

As an example of array multiplication, consider Figure 5.3.5.

DESIGN　The object of the game here is to use as much of the previous code as possible. This is one of the major advantages of programming using general modules capable of being inserted where they are needed. We realize we need modules similar to the modules presented in the previous problem:

　　1.　Enter the arrays from the keyboard.

Figure 5.3.4   Two-Dimensional Arrays as Function Arguments

```c
/*-------------------------------------------------*/
#include <stdio.h>
/*-------------------------------------------------*/
/*      function prototypes                         */
/*-------------------------------------------------*/
void getarray(int mat[][10], int *rows, int *cols);
void printarray(int mat[][10], int *rows, int *cols);
void addarrays(int mata[][10],int matb[][10],int matc[][10],
      int *rows,int *cols);

main()
{
   int
      mata[10][10], matb[10][10], matc[10][10];
   int
      rowsa, colsa, rowsb, colsb, i,j;

   getarray(mata,&rowsa,&colsa);
   getarray(matb,&rowsb,&colsb);
   if((rowsa==rowsb) && (colsa==colsb))
   {
      addarrays(mata,matb,matc,&rowsa,&colsa);
      printarray(mata,&rowsa,&colsa);
      printarray(matb,&rowsb,&colsb);
      printarray(matc,&rowsa,&colsa);
   }
   else
   {
      printf("These arrays cannot be added. The same number of \n");
      printf("rows and columns are required.\n");
   }
}

void getarray(int mat[][10], int *rows, int *cols)
{
/*-------------------------------------------------*/
/*  Function getarray reads arrays from the keyboard */
/*  it receives a two-dimensional array and two      */
/*  pointers to rows and columns of the array as     */
/*  arguments.                                       */
/*-------------------------------------------------*/
   int
      i,j;

   printf("How many rows ");
   scanf("%d",rows);
   printf("How many columns ");
   scanf("%d",cols);
```

(continued)

Figure 5.3.4 Two-Dimensional Arrays as Function Arguments (*continued*)

```
    printf("Please enter the elements of the array, row by row\n");
    for (i=0;i<*rows;i=i+1)
        for (j=0;j<*cols;j=j+1)
        scanf("%d",&mat[i][j]);
}
void printarray(int mat[][10], int *rows, int *cols)
{
/*----------------------------------------------------*/
/*  Function printarray prints the values of an       */
/*  integer array on the screen. It receives a two    */
/*  array and pointers to the number of rows and      */
/*  columns as arguments.                             */
/*----------------------------------------------------*/
    int
        i,j;

    printf("\nHere is your array: \n\n");
    for (i=0;i<*rows;i=i+1)
    {
        for (j=0;j<*cols;j=j+1)
        {
            printf("%3d ",mat[i][j]);
        }
        printf("\n");
    }
}

void addarrays(int mata[][10],int matb[][10],int matc[][10],
               int *rows,int *cols)
{
/*----------------------------------------------------*/
/*  Function addarrays adds two arrays mata and matb */
/*  and places the sum in matc. It does no checking  */
/*  for the sizes of the arrays to see if the         */
/*  addition can be performed. It receives the arrays*/
/*  along with the rows and columns in the arrays as */
/*  arguments.                                        */
/*----------------------------------------------------*/
    int i,j;
    for(i=0;i<*rows;i=i+1)
        for(j=0;j<*cols;j=j+1)
            matc[i][j] = mata[i][j] + matb[i][j];
}
```

2. Perform the matrix multiplication.

3. Display the results on the terminal screen.

The **getarray** and **printarray** functions can be used exactly as they are. The **addarrays** routine and the **main** routine will have to be modified slightly to perform the array multiplication.

Figure 5.3.5 Array Multiplication

$$\begin{bmatrix} 2 & 3 & 4 \\ 1 & 5 & 3 \end{bmatrix} \begin{bmatrix} 1 & 1 \\ 2 & 6 \\ 3 & 1 \end{bmatrix} = \begin{bmatrix} 20 & 24 \\ 20 & 34 \end{bmatrix}$$

CODE The entire matrix multiplication program is shown in Figure 5.3.6. Study this code to see the changes made.

Observe that the **multiplyarrays** routine includes a segment that zeros the space the product array will occupy. This is necessary because of the way the sums are accumulated to form the product. The **getarray** and **printarray** functions are exactly the same as they were in the previous example, in which arrays were added. It should be clear that the code from these routines can be used anytime such segments are needed. This is the primary advantage of writing very general code. In fact, if we were so inclined, we could construct a library of functions and include these routines.

Strings and Functions

As we learned earlier, a string is merely an array of characters. As such, strings may be handled in much the same way as we dealt with one- and two-dimensional arrays. The reader is also referred to Section 3.4.3, in which strings were discussed at length. Our primary purpose in this section is to illustrate the relationship between strings and functions.

▶ PROBLEM To illustrate the handling of strings by functions, consider the problem of counting the number of occurrences of the letters of the alphabet in a body of text. We will develop a project that prompts the user to enter a body of text from the keyboard. The program should count the number of times each letter of the alphabet occurs in the text.

ANALYSIS Our analysis of this problem indicates we will need a function to input the string the user wishes to analyze. We will also need an array to count

Figure 5.3.6 Matrix Multiplication

```c
/*----------------------------------------------------*/
#include <stdio.h>

/*----------------------------------------------------*/
/*        function prototypes                      */
/*----------------------------------------------------*/
void getarray(int mat[][10], int *rows, int *cols);
void printarray(int mat[][10], int *rows, int *cols);
void multiplyarrays (int mata[][10],int matb[][10],int matc[][10],
      int *leftindex,int *middleindex,int *rightindex);

main()
{
   int
      mata[10][10], matb[10][10], matc[10][10];
   int
      rowsa, colsa, rowsb, colsb, i,j;

   getarray(mata,&rowsa,&colsa);
   getarray(matb,&rowsb,&colsb);
   if(colsa==rowsb)
   {
      multiplyarrays(mata,matb,matc,&rowsa,&colsa,&colsb);
      printarray(mata,&rowsa,&colsa);
      printarray(matb,&rowsb,&colsb);
      printarray(matc,&rowsa,&colsb);
   }
   else
   {
      printf("These arrays cannot be multiplied. We require\n");
      printf("the same number of columns in the first array\n");
      printf("as rows in the second array.\n");
   }
}
void getarray(int mat[][10], int *rows, int *cols)
{
/*----------------------------------------------------*/
/* Function getarray reads arrays from the keyboard. */
/* It receives a two-dimensional array and two       */
/* pointers to rows and columns of the array as      */
/* arguments.                                         */
/*----------------------------------------------------*/
```

(continued)

Figure 5.3.6   Matrix Multiplication (*continued*)

```
    int
       i,j;

    printf("How many rows ");
    scanf("%d",rows);
    printf("How many columns ");
    scanf("%d",cols);
    printf("Please enter the elements of the array, row by row\n");
    for (i=0;i<*rows;i=i+1)
       for (j=0;j<*cols;j=j+1)
          scanf("%d",&mat[i][j]);

}
void printarray(int mat[][10], int *rows, int *cols)
{
/*-----------------------------------------------------*/
/* Function printarray prints the values of an         */
/* integer array on the screen. It receives a two      */
/* array and pointers to the number of rows and        */
/* columns as arguments.                               */
/*-----------------------------------------------------*/
    int
       i,j;

    printf("\nHere is your array: \n\n");
    for (i=0;i<*rows;i=i+1)
    {
       for (j=0;j<*cols;j=j+1)
       {
          printf("%3d ",mat[i][j]);
       }
       printf("\n");
    }
}
void multiplyarrays(int mata[][10],int matb[][10],int matc[][10],
       int *leftindex,int *middleindex,int *rightindex)
{
/*-----------------------------------------------------*/
/* The function multiplyarrays will find the array     */
/* product of any two compatible arrays. It is         */
/* assumed that the calling function checks for        */
/* compatibility of the arrays and only calls this     */
/* function if the arrays can in fact be multiplied. */
```

(continued)

Figure 5.3.6   Matrix Multiplication (*continued*)

```
/* The function accepts three matrices as arguments  */
/* along with the appropriate dimensions of the      */
/* arrays. The work is accomplished in three loops.  */
/*---------------------------------------------------*/
    int
        i,j,k;

    for (i=0;i<*leftindex;i=i+1)
        for (j=0;j<*rightindex;j=j+1)
            matc[i][j] = 0;

    for(i=0;i<*leftindex;i=i+1)
        for(j=0;j<*rightindex;j=j+1)
            for(k=0;k<*middleindex;k=k+1)
                matc[i][j] = matc[i][j] + mata[i][k] * matb[k][j];
}
```

the number of occurrences of each letter of the alphabet in the string. Moreover, the user might wish to enter the characters of the string in both uppercase and lowercase, so we require a function to fix the case (either all upper or all lower). We will use the fact that the lowercase letters of the alphabet lie between ASCII 97 and 122, while the uppercase letters lie between ASCII 65 and 90. To actually count the characters, the ASCII values of the characters themselves can be used as an index into an array. Anytime a character is seen, we subtract 97 from its ASCII value, and increment that position of the counter array. If 'a' were the character in question (ASCII 97) then the array position with index 0 would be incremented.

DESIGN   Our preliminary design of the solution to the problem includes the following steps:

1. Initialize an array that will hold the character counts.

2. Get the string from the keyboard.

3. Convert the string to all lowercase characters (all uppercase would work just as well).

4. Scan the string, character by character, and match characters with the alphabet. When a particular character occurs, increment the appropriate position in the counter array.

5. Display the summary information on the screen.

To enable the function **fixcase** to convert the characters from uppercase to lowercase, we use the fact that all uppercase characters have ASCII values between 65 and 90, inclusive. The lowercase characters have ASCII values between 97 and 122, inclusive. To change a character from uppercase to lowercase we add 32 to its ASCII value.

In order to count each occurrence of a character, suppose for a moment that an **'a'** is detected. We wish to add one to the first position in the counter array, **countarray[0]**. Since **'a'** has ASCII value 97, the value **'a' - 97** will be zero and may be used as an index into the array in precisely the right position. This is the technique that will be used to count each of the characters.

CODE The entire character-counting program, including all necessary functions, is shown in Figure 5.3.7. Make note of the array indexing used in this example.

TEST A sample execution of the program in Figure 5.3.7 follows.

```
Please enter a sentence, up to 500 characters long

NOW is the TIME for all good persons to COME to the aid
    of their PARTY.
you entered 71 characters
a    3    b    0    c    1    d    2    e    6
f    2    g    1    h    3    i    4    j    0
k    0    l    2    m    3    n    2    o    9
p    2    q    0    r    4    s    3    t    7
u    0    v    0    w    1    x    0    y    1
z    0
```

The function counts the occurrences of the characters in the text correctly whether they are uppercase or lowercase.

▶ Exercises 5.3

5.3.1 Refer to the bubble sort algorithm presented in Chapter 4. Modify the code for this algorithm so that the bubble sort algorithm is a function that may be called from a **main** function. Pass an array and a number of elements to the function. The function's explicit return value should be the number of comparisons made to perform the sort.

5.3.2 Refer to the exchange sort algorithm presented in Chapter 4. Modify the code for this algorithm so that the exchange sort algorithm is a function. Pass an array and a number of elements to the function. The return value from the function should be the number of data exchanges made to perform the sort.

Figure 5.3.7   Counting Occurrences of Characters in Text

```c
#include <stdio.h>

  /* ----------------------------------------------------------*/
  /*                 function prototypes                       */
  /* ----------------------------------------------------------*/
  void getthestring(char string[]);
  void countcharacters(char string[],int array[],int length);
  void fixcase(char string[]);
  void initialize(int array[], int numberelements);

  main()
  {
     char
        mystring[500];
     int
        countarray[26],i,j,k,length;
     initialize(countarray,26);
     getthestring(mystring);
     length = strlen(mystring);
     printf ("\nyou entered %d characters \n\n",length);
     fixcase(mystring);
     countcharacters(mystring,countarray,length);

     for(i=0;i<26;i=i+1)
     {
        printf("%c %3d    ",i+97,countarray[i]);
        if ((i+1)%5 == 0) /* make 5 characters per line       */
           printf("\n");
     }
     printf("\n");
  }

  void getthestring(char string[])
  {
  /* ----------------------------------------------------------*/
  /*   This function reads a string from the keyboard using   */
  /*   the gets function.                                     */
  /*---------------------------------------------------------- */
     printf("Please enter a sentence, up to 500 characters long\n\n");
     gets(string);
  }
```

(continued)

Figure 5.3.7   Counting Occurrences of Characters in Text (*continued*)

```
void countcharacters(char string[],int array[],int length)
{
/*------------------------------------------------------------- */
/* This function counts the characters in the text. It does*/
/* this by using the character itself as an index into an  */
/* array of length 26—one for each character of the        */
/* alphabet.                                                */
/*-------------------------------------------------------------*/
    int
        i,j;
    for (i=0;i<length;i=i+1)
        for (j=97;j<123;j=j+1)
            if(string[i] == j)
            {
                array[j-97] = array[j-97] + 1;
                j=123;
            }
}

void fixcase(char string[])
{
/*-------------------------------------------------------------*/
/* This function converts all uppercase characters to     */
/* lowercase by adding 32 to their ASCII values.          */
/*-------------------------------------------------------------*/
    int
        i=0;
    while(string[i] != '\0')
    {
        if ((string[i] >= 65) && (string[i] <= 90))
            string[i] = string[i] + 32;
        i = i + 1;
    }
}
void initialize(int array[], int numberelements)
{
/*-------------------------------------------------------------*/
/* This function initializes the counter array.           */
/*-------------------------------------------------------------*/
    int
        i;
    for(i=0;i<numberelements;i = i + 1)
        array[i] = 0;
}
```

5.3.3 Write a function that will find the trace of a square array. The trace is defined to be the sum of the elements on the main diagonal of the array. Pass an array and a dimension (passing **n** means the array is **n** by **n**), and return the value of the trace as the function's return value.

5.3.4 Write a program to test what the **sizeof** function returns when it is applied to a one-dimensional array. Repeat the exercise for a two-dimensional array. Repeat again for a string.

5.3.5 Modify the palindrome exercise from Section 4.4. Specifically, write a function that will take a string as an argument, and return as its return value a 1 if the string is a palindrome, and 0 otherwise.

5.3.6 Improve your palindrome function so it will eliminate all blanks and special characters, and will convert all characters to lowercase before examining the string to see if it is a palindrome.

5.3.7 Write a function that will reverse the characters in a string. Specifically, you must establish a pointer to the beginning of the string, a pointer to the end of the string, and increment the beginning pointer while decrementing the end pointer to perform this task.

5.3.8 Write a program that will verify the close relationship between pointers and arrays. Specifically, verify that the array expression **a[i]** is equivalent to the pointer expression ***(a+i)**. Does the data type of **a** make any difference to this experiment? Why or why not?

5.3.9 In C, a two-dimensional array is merely an array of one-dimensional arrays. Select a data type, print the values of the addresses of the rows of the two-dimensional array, and verify using **sizeof** that the addresses are correctly calculated.

5.4 SOFTWARE ENGINEERING

SECTION TOPICS

Structured Programming and Modularity

Debugging

Program Documentation

Software Testing Strategies

In this section we will discuss some of the fundamental principles associated with the construction of good software. A crisis exists in the world of computer science—a crisis that cannot be solved in a first course in computer science, but nonetheless a problem that prospective computing professionals must be aware of. The problem is the need for good quality software to drive the incredible advances in hardware technology seen in recent years. It has been estimated that hardware development is at least 10 years ahead of software development.

Several fundamental principles associated with software development have their roots in an engineering discipline. In this section we will touch on some of the more elementary aspects of software engineering and provide for the student some engineering principles that can be used even in the most elementary software creation endeavors.

Structured Programming and Modularity

In previous sections we discussed problem solving and the need for careful analysis and design before writing any code. With your accumulated experience in studying and writing some examples, you should be convinced that dividing a task into manageable chunks is a good idea. But what should be in the chunks? How should the program be structured for optimal efficiency? Experts agree on several rules that make for good design.

- Each of the modules in the decomposition of the problem should perform only one task.

- No function should be too long. If a function is overly long, perhaps it can be broken down into subtasks.

- In any case, flow of control through the hierarchy of modules must be from top to bottom. Flow of control within modules must also be from top to bottom.

- Each function should have one reason for existence. Functions should not be required to perform several different tasks.

- Each function should be provided exactly the information it needs to perform its task, and no more. Information should be provided to a function through its argument list.

- A programming project should minimize the use of global variables. If one function can change the value of a global variable, the effect on another function can cause errors.

- If a function is provided exactly the information it needs through its argument list, it can be debugged independently of the other functions in the project.

- Functions should be added to a project one at a time. One should strive to keep a working model of the project at all times. If several functions are added at once and the project fails, the debugging process is more difficult since we do not know which of the added modules caused the error.

- The **main** function should perform only the tasks of allocating memory that is to be used in the program, and (perhaps) performing the input and output associated with the project. The only other task **main** should perform is calling the respective functions at the appropriate times.

• The **#defines** should be used to specify constants used in the program, and these should be at the beginning so they may be easily modified.

• Function prototypes should be used even if they are not required by the particular implementation of C. Function prototypes require an additional level of discipline by the programmer and promote good programming practice.

• Programmers should use the call by value paradigm for passing parameters whenever possible to avoid unwanted and adverse side effects.

• Programmers should pay careful attention to the data flowing into and out of the module. Careful attention to data structure is an extremely important part of the development process. It has been said that there are many children running around the streets of London barefoot because their parents didn't pay attention to appropriate data structure in program design.

As with any problem-solving process, these rules must be taken for what they are worth. If there are other considerations in code creation, then of course certain of these rules may not be followed. For example, if it is absolutely essential that a program operate as fast as possible, then one might reconsider a modular structure since a certain amount of overhead is associated with function calls. Similar considerations may mandate other changes to the guidelines previously specified.

Debugging

One of the most difficult tasks facing a programmer is that of debugging a program that will not work correctly. Several steps can be performed which will make this mundane but very important task somewhat easier.

• Good analysis and good design make good code. Good code is easier to debug.

• Modules (functions) should perform only one task. Such a module will be easier to debug.

• Modules should be added to the project one at a time. Strive to keep a working project at all times. Then when a module is added, that module can be error checked independently of the other modules in the project.

- Realize that debugging follows as a natural consequence of testing. Since testing is an integral part of the software development process, debugging also becomes an important part of the development process.

- One should carefully examine the nature of the error, and form a reasonable hypothesis as to its cause. In this way we avoid a random hit-or-miss approach to debugging, which is often counterproductive.

- One of the simplest and yet often most effective methods of debugging is the "wolf fence" approach to debugging (after Edward J. Gauss, *Communications of the ACM,* November, 1982). The approach works something like catching a wolf in Alaska. First, it is known that there is a wolf in Alaska. We have heard the howls. (Our program has an error.) We build a fence across Alaska, and again listen for the howls. (We place an appropriate print statement in our program code and again run the program.) We determine which side of the fence the wolf is on. We construct another fence across the portion of Alaska the wolf is known to be in. In this way, by continually subdividing the portion of Alaska the wolf is known to be in, we soon have the wolf confined to a small pen, and by so doing, the wolf may be captured. By continually placing print statements at appropriate locations in our module (which is assumed to be of reasonable length) we soon isolate the cause of the error. This method will be effective if the module size is reasonable, and if modules are added to the project one at a time as advocated earlier. Incidentally, the authors of this text have nothing against wolves. In fact, they believe wolves to be magnificent and beautiful creatures who should be given every opportunity to survive.

- If automated debugging assistance is available, it may be used unless the overhead associated with its use is prohibitive. Many debuggers are memory and processor hogs that may not be effectively used on some personal computers.

- If all else fails, get help. If you have not had the experience of working with your code for hours without being able to isolate the error, only to have a colleague (student or faculty) glance over your shoulder and point out the error, you will. While this may be frustrating to you, it does point out that if one is too familiar with the code, often he or she cannot "see the forest for the trees." Many times it takes a fresh look at the code to find the error. Explaining what you are trying to do to a friend will often help you find the error. If all else fails, put the code aside for a period of time and return to it later with an open mind.

Many times debugging is difficult for a number of reasons, such as those contained in the following list.

- The cause of the problem and the manifestation of the error may appear to be in different parts of the code.

- If a first error is fixed, a second error may also disappear.

- Inaccuracies may be due to causes beyond your control, such as round-off error, or single versus double precision arithmetic.

- Errors may be caused because of human inconsistencies. Persons may incorrectly enter data, or include characters in numeric data streams, etc. It is therefore important to "user-proof" your code as much as possible.

- If global variables are used, or if many modules operate (reference) the same data locations, the error may appear to be intermittent. It may be difficult to reproduce the error from execution to execution, depending on the complexity of the test data. For this reason, modules should be as independent as possible, and should be passed only the information they need in the argument list.

Program Documentation

Program documentation falls into two categories: internal and external. Both of these categories are important to software that has a life expectancy longer than just completing an assignment for your professor. Even if you are the author of the software and if the program code is untouched for a month or more, you will have difficulty figuring out what certain portions of your code do, or why you chose to perform a particular task the way you did without some documentation. One respected software professional has indicated that program documentation is adequate if the total body of code is 90 percent documentation and 10 percent native program code. We may not go so far as to recommend this volume of documentation, but rest assured, we believe that program documentation is extremely important. The following paragraphs contain some guidelines for creating internal documentation.

- It is not recommended that every line be documented. In attempting to study code with this volume of documentation, the comments detract from the code. The documentation is supposed to be a help, not a hindrance.

- Variable names, function names, constants, should be chosen with descriptive names. Do not use variable names like **x**, **a**, **b**, etc.; rather, choose names like **AreaOfCircle**, **SquareRoot**, and so on. Since C allows a combination of uppercase and lowercase characters, uppercase characters may be selectively placed to improve readability. Moreover, the underscore character is an appropriate character, so if the user prefers, variable names such as **area_of_circle** or **square_root** may be used.

• Each time a new thought is encountered, it must be documented. Whether the thought is a new function, module, or other block of code, a block of documentation at the beginning of the module is appropriate. The documentation should carefully specify the inputs to the block, and should describe the effect or the output of the block. If global variables are used, and if the block modifies the global variables, this fact should be clearly indicated in the documentation.

• The documentation block should be clearly marked so that it is set off from the rest of the code. The block must begin with `/*` and end with `*/`, but other characters may be used to indicate clearly to the code reader what is documentation and what is not, perhaps similar to the following:

```
/*-------------------------------
    a block of documentation
-------------------------------- */
```

• Another critical aspect of writing good code is indentation. Each block, whether an `if . . . else . . .` construct or a `while` loop, should be clearly visible to the reader. One should be able to place a ruler alongside the code and be able to tell the extent of each of the blocks in the program source code. Judicious choice of white space also improves readability.

External documentation for a project should include a user's manual consisting of the analysis and design of the program, including, but perhaps not limited to, the following items.

• The requirements of the program should be clearly documented.

• The general program design.

• All refinements of the basic algorithm design.

• A hierarchy chart showing the logical invocations of the functions.

• A description of the role each function plays.

• A copy of the source code.

• A description of the testing strategies employed.

• A copy of all test input to the program.

• A statement of "how to run this program," telling what is expected of the user.

If appropriate internal and external documentation habits are formed at an early stage in your career, many headaches will be avoided in the future. Take our word for it.

Software Testing Strategies

A thorough discussion of software testing is beyond the scope of this text, but certain fundamental principles can be discussed and will provide the student with a better opportunity to deliver software with fewer errors.

Software is ordinarily tested using two strategies: so called "black-box" testing and "white-box" testing. Black-box testing strategies have little concern for the internal structure of the program or module being tested. The software is treated like a black box and the only concern is that the box performs as it should. The only thing examined is the output of the box for various inputs. For the most part, black-box testing ignores the internal control structure and focuses on the information provided to and received from the module. Black-box testing would strive to uncover

1. functional deficiencies
2. interface errors (module testing)
3. data errors
4. performance errors
5. initialization and termination errors

As an example of a black-box test, suppose a particular program or module is required to accept numeric input in the range [a,b]. Test cases should be selected from three classes: less than **a**, between **a** and **b**, and greater than **b.** In each case, two invalid and one valid test case should be provided. Moreover, the boundaries should be given special attention, since errors often occur on the boundaries of the acceptable data sets. As an additional example, suppose a particular program is to search and find numbers on a range [a,b]. Again, two invalid test cases and one valid case should be provided. However, make sure the values **a** and **b** themselves are involved in the test. Additionally, values just below and just above **a** and **b** should be tested.

There are several approaches to white-box testing. In fact, software testing strategies have received considerable attention from computing professionals in recent years. Ideally, a testing strategy would involve testing all possible processing paths through a particular module. In many cases, particularly if the module is reasonably large or contains many loops and decisions, this exhaustive path testing strategy is impractical, since the number of paths can become an extremely large number, and designing test cases for each of the paths would become prohibitive. However, it is possible to test a basis set of *independent* paths through a particular module. The basis path testing strategy was first proposed by McCabe (R.S. Pressman, *Software Engineering,* McGraw Hill, 1992). A basis set is a collection of program paths which, when executed, will result in the execution of every program statement at least once. To guarantee that you have a basis set of independent paths, each new path through the program or module must introduce at least one new processing statement or one new condition not included in previous paths.

To accomplish the basis path testing strategy, begin with the pseudo-code or with an ANSI flowchart for the particular module being tested. In terms of the flowchart, an independent path must move along one control flow path not previously covered before this path was defined. One must then identify a collection of independent paths through the flowchart, and design test cases that will force (at least) the execution of the statements along this path. But how many paths should we look for? The answer is remarkably simple. It has been shown that all we need to do is count the number of *simple* conditions in the flowchart, and add one to this number to obtain the correct number of paths. The proof of this fact has its basis in graph theory and is beyond the scope of this text. The complex condition (a < b) && (c < d) must be reduced to two simple conditions in order to correctly determine the desired number of paths.

McCabe pointed out that if we choose a basis set of independent paths we will guarantee that each processing statement and each decision will have been executed at least once by designing test cases to exercise each independent path. It is possible that fewer tests will accomplish the same thing. McCabe's testing strategy provides an upper bound on the number of tests necessary to make sure that all program statements have been executed.

▶ Exercises 5.4

5.4.1 Consider the flowchart on page 230. Number each processing statement and simple decision, and determine the number **P** of independent paths through the flowchart. List **P** independent paths through the structure.

5.4.2 Consider the following problem (adapted from Myers, G., *The Art of Software Testing,* Wiley-Interscience, 1979).

A program is to accept three integers as input. These integers represent the sides of a triangle when connected end to end. The program is to produce the following output:

- the triangle is equilateral
- the triangle is isosceles
- the triangle is scalene
- no triangle exists
- the input data are in error

Develop a detailed procedural design for this program using ANSI flowcharts and then implement the program in the C programming language. Use McCabe's basis path testing procedure and determine a basis set of independent paths through the program. Finally, develop a set of test cases that will execute each of the paths. What are the results?

Flowchart to Accompany Exercise 5.4.1

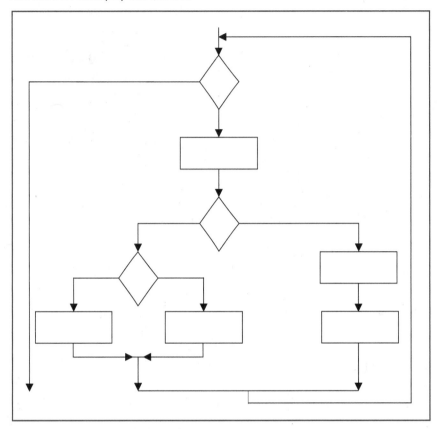

5.4.3　Compare and contrast the two testing strategies, black box and white box. What are the advantages and disadvantages of each? In practice, a combination of white-box and black-box strategies is recommended. Why?

▶ Key Words

addressing
address operator (**&**)
character strings
dereference operator (*****)
function arguments—call by value
　(**x**), call by reference (**&x**)
functions

software engineering (modularity,
　structured design, debugging,
　documentation)
storage types (global, static,
　automatic, dynamic)
testing strategies

▶ Chapter Concepts

5.1 The concept of modular design and implementation is reinforced throughout this chapter. When large problems are encountered you should divide the problem into smaller pieces and solve each of the smaller pieces. Each small solution, when combined, will solve the original large problem.

5.2 Call by value passes only the value of a storage location to a function, thus the function is able to only use the value, not to change the value in the original storage location. Call by reference, sometimes named call by address, passes the address of a value to the function. Thus the function can change the value at the original location by using the dereferencing operator.

5.3 A basic concept discussed in the chapter is that of causing a variable to contain the address of an array or structure. Address arithmetic is discussed, that is, `array[3]` is the same as `*(i+3)` if `i` has the address of the array.

5.4 The array name is actually the address of the first element of the array. This fact is used in item 5.3 and plays a role when arrays are passed to functions. Since array names are addresses, the pointer arithmetic can be used to access array elements in functions using the dereferencing operators or using indexing variables in a traditional manner.

5.5 Two- and higher-dimensioned arrays are possible in C. Arrays are used when dealing with homogeneous data. An example is the use of character strings where each string is a single-dimensioned array. If several names are to be stored, the individual names are addressed through the row and each character of a name is accessed through the column.

5.6 Software engineering concepts of program analysis, design, implementation, documentation, and debugging are included in this chapter. You should pay careful attention to these topics since your programs will be far more valuable if they are carefully designed, documented, and implemented.

▶ Programming Projects

5.1 Redo each of the programming projects from Chapter 4 in a modular structured fashion.

5.2 A two-dimensional array is an array of arrays. The arrays in question may not be the same sizes, which leads to the concept of ragged (two-dimensional) arrays. Since a string is an array, an array of strings may be conceptualized as a ragged array. Modify the bubble sort function of exercise 5.3.1 so that the bubble sort algorithm will sort strings into ascending (alphabetical) order.

5.3 Repeat project 5.2 for the selection sort algorithm.

5.4 You are working for an insurance company that pays dividends to the nearest integer. Write a program that reads in a series of dividends and reports the frequency dividends. For example, the following input data

```
16 45 22 67 45 23 22 45 67 13
```

would cause the output

dividend	frequency
16	1 times
45	3 times
22	2 times
67	2 times
23	1 times
13	1 times

5.5 You did a nice job on project 5.4, but now management would like the same data, but sorted on the frequency of occurrence. Thus the data output should appear as

dividend	frequency
45	3 times
22	2 times
67	2 times
23	1 times
16	1 times
13	1 times

where the items that occur the same number of times appear in the order first received.

5.6 Assume you are working for an actuarial company that requires a computer program to compute a variety of statistical analyses. Specifically, the data will consist of a list of integer numbers representing life expectancy. You are to create separate functions to compute the mean, mode, median, standard deviation, and variance. Recall that the mean is just the average. The median is defined to be the value in an ordered set of values below and above which there is an equal number of values, or which is the arithmetic mean of the two middle values if there is no one middle number. The mode is the most frequent occurring value in a set of values. The standard deviation is found by the equation

$$\mathbf{sd} = \sqrt{\frac{\sum_{k=1}^{n} (\mathbf{d_k} - \mathbf{m})^2}{n}}$$

where $\mathbf{sd}$ is the standard deviation, $\mathbf{m}$ is the mean, $\mathbf{d_k}$ is the kth data item, and $\mathbf{n}$ is the number of data items. The standard deviation is a value that predicts how far a particular data item is from the mean. The variance is the square of the standard deviation. Be sure to use good programming practices since this project can be done rather easily if the correct organization is used. Many of the computed values are used in later calculations.

5.7 The game of tic-tac-toe can be represented by a two-dimensional array of three elements in each dimension. Write an interactive program that will read in a person's move in terms of the coordinates to place an **x** or **o**. For example, 1,3 would imply an **x** should be placed in the upper-right corner. The program should then generate its move. Determine if the computer wins or the person wins after each move. Using modular programming and careful analysis and design, write functions to read a person's move, generate the computer's move, and determine who wins. Initially the board should be presented as

```
- - -
- - -
- - -
```

and if the 1,3 was read in, the board should be presented as

```
- - x
- - -
- - -.
```

The program should generate a move, say 2,2. The board is then presented as

```
- - x
- o -
- - -.
```

The board should be printed after every move.

5.8 Matrices (two-dimensioned arrays) are used in a variety of mathematics, engineering, and robotics applications. Often it is important to ascertain certain facts. Read in a set of data to fill a matrix of size 6 by 6 and determine if:

- The main diagonal is all 0. The main diagonal is defined as the (1,1), (2,2), (3,3), . . . positions of the matrix.

- The matrix is symmetric—that is, if the upper-right portion is a mirror image of the lower left. For example if the **(2,1)** position is equal to the **(1,2)** position, the matrix is symmetric with respect to these two positions. You have to determine if the matrix is symmetric with respect to all the positions above and below the main diagonal.

- The matrix is lower triangular—that is, if the lower-left portion is all 0. Lower triangular is defined as **a[i][j] = 0** whenever **i < j**.

5.9 Suppose you are at a shooting range where it is difficult to see the results of a target. That is, you can clearly see the target, but it is difficult to determine the accuracy of a shot. Suppose the target is constructed with sensors that return the coordinates of the shot. Your problem is to determine if the coordinates returned represent a miss, a hit in the outer ring, a hit in the inner ring, or a bullseye. Let the radius of the bullseye be 2 inches, the radius of the inner circle be 5 inches, and the radius of the outer circle be 10 inches. A coordinate returned by the sensors will lie in the bullseye region, inner circle, outer circle, or missed target. Your task is to read the coordinate that might be returned by the sensor and determine where the shot landed.

5.10 Suppose you are working for an engineering firm. Consider the accompanying diagram where R_i is the resistance of the system, R_1 is the resistance of the load (like a speaker of a stereo system), and V_s is the voltage source (power). We know current, I, is found by

$$I = \frac{V_s}{R_i + R_1}$$

and the power absorbed, P, is found by

$$P = I^2 R_1$$

A. Compute I and P for

$$\frac{R_i}{2} < R_1 < 2^* R_i$$

where R_i is 1000 ohms and V_s is 5 volts.

B. Using the information found in exercise A report the value of R_1 for maximum P.

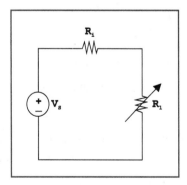

CHAPTER
6

Recursion

CHAPTER TOPICS

Introduction to Recursion

Examples of Recursion

Operating System Support of Recursive Programs

Recursive Sorting and Searching

INTRODUCTION

Chapter 6 presents a sophisticated problem-solving technique that has served as the foundation for many elegant problem-solving methodologies. Recursion is sufficiently powerful and complex to warrant a chapter dedicated solely to this topic. You will be presented problems and definitions to help you "think recursively." Recursion allows you to solve difficult problems with simple, elegant solutions. We believe you learn by doing, so after the introduction in the first section, we present several simple recursive algorithms. The solutions demonstrate good programming skills as presented in the previous chapters and establish techniques to assist you in mastering recursion. Section 6.3 will briefly discuss run-time support, provided by the operating system, that will enhance your understanding of recursion. The chapter will conclude with Section 6.4, which discusses recursive solutions of sorting and searching introduced in Chapter 4.

6.1 INTRODUCTION TO RECURSION

SECTION TOPICS

Recursion Defined

Recursive Control

Recursion Defined

What is recursion? We have seen in previous chapters that functions in C can call or invoke other functions. Recursion occurs when a function, either directly or indirectly, calls itself. Consider Figure 6.1.1, which shows the basic control structure in a direct recursive call.

Figure 6.1.1   Recursive Control Flow

```
main()
{
    declaration of variables
    some program statements
    x = sub(y); /* the invocation of function */
    other statements
}

sub(y)
declaration of y
{
    possibly declare some other variables
    possibly do some work
    x = sub(y); /* invoke sub from within sub */
            /* the sub (y) is the recursive call reinvoking this function */
    possibly do some other work
}
```

Recursive Control

Control flow of the program in Figure 6.1.1 is sequentially top to bottom starting in **main** until the statement **x=sub(y)** is executed, causing control to flow to the **sub** function. In the **sub** function control flows sequentially top to bottom until the statement **x = sub(y)** is encountered, where control is moved to the top of the function beginning a new invocation just as it is when **sub** is first invoked from **main**. Let us now define what is meant by *invocation*. When a function is "called" as in **y = sub(x)**, we say that the function has been *invoked* or that an invocation has occurred. While there may exist only one physical coding appearance of the function, through recursion there may be several invocations of that function active at a given time. When a function invokes another function, the values of variables and the control point of the first invocation are saved so when control is returned from the second invocation, the first invocation proceeds from where it left off, just like **main** will proceed from the statement that invoked **sub** when the original invocation of **sub** finishes. In this second invocation, control will start at the first statement, proceeding sequentially from top to bottom until the statement **x = sub(y)** will once again be encountered. When it is executed, a third invocation of the function is created and the second invocation is saved. That is, all the current values of variables and the control point are stored, so that the second invocation may become active again after the third invocation completes. The number of invocations of a function is called the *recursive depth* or *depth of recursion* and can be, in general, any number of levels deep, until the computer's memory is exhausted. It is possible to write programs that contain infinite recursion similar to infinite loops that will continually perform recursive calls until memory is exhausted. You must be very careful to identify the conditions that will allow the program to return from a recursive call.

If the program in Figure 6.1.1 were actually coded in C and run, what do you suspect would be the outcome? If you answer "probably infinite recursion," you would be correct. The function **sub** continually calls itself with no way of ever returning, and actually the "do some other work" in **sub** will never be executed since the function call will always cause control to start at the top of a new invocation of the function. So, we need to do some refinement of the pseudocode before we can attempt to write the program and execute it.

An excellent way to learn to write recursive programs is to study recursive definitions. Programs can be constructed directly from the recursive definition. A recursive definition as well as the program must contain two features:

- a stopping point or an anchor for the recursion
- a redefinition of the problem as a simpler form of itself

In order for recursion to execute properly, we need to define a problem in terms of itself in a simpler form.

▶ **PROBLEM**   Consider the factorial problem. The function **n!** (n factorial) is defined to be

$$n! = n*(n-1)*(n-2)*(n-3)* . . . * 3*2*1$$

We wish to write a function to calculate factorial.

ANALYSIS   From the definition, we observe that **5!** is

$$5*4*3*2*1 = 120$$

We also cleverly observe that

$$5! = 5*4!$$

and that from the definition

$$1! = 1$$

In making these observations, we have reduced the problem of calculat-

Figure 6.1.2 Definition Example

```
Suppose n is 5, then 5! is:
      5! = 5 * (5-1)! or 5 * 4! but
      4! = 4 * (4-1)! or 4 * 3! but
      3! = 3 * (3-1)! or 3 * 2! but
      2! = 2 * (2-1)! or 2 * 1! and
we know 1! = 1 since this is in our definition, so
      2! = 2 * 1! or 2 * 1 = 2 and
      3! = 3 * 2! or 3 * 2 = 6 and
      4! = 4 * 3! or 4 * 6 = 24 and
      5! = 5 * 4! or 5 * 24 = 120 the desired result.
```

ing **5!** to a problem of calculating **4!**, which is a simpler form of the factorial problem.

The recursive definition of the factorial function is

```
1! = 1
n! = n * (n-1)!
```

Consider the definition carefully. The first line provides an anchor or stopping point for the recursion. We need to program the conditions that will allow the recursion to terminate, that is, the condition that causes a function to stop calling itself. The second line of the definition redefines the problem as *a simpler instance of itself.* These two features are necessary in every recursive definition. If these two aspects of the definition exist, a recursive function can be written from the definition. Figure 6.1.2 demonstrates how the factorial function works.

CODE   A complete program for finding factorial is given in Figure 6.1.3, where line numbers are not part of the program but are included for discussion purposes.

TEST   The results of this program are

```
find the factorial of what?
5
the factorial of 5 is 120
```

The aspects of recursion discussed in this example are common to all recursive functions. Notice how the program does exactly what the definition indicated it should. Line 15 of the function **factorial** corresponds to **1! = 1** and line 17 is **n! = n * (n-1)!**, factorial (**n- 1**), where the **(n-1)!** is the recursive call to the function. Line 17 invokes function

Figure 6.1.3   Factorial Example

```
1    #include <stdio.h>

2    int factorial(int n);

3    main()
4    {
5        int
6            n, result;
7        printf("Find the factorial of what?\n");
8        scanf("%d",&n);
9        result = factorial(n);
10       printf("the factorial of %d is %d\n",n,result);
11   }
12   int factorial(int n)
13   {
14       if (n == 1)
15           return (1);
16       else
17           return (n * factorial(n-1));
18   }
```

factorial from within **factorial** causing a new invocation of **factorial** to occur. You now see why we must redefine the problem as a simpler instance of itself, since ultimately **n** must become **1** (in this example). Initially, the sample run was executed with **5** passed to the recursive function. Since **5** is not equal to **1**, line 16 was executed with the statement

```
return(5 * (5-1)!) or return(5 * 4!) /*4! invokes the
        function again*/
```

Now **4!** is a simpler instance of the same problem; **4!** is simpler than **5!**. Thus, we have redefined the problem as a simpler instance of itself. So the **4!** call reinvokes the exact same function, with **4** as the value of the argument **n**. Since **4** does not equal **1**, line 17 of code is again executed reinvoking the function

```
return(4 * 3!) which is return(n*factorial(n-1))
```

which is again redefining the problem as a simpler instance of itself. In this invocation, **n** has become **3**, which is not equal to **1**; line 16 is once again executed.

```
return(3 * 2!)
```

and similarly will again be executed

```
return(2 * 1!)
```

Now, in this invocation of the function, **n** has become **1** and is equal to **1** so **1** is returned as the value computed by the function. Where is this value returned to? To the previous invocation, that is, to the **return** statement that invoked the function. So now control is back in the **return(2 * 1!)** which has become **return(2 * 1)** as a result of the value returned. That is, in the **return(n * factorial(n-1))**, the **factorial(n-1)** is effectively replaced with the value returned from the previous invocation. This value is given to the **return(3 * 2!)**. Since **2!** has just been computed as **2**, the **return(3 * 2!)** is **return(3 * 2)** or simply **return(6)**. The **6** is then passed back to the statement that invoked this instance of the function, the instruction **return(4 * 3!)**, which has become **return(4 * 6)** from evaluation of **3!**, and **24** is returned back to its invocation statement, **return(5 * 24)**. The **120** is then returned to the **main** routine that started the whole thing. Figure 6.1.4 diagrams what has just been described.

Consider what happens when one function calls another function. Look at the program in Figure 6.1.5.

When **sub1** is invoked from **main**, what happens to **main**'s variables? Are they destroyed? Are they changed? The answer, of course, is that they are simply saved until control is returned to **main**. The **y** in **sub1** is a different **y** than the **y** in **main**, or the **y** in **sub2** for that matter. The calling function's variable values are stored while the called function executes and are restored when control is returned. In Figure 6.1.5, we have created three distinct **y**'s, each with unique stor-

Figure 6.1.4 Diagram of Factorial Function

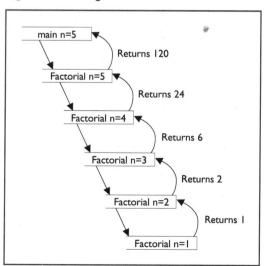

Figure 6.1.5   Function Calls

```
1    #include <stdio.h>
2    main()
3    {
4       int x=5,   /* saved when sub1 is called, restored when sub1 finishes */
5           y=6,   /* also saved and restored                              */
6           z=7;   /* also saved and restored when sub1 is called          */
7       sub1(x);   /* invokes sub1, passing the value of x to sub1         */
8    }

9    sub1(int xx) /* function sub1, value of x is placed in storage for xx */
10               /* int xx is parameter xx storage request                */
11   {
12   int y = 17,  /* local variables, storage created each time sub1 entered */
13       z = 22;  /* value placed in that storage upon creation             */
14       sub2(xx); /* sub2 called, y and z are saved and restored when sub2 */
15   }            /* finishes its execution, sub1 is present but sleeping   */
16   sub2(int xx) /* function sub2, value of xx is passed to this xx        */
17               /* this is a new xx than the one in sub1                  */
18   {
19       int y = 1,/* variables local to sub2                              */
20           ww = 2;/* allocated when sub2 is entered, destroyed when sub2  */
21   }            /* finishes                                              */
```

age location and therefore capable of storing distinct integer values. Now consider what happens when recursion is present. Reconsider Figure 6.1.3, which has a control flow sequence for $n = 5$ (illustrated in Figure 6.1.6).

Figure 6.1.6 represents the invocations of **factorial** that exist at the deepest level of recursion for $n = 5$. When the fifth call occurs, the variables that exist in the fourth call are stored; they remain inactive until program control is returned to that invocation. We no longer think of a function as being only a body of code, but rather code and an invocation of that code. So, in the factorial program, **factorial** is invoked a total of five times. If n were a greater value, **factorial** would be invoked more before the solution would be returned, that is, the depth of recursion would be greater. You can think of the recursive invocations of a function as though they were distinct functions being called or invoked from other functions. The variables of preceding invocations are saved and ultimately restored when control returns to that invocation. The key to the success of recursion is that each call brings some value closer to a stopping point. That is, there must be a stopping condition and a redefinition of the problem that works toward that stopping point.

Figure 6.1.6 Recursion Unraveled

```c
#include <stdio.h>
main()
{
   int
      n, result;

   printf("find the factorial of what?\n");
   scanf("%d",&n);
   result = factorial(n);
   printf("the factorial of %d is %d\n",n,result);
}

int factorial(int n) /* first call when n = 5 */

{
   if (n == 1) return (1);
   return (n * factorial(n-1)); /* this stmt gets executed    */
}  /* factorial is the call, and receives the value upon return */

int factorial (int n) /* second call when n = 4 */

{
   if (n == 1 ) return (1);
   return (n * factorial(n-1)); /* this stmt gets executed    */
}  /* factorial is the call, and receives the value upon return */

int factorial(int n) /* third call when n = 3 */

{
   if (n == 1) return (1);
   return (n * factorial(n-1)); /* this stmt gets executed    */
}  /* factorial is the call, and receives the value upon return */

int factorial(int n) /* fourth call when n = 2 */

{
   if (n == 1) return (1);
   return (n * factorial(n-1)); /* this stmt gets executed    */
}  /* factorial is the call, and receives the value upon return */

int factorial(int n) /* fifth call when n = 1 */

{
   if (n == 1) return (1); /* this stmt gets executed    */
   return (n * factorial(n-1));
}
```

Let us now consider some additional examples of recursive definitions in order to help you practice the first step in writing recursive routines, that of writing recursive definitions.

▶ **PROBLEM**　Suppose we consider the sequence 2, 4, 6, 8, 10, ... Write a recursive definition that will generate these numbers.

ANALYSIS　We will anchor the recursion when the value of the sequence is 2. Let **n** represent the number of numbers to generate in the sequence. Now, given the first number, how can we generate the next number? The next number is two more than the previous number, which we may write

```
S(n) = S(n-1) + 2 for n > 1.
```

Here the **S(n)** represents the nth number of the sequence. Thus

```
S(1) = 2                /* the anchor for the recursion */
S(n) = S(n-1) + 2 /* the recursive definition     */
```

DESIGN
```
S(5) = S(4) + 2   /* from the rule */
S(4) = S(3) + 2
S(3) = S(2) + 2
S(2) = S(1) + 2
S(1) = 2          /* from the stopping point */
S(2) = 4 from S(2) = S(1) + 2 or S(2) = 2 + 2
S(3) = 6 from S(3) = S(2) + 2 or S(3) = 4 + 2
S(4) = 8 from S(4) = S(3) + 2 or S(4) = 6 + 2
S(5) = 10 from S(5) = S(4) + 2 or S(5) = 8 + 2
```

We have generated, recursively, the desired sequence of terms. The program in Figure 6.1.7 implements this definition. Notice, in this case, the recursive definition states a rule for generating the next term from the previous one, that is, the nth term from the (n−1)st term. This satisfies our idea of recursion, that of defining the problem in terms of itself. The recursion continues until **n = 1** and generates the values as the recursion "unwraps" or returns from each recursive call.

CODE　The complete program in Figure 6.1.7 implements the preceding design. Note that **main** simply invokes the recursive function.

TEST　The output of the above program is exactly

```
num 1 of sequence is 2
num 2 of sequence is 4
num 3 of sequence is 6
num 4 of sequence is 8
num 5 of sequence is 10
```

Figure 6.1.7   Sequence of Five Numbers, Recursively Generated

```
#include <stdio.h>

#define N 5    /* find the first 5 numbers of the sequence */
int S(int);
main()
{
    S(N);       /* invoke the function the first time */
}

int S(int n)  /* ANSI standard parameter declaration */
{
    int nums;
    if (n == 1) /* recursive stopping point */
    {
        printf("num %d of sequence is %d\n",n,2);
        return (2);
    }
    nums = S(n-1) + 2; /* recursive call */
         /* print each number as it is found */
    printf("num %d of sequence is %d\n",n, nums);
    return (nums);      /* return the current value */
}
```

An interesting thing about the program in Figure 6.1.7 is that it performs essentially the same function as a simple **for** loop would perform. Computer science theorists have shown that virtually any problem that can be solved using iterative methods (loops, etc.) can be solved using recursive solutions. It might be interesting for you to try to write recursive solutions for problems ordinarily attacked by iteration. We must also ask the obvious question: What is a nonrecursive definition for the above sequence?

▶ **PROBLEM**   Consider the sequence of numbers

$$1, 3, 7, 15, 31, \ldots$$

We wish to write a recursive C function that will generate this sequence.

ANALYSIS   This sequence is defined recursively by

```
T(1) = 1                 /*the stopping point          */
T(n) = 2 * T(n-1) + 1    /*redefined as a simpler problem */
```

DESIGN The recursive definition is effectively the design of the algorithm in this case. We must write a function that returns a value given by the definition.

CODE The implementation of the preceding recursive definition is shown in Figure 6.1.8.

TEST The output of Figure 6.1.8 is

```
num 1 of sequence is 1
num 2 of sequence is 3
num 3 of sequence is 7
num 4 of sequence is 15
num 5 of sequence is 31
```

We have found, by looking at these examples, that sequences of numbers and simple recursive definitions provide a pattern for imple-

Figure 6.1.8 Sequence Recursively Generated

```c
#include <stdio.h>
#define N 5        /* find the first 5 of the sequence */
int T(int n);
main()
{
    T(N);      /* the invocation to start generating the sequence   */
}

int T(int n)
{
    int nums;
    if (n == 1)          /* testing for the stopping point */
    {
        printf("num %d of sequence is %d\n",n,1);
        return (1);
    }
    nums = 2 * T(n-1) + 1;  /* the recursive call */
    printf("num %d of sequence is %d\n",n, nums);
                        /* print as the recursion unwraps */
    return (nums);
}
```

mentation. That is, the programs in Figures 6.1.7 and 6.1.8 are almost identical, so any sequence of numbers defined with this two-statement pattern is programmed by these instructions. A third example of recursion using this pattern is the Fibonacci numbers generated later in this chapter. Also, in the next section are examples of other problems solved recursively requiring slightly more sophisticated definitions. But the basic principles of recursion are always present: that of a stopping point and redefining the problem as a smaller instance of itself. The smaller instance of itself simply allows the recursive calls to work toward a stopping point. If this simplifying characteristic is absent or the stopping point somehow missed, the recursive calls would continue until memory was exhausted which is a common problem not unlike infinite loops, called infinite recursion. You can avoid this problem by carefully selecting a stopping condition for the recursion and ensuring that the recursive function invocations move toward the stopping point.

▶ Exercises 6.1

6.1.1 Write a recursive definition of the sequence

3, 6, 9, 12, 15, . . .

6.1.2 What is the sequence defined by the recursive definition

```
S(1) = 4
S(n) = S(n-1) * 4
```

6.1.3 Identify the stopping point and the recursive call in the following function X.

```
int X(int m, int n)
{
    if (n == 0) return(m);
    if (n > m) X(n,m);
}
```

6.1.4 Identify the error and describe the effect of the following function.

```
int X (int m)
{
    X(n);
}
```

6.1.5   Identify the error and describe the effect of the following function. Assume **m** has the value 10 the first time the function is invoked.

```
int X (int m)
{
    if (m <= 0) return(1);
    printf("value is %d\n", X(m+1));
}
```

6.1.6   Identify the error and describe the effect of the following function. Assume **m** has the value 10 the first time the function is invoked.

```
int X (int m)
{
    int p = 5;
    if (p <= 0) return(1);
    printf("value is %d\n", X(m-1));
}
```

6.1.7   Trace the execution of the following program to determine its output.

```
#include <stdio.h>
int gen(int);
main()
{
    int x = 10;
    gen(x);
}

int gen(int y)
{
    if (y > 20) return(1);
    gen(y+2);
    printf("value is %d\n",y);
}
```

6.1.8   How many invocations are made to function **gen** in exercise 6.1.7?

6.1.9   Given the following recursive definition, implement the corresponding program.

```
S(1) = 5
S(n) = 2*S(n-1) + 1
```

6.1.10   What will be the maximum depth of recursion required to generate the numbers described in exercise 6.1.9?

6.2 EXAMPLES OF RECURSION

SECTION TOPICS

Fibonacci Numbers

String Reversal

Maxsort

Base Conversion 10 to 16

Greatest Common Divisor

This section will develop some standard algorithms that are often used to demonstrate recursion. The best way to learn recursion is by doing, so this section provides an opportunity for practicing recursion. You should attempt to solve the problems first by developing an algorithm you think will perform the desired function. If you have sufficient time, you may put your algorithm on the computer and see how it works. Initially you might be surprised at the results, but after practice, recursion will come more naturally. After you have developed your solutions, compare your techniques to the ones presented here.

Fibonacci Numbers

We first investigated the Fibonacci numbers iteratively in exercise 4.1.2. We now consider this interesting sequence of numbers from a recursive point of view.

▶ **PROBLEM** Our first example considers the sequence of numbers where the first two numbers are 1 and each successive number is found by adding the previous two. The sequence is

1, 1, 2, 3, 5, 8, 13, 21, . . .

This problem is similar to the sequences presented in Section 6.1. These are well-known numbers called the Fibonacci sequence, named after their discoverer, Fibonacci, also known as Leonardo of Pisa. The sequence results from the recreational problem: "How many pairs of rabbits can be produced from a single pair in one year if it is assumed that every month each pair begets a new pair which from the second month becomes productive?" The months and number of rabbits are shown below:

```
Month:          1 2 3 4 5 6  7  8  9 10 11  12
No. of pairs:   1 1 2 3 5 8 13 21 34 55 89 144
```

Many properties of Fibonacci numbers have been discovered by mathematicians over the years. For example,

```
F(n+1) * F(n-1) = (F(n))² + (-1)ⁿ
```

ANALYSIS   Now that you are excited about Fibonacci numbers, what is the recursive definition of these numbers? If `F(n)` represents the nth Fibonacci number, then

```
F(1) = 1
F(2) = 1
F(n) = F(n-1) + F(n-2) for n > 2
```

In this case we have two initial conditions. Notice that the computation of each Fibonacci number requires two recursive calls. One with parameter `(n-1)` and the second with parameter `(n-2)`.

DESIGN   Consider finding the first 5 Fibonacci numbers. This is the case where n=5. From the definition we know that

```
F(5) = F(4) + F(3)
F(4) = F(3) + F(2)
F(3) = F(2) + F(1)
```

where `F(2)` and `F(1)` are known. Each `F(3)`, `F(4)`, and `F(5)` represents a recursive function invocation. Thus, we write the program such that it starts at `n`, works to n = 2 and n-1 = 1 and returns Fibonacci numbers as the recursion unwraps. Figure 6.2.1 gives the implementation.

CODE   The code in Figure 6.2.1 is a complete implementation of the Fibonacci sequence problem.

TEST   The output of Figure 6.2.1 is possibly a little surprising. It is

```
Fibonacci number 2 is 1
Fibonacci number 1 is 1
Fibonacci number 3 is 2
Fibonacci number 2 is 1
Fibonacci number 4 is 3
Fibonacci number 2 is 1
Fibonacci number 1 is 1
Fibonacci number 3 is 2
Fibonacci number 5 is 5
```

We see some of the Fibonacci numbers are repeated, which is to be expected since there are two recursive calls required to compute each number and we print after each recursive call. For example, `F(5) = F(4) + F(3)`, but `F(4) = F(3) + F(2)`, so to compute `F(5)`, `F(3)` is computed

Figure 6.2.1   Recursive Fibonacci Numbers

```
#include <stdio.h>

#define N 5    /* find the first 5 Fibonacci numbers */
int F(int n);
main()
{
    F(N);    /* invoke the function to compute numbers              */
}

int F(int n)
{
    int nums;
    if (n == 1)          /* the stopping point                      */
    {
        printf("Fibonacci number %d is %d\n",n,1);
        return (1);
    }
    if (n == 2)       /* both stopping points are necessary since the   */
                      /* definition uses both f(n-1) and f(n-2)         */
    {
        printf("Fibonacci number %d is %d\n",n,1);
        return (1);
    }
    nums = F(n-1) + F(n-2);   /* the recursive call                     */
    printf("Fibonacci number %d is %d\n",n,nums);
    return (nums);
}
```

two distinct times, once to compute F(5) and a second time in the computation of F(4). Thus, our standard program, which prints the result of each recursive call, prints some of the Fibonacci numbers multiple times. It should be noted that while the generation of Fibonacci numbers provides a nice recursive example, recursion is not the best technique for solving this problem due to the repetition of solutions. Once F(3) has been found, it should be unnecessary to recompute it. An iterative solution would possibly be more efficient to calculate Fibonacci numbers. Can you write such an iterative function?

String Reversal

As another example of recursion, consider the problem of reversing a string of characters.

▶ **PROBLEM** The program should receive a string like **"abcdef"**, of arbitrary length, and display **"fedcba"**, the string in reverse order. Note that the problem statement only addresses the appearance of the string in reversed order, not reversing the string in the computer's memory.

ANALYSIS The goal is to develop a recursive solution to the problem. Clearly, we could read the string into an array, and simply display the array in reverse order. But, since we would like to use recursion, how can we solve the problem? We start at the end of the string and recursively move to the beginning, printing each character as we work toward the beginning of the string recursively which will cause the string to display reversed. Note that the string is only *displayed* in reversed order; we have *not* caused the string to be stored in reverse order in memory.

DESIGN A string of length 1 will be the anchor for the recursion. Remember, when we make a recursive call, the values of the current variables are stored in a manner where the last one in is the first one out, much like trays are placed in a cafeteria. The *last in, first out* way of storing information is called a stack. We can traverse recursively from the end of the string to the beginning, displaying each character as we go. When we get to the beginning of the string all the characters will have been displayed in reverse order. A recursive definition, using **n** as the length of the string, is:

1. If (**n < 0**) return.
2. Print the current string character as the recursion unwraps.
3. Invoke the function with **n-1**, causing the original **n** to be saved.

Recall that a character array is used to store a string, so we display the string in reversed order by displaying each character of the array separately, that is, we consider the string as elements of an array rather than as a complete string.

CODE The complete program for string reversal is given in Figure 6.2.2.

TEST The output of the program in Figure 6.2.2 is:

```
Please enter a string of less than 31 characters
abcde
string = abcde
reverse string = edcba
```

Again, it should be pointed out that recursion is not the best method for solving this problem, just as it was not the best for the Fibonacci number problem. This example provides an opportunity to compare recur-

Figure 6.2.2 Recursive String Reversal

```
#include <stdio.h>
void rev_str (int l, char s[]);
main()
{
    char
        in_string[30]; /* string to be reversed */
    int
        n;              /* the length of the string */
    printf("Please enter a string of less than 30 characters \n");
    scanf("%s",in_string);
    printf("string = %s\n",in_string);
    printf("reverse string = ");
    n = strlen(in_string);  /* includes end of string marker, so pass n-1 */
    rev_str(n-1,in_string); /* n-1 since we do not want to include the
                            \0 end of string marker */
}
void rev_str (int l, char s[])
{
    if (l < 0) return; /* stopping point */
    printf("%c",s[l]); /* l is the length of string so prints last character */
    rev_str(l-1,s);    /* recursive call with length one less */
}
```

sion and iteration. Clearly, the same effect can be accomplished by a loop counting from **n** to **0**, displaying characters as we go. So, recursion is another form of iteration, but an added advantage is gained with recursion. The intermediate values of the recursive functions are saved. Their values will be available for computations as the recursion *unwraps*. This proves to be a very powerful tool.

Recursion provides a rather simple solution, one that requires little coding, even in this rather simple example. A solution using recursion is often faster and easier to code as exemplified by the tree traversals of Chapter 7 which provide examples of important, efficient algorithms easily programmed recursively.

Consider the flow of execution of the program in Figure 6.2.2. The function **rev_str** is invoked with **s="abcde"** and **l=4**, the length of the string. Remember, strings are stored in arrays and therefore the length is computed beginning from index **0**. A five-character string will be in positions **0** through **4** of the array. Since **l** is not less than **0**, the return is not executed. The print is executed, displaying the **s[l]** character, which is the last character of the string since **l** is **4**. The function is then invoked with **1-1** or **3** as a simpler problem. Shortening the string is simplifying the problem. Again, the **if** fails, allowing the print to execute, displaying the second to the last character, which is the last character for this invocation. The function is again invoked with **1-1** being **2**. This pattern continues until **1** becomes −1, exhausting the string of characters. Notice that the storage of the string has not changed; the string is stored in **s** in the same order upon completion of the function, we have simply printed it in reverse order. Figure 6.2.3 diagrams what has just been described.

    This example differs from preceding examples in that the *work* in the routine is performed on the way in to the recursion rather than on the way out. There is no inherent advantage to one over the other; when the work is done is simply a matter of style or restraints of the problem.

Maxsort

Sorting has been studied extensively by computing professionals so it is not surprising that many sorting algorithms exist. The next problem considers a recursive version of the maxsort algorithm.

Figure 6.2.3   Recursive String Reversal Unwrapped

```
invoke rev_str s="abcde"
                     1 = 4
print s[1] --- the e
    invoke rev_str s="abcde"
                         1 = 3
    print s[1] --- the d
        invoke rev_str s="abcde"
                             1 = 2
        print s[1] --- the c
            invoke rev_str s="abcde"
                                 1 = 1
            print s[1] --- the b
                invoke rev_str s="abcde"
                                     1 = 0
                print s[1] --- the a
                    invoke rev_str s="abcde"
                                         1 = -1
                        return
                    return
                return
            return
        return
    return
return
```

▶ **PROBLEM**   Use a recursive implementation of the maxsort algorithm to sort a collection of integers into ascending order.

ANALYSIS   Again, we will use the number of numbers to be sorted as the size of the problem. Initially, there will be **n** number of numbers to sort; after a recursive call there needs to be **n–1** number of numbers to sort. When there are no more numbers (**n = 0**), the recursion will stop. The previous sentence satisfies the recursive stopping point.

DESIGN   The problem is solved by finding the position of the largest number in the first **n** numbers. Exchange that number with the **n**th number and recursively call the procedure with **n–1** causing the routine to find the position of the largest number in **n–1** numbers. Exchange that number with the number in **n-1** position, which is the **n**th position of the recursive call.

A function is used to print the unsorted and sorted numbers. Whenever similar multiple tasks are performed, or just for readability, functions should be used. This program also demonstrates the use of another function, **find_max**, called from the recursive function, but not part of the recursion. This reinforces the concept of recursive calls being function invocations like invoking any other function. Other functions can be invoked from recursive functions like any other function; after all, a recursive function is any other function that simply calls itself.

CODE   A complete program implementing the maxsort algorithm is contained in Figure 6.2.4.

TEST   A sample input data set follows:

```
23 12 34 10 56 4 8 15 25 12 9
```

The corresponding output created is:

```
there are 11 elements to be sorted

the unsorted data:
23 12 34 10 56 4 8 15 25 12 9

the sorted data:
4 8 9 10 12 12 15 23 25 34 56
```

The working of the program in Figure 6.2.4 is now demonstrated. Suppose we consider the input data given above:

```
index      0  1  2  3  4  5 6 7  8  9  10
contents   23 12 34 10 56 4 8 15 25 12 9
```

The array positions are numbered for readability. The program begins execution by reading in the numbers from the keyboard and invoking the function to print the array. The variable **noelts** counts the number of

Figure 6.2.4   Recursive maxsort

```
#include <stdio.h>
void writearray (int a[], int noelts);
int findmax (int a[], int n);
void maxsort (int a[], int n);
main()
{
   int
      a[1000],    /* sort up to 1000 numbers        */
      i,j,        /* index variables into the array */
      noelts = 0; /* number of elements to sort     */
   while(((scanf("%d",&a[noelts])) != EOF) && (noelts < 1000))
      noelts = noelts + 1; /* noelts++ could be in the while */
                /* read in the numbers            */
   noelts = noelts - 1; /* it was one too big      */
                   /* as before the above line could be noelts-- */
   printf("there are %d elements to be sorted\n\n",noelts);
   printf("the unsorted data:\n");
   writearray(a,noelts);     /* function to display array contents */
   maxsort(a,noelts);      /* function that will perform sorting */
   printf("the sorted data:\n");
   writearray(a,noelts);   /* function to display array contents  */
}
/*******************************************************************/
/* This function is invoked twice to display the array contents before */
/* and after the sorting has taken place.                          */
/*******************************************************************/
void writearray(int a[], int noelts)
{
   int
      i;
   for (i=0;i<noelts;i=i+1)                  /* iterate through the array */
      printf("%d ",a[i]);
   printf("\n\n");
}
/*******************************************************************/
/* This function finds the position of the maximum element and is      */
/* invoked by maxsort.                                             */
/*******************************************************************/
int findmax(int a[], int n)
```

(continued)

Figure 6.2.4 Recursive maxsort (*continued*)

```
{
   int
      max=0,   /* max holds the location of the largest number       */
      i;       /* i just steps through the array looking for largest  */
   for(i=1;i<n;i=i+1)
      if (a[i] > a[max]) max = i;
   return(max);
}



/*********************************************************************/
/* This is the heart of the sorting. It searches through the array of  */
/* numbers each time correctly placing the maximum number of the section*/
/* of the array considered. The function is recursively invoked with   */
/* smaller value of n, indicating less of the array to be searched.     */
/*********************************************************************/


void maxsort(int a[], int n)
{
   int
      temp, /* a temporary variable used for exchanging numbers */
      max;  /* the maximum value in this section                */
   if (n == 2)
   {
      if (a[0] > a[1]) /* handle the last two as a special case */
      {
       temp = a[1];    /* perform the interchange              */
       a[1] = a[0];
       a[0] = temp;
      }
   }
   else
   {
      max = findmax(a,n);   /* locate the position of the max element */
      temp = a[n-1];        /* exchange the last element with the max */
      a[n-1]=a[max];
      a[max]=temp;
      maxsort(a,n-1);       /* recursive call with smaller list */
   }
}
```

numbers which is passed to the function **maxsort**. Then **maxsort** first calls **findmax** which returns the location of the largest number in variable **max**.

```
index        0   1   2   3   4   5  6  7   8   9   10
contents    23  12  34  10  56  4  8  15  25  12  9
                                ↑ max = 4            ↑ n = 10
```

The number at **max**'s position is interchanged with the number in **n**'s position, yielding:

```
index        0   1   2   3   4  5  6  7   8   9   10
contents    23  12  34  10  9  4  8  15  25  12  56
```

The **maxsort** function is reinvoked with **n-1** as a parameter. Again, the first instruction is the call of **findmax** which locates the largest number, this time from array positions **0** through **9**.

```
index        0   1   2   3   4  5  6  7   8   9   10
contents    23  12  34  10  9  4  8  15  25  12  56
                     ↑max = 2                ↑
```

                        n = 9 from n-1 parameter

Again, the number at **max**'s position is interchanged with the number at **n**'s position, yielding:

```
index        0   1   2   3   4  5  6  7   8   9   10
contents    23  12  12  10  9  4  8  15  25  34  56
```

Now the array is sorted in the last two positions, that is, the last two numbers are in their proper sorted location. This pattern is continued until **n** is less than **0**, thus sorting the complete array.

This program differs from the string reversal program in that the numbers in the computer's storage are being changed. It is emphasized that recursion is the invocation of a function as though it were a distinct and separate function. Therefore, all concepts related to passing values to a function covered in Chapter 5 are relevant. Call by address and call by value are to be considered when using recursion. In this case, the array is passed by address, so changes to the array remain from one function invocation to another.

Base Conversion 10 to 16

When dealing with computers, it is sometimes necessary to examine the contents of memory before any conversions are done. That is, to look at memory in its internal state. We have already learned that memory contains data as a string of binary digits. By associating binary digits in groups of four, base 16 numbers can directly be written. For example, the number correspondence is shown:

```
base two number: 1101 0010 1001 1110 1111 1010
in base sixteen:  D    2    9    E    F    A
```

So the ability to convert between common base 10 and binary/hexadecimal, which is what the computer uses, is important. We would like a program that receives a base 10 number and converts it, recursively, to base 16.

▶ **PROBLEM**   Write a program that will convert decimal numbers to hexadecimal.

ANALYSIS   The technique and motivation for this problem was presented in Chapter 1. Consider the number 4074. To convert to base 16, we divide by 16, that is, 4074 divided by 16 yielding quotient 254 and remainder 10. So, the last digit is A, which we use to represent 10 in base 16. We then repeat by dividing 16 into the quotient, 254, of the previous operation. Thus, 254 divided by 16 yields quotient 15 and remainder 14. The second digit is E, the representation for 14. Now 16 is divided into 15, yielding quotient 0 and remainder 15, which is F, the third digit. Thus, the base 16 number is FEA, found from the remainders of the successive divisions.

```
4074 / 16  = 254 remainder = 10 or A
256 / 16   = 15 remainder  = 14 or E
15 / 16    = 0 remainder    = 15 or F
```

DESIGN   The stopping point occurs when the quotient is 0 and the simpler problem is usage of the quotient as the dividend in successive divisions. The division process is accomplished in a straightforward manner, but we need a method to translate the remainders into their base 16 representation. The **trans** array will accomplish this task. The integer remainder will index this character array providing the appropriate character to be displayed on the output. The program in Figure 6.2.5 implements this description.

CODE   The complete program with recursive function for base 10 to 16 conversion is provided in Figure 6.2.5.

TEST   Recursion provides a nice solution and a convenient way to make one quotient become the dividend for the next division by parameter passing. This is accomplished by the function call where the quotient is passed

Figure 6.2.5   Recursive Base Conversion—10 to 16

```c
#include <stdio.h>

#define number 12266      /* convert this decimal number to base 16 first */
#define number2 4074      /* convert this number second                   */
#define number3 16        /* convert this number next                     */
#define number4 10        /* convert this number last                     */
void conv(int n);
char                      /* the translation array                        */
trans[16]={'0','1','2','3','4','5','6','7','8','9','A','B','C','D',
      'E','F'};
main()
{ /* clearly we could have done some "scanf's" to read in the numbers   */
  /* but this demonstrates the numbers being converted                  */
    printf("%d base 10 in base 16 is:\n",number);
    conv(number);          /* go convert the number                      */
    printf("\n");
    printf("%d base 10 in base 16 is:\n",number2);
    conv(number2);         /* convert the second number                  */
    printf("\n");
    printf("%d base 10 in base 16 is:\n",number3);
    conv(number3);         /* convert the third number                   */
    printf("\n");
    printf("%d base 10 in base 16 is:\n",number4);
    conv(number4);         /* convert the fourth number                  */
    printf("\n");
}
/****************************************************************************/
/* The conv function will perform the success divisions and using the   */
/* global trans array display the appropriate base 16 digit.            */
/****************************************************************************/
void conv(int n)      /* the convert function */
{                     /* the number to convert */
    if (n > 0)  /* the stopping point */
    {
        if ((n/16) > 0)      /* the problem redefined as a smaller instance */
           conv(n/16);       /* the division is done, its result is passed to */
                             /* the next invocation of conv                 */
        printf(" %c ",trans[n%16]); /* print the proper character from table */
    }
}
```

into what becomes the dividend for the next invocation of the function. The output created by the program in Figure 6.2.5 is:

```
12266 base 10 in base 16 is:
 2  F  E  A
4074 base 10 in base 16 is:
 F  E  A
16 base 10 in base 16 is:
 1  0
10 base 10 in base 16 is:
 A
```

Since base 16 numbers require letters as digits of the number, we construct a character array that holds the appropriate characters to be printed. There is a distinct difference between the number 2 and the character 2 as far as the computer is concerned. We have discussed how integers are stored in the computer as compared to characters or floats. We present the base 16 numbers as character strings rather than actual numeric strings of digits. This requirement is present since base 16 demands the use of A, B, C, D, E, and F to represent all base 16 numerals. The remainders from the divisions are used to index into that character array. For example, when 14 is the remainder, given by the modulus operator %, we place **trans[14]**, which is E, into the string representing the base 16 number.

The problem is made smaller for the recursion by passing the integer quotient to the next invocation of the function, which makes the next recursive call work on a smaller number. A smaller number represents a simpler problem, allowing the recursion to approach the stopping point as required.

There are other ways of doing this conversion, but recursion offers a simple, precise way of solving the problem. Recursion is efficient both in terms of the amount of coding necessary and the execution time of the program.

Greatest Common Divisor

Mathematics often requires the largest number that will divide evenly into two other numbers. This is the requirement of the greatest common divisor (**gcd**). For example, the **gcd** of 24 and 18 is 6 because 6 is the largest number that will divide into both 24 and 18 evenly.

▶ **PROBLEM**   Write a computer program that will find the greatest common divisor of any two positive integers.

ANALYSIS   Euclid discovered that for any two positive integers **a** and **b**, a = q*b + r, where **q** is the quotient of the division and **r** is the remainder of the division (a/b). He also showed that the greatest common divisor function gcd satisfies the equation gcd(n,a) = gcd(n,r). We therefore compute the remainder r and use r in the next iteration of the computation, until the remainder is 0. To illustrate, suppose we seek the gcd of 1024 and 50. The following steps are performed using Euclid's algorithm and C's modulus operator to obtain the remainder involved in each division:

```
1024 % 50 = 24
50 % 24 = 2
24 % 2 = 0 so 2 is the gcd!
```

DESIGN   The stopping point occurs when the result of the % operation is 0. The recursive call uses the previous result of the % operation with the smaller of the original two numbers. That is,

```
if n = 0 return m, otherwise return gcd (n, m%n)
```

CODE   The complete program with recursive function to calculate the greatest common divisor is given in Figure 6.2.6.

The program includes the use of argv and argc for including command line parameters with the program invocation. The integer variable argc holds the number of parameters on the command line. So, if the program were compiled to rungcd, the proper invocation would be rungcd 18 12 to find the greatest common divisor of 18 and 12. The variable argc would be 3 in this case, indicating there were three parameters on the command line. The count clearly includes the name of the program to run as well as arguments passed to the program. The variable argv is a character string array (a two-dimensional array) containing the individual arguments as character strings. Notice that it is declared as an address of a single-dimensioned array, which effectively makes it a two-dimensioned array since array names are the address of the array. In our example, argv[0] is rungcd, argv[1] is 18 as a character string, and argv[2] is 12 as a character string. Since it is assumed that the second two parameters are integers, the built-in function atoi is used to convert the internal string representation of the numbers to an integer representation. When the required input for a program is known in advance, the command line offers a convenient method of providing the data. Notice that input/output routines are avoided using this technique; no scanf or get function is necessary.

TEST   A sample execution sequence of the above program follows on page 264.

Figure 6.2.6   Recursive Greatest Common Divisor

```c
#include <stdio.h>
#include <stdlib.h>
#define MAX 32767         /* the largest integer that can be stored in 2 bytes  */
int gcd (int m, int n);  /* just to be sure too large a number is not used     */
                         /* this has been covered before but reviewed here!    */
                         /* argc is the number of command line parameters      */
main (int argc, char * argv[])/* each command line parameter in character
                         string form                                           */
{
   int
      m,n;               /* m and n are the numbers, gcd is a function          */
                         /* returning an integer.                               */
   if (argc != 3) /*check to make sure the program was invoked correctly */
   {                /* pgm num1 num2 is invocation requirement                  */
     printf( "Usage: gcd m n \n");
     exit(1);
   }
   m = atoi(argv[1]);      /* convert the second command line arg to int   */
   if (m < 1 || m > MAX)    /* check the range                              */
   {
      printf( "m must be between 1 and %d\n",MAX);
      exit(1);
   }
   n = atoi(argv[2]);      /* convert the second command line arg to int*/
   if (n < 1 || n > MAX)    /* check the range                              */
   {
      printf( "n must be between 1 and %d\n",MAX);
      exit(1);
   }
   printf("the gcd of %d and %d is %d\n",m,n,gcd(m,n)); /* invoke function*/
}
/*************************************************************************/
/*This is the complete function to compute the gcd. All the stuff above is */
/*flower to verify the input data and to insure the program is invoked    */
/*correctly. Note the preciseness of the function and its ease of coding.  */
/*Often recursive solutions yield elegant, simple functions.              */
/*************************************************************************/
int gcd (int m, int n)
{
   if (n == 0) return(m);   /* stopping point                             */
   if (n > m) gcd(n,m);     /* make the largest number first parameter    */
   if (n > 0) gcd(n, m % n);/* recursion with a smaller problem           */
}
```

263

Suppose the program was compiled to an executable file called **rungcd**. The program will be invoked with **rungcd 18 8** and will respond with **the gcd of 18 and 8 is 2**. The **18** will be assigned to m and 8 to n as a result of **argv** and the **atoi** function. After the **gcd** function is invoked m is **18** and n is **8**. Since n is greater than 0, the **gcd** function is invoked again with n's value, **8**, passed to m and **18%8** passed to n. So m is **8** and n is **2** for the second invocation of **gcd**. Since n again is not 0, the function is invoked a third time with 2 being passed to m and **8%2** or 0 passed to n. Now n is **0** so the function simply returns to the previous invocation the current value of n which is 2 as the **gcd**. This value is returned through each of the invocations and is ultimately printed in the **main** function.

▶ Exercises 6.2

6.2.1 Write a recursive function which will produce the output

10

9

8

7

6

5

4

3

2

1

Blast off!

6.2.2 How many recursive calls are necessary to find the first six Fibonacci numbers?

6.2.3 Write a recursive program that will convert base 16 numbers back to base 10.

6.2.4 Write the string reversal program that reverses the string in the computer's memory.

6.2.4 It has been shown that if a and b are any two positive integers with a > b, then

```
gcd(a,b) = gcd(a,a-b)
```

Use this fact to write a recursive function that will calculate the greatest common divisor by this "successive subtractions" method.

6.2.5 The insertion sort algorithm is predicated on the following facts:

- an array of one number is sorted
- if we have an array of **k** numbers which is sorted, and we are given an additional number, we may obtain an array of **k+1** sorted numbers by inserting the **k+1**st number in the correct position in the already sorted list of **k** numbers.

This definition is inherently recursive—write a C function to perform the insertion sort using a recursive algorithm. (See Chapter 5 for an iterative insertion sort.)

6.3 OPERATING SYSTEM SUPPORT OF RECURSIVE PROGRAMS

SECTION TOPICS

Run-Time Memory Organization

Activation Records

Scope

To help you better understand how the computer operating system supports recursion, we now explain the way a program is stored during its execution by the operating system. You should gain some insight into the run-time environment constructed to support a program's execution from this section. We are presenting only a brief outline of the support; the reader should not conclude that this is all there is to it, but consider operating system courses or courses on system software for a thorough discussion.

Run-Time Memory Organization

Figure 6.3.1 shows a typical run-time organization of memory after a program is loaded and begins execution.

Figure 6.3.1 shows the memory organization used to place a program in the computer's memory at the time the program begins execution. The program instructions are stored first, followed by any static data. In C, any variables declared as **static int;** would appear in this area. The stack area dynamically holds activation records of functions. A new acti-

Figure 6.3.1   Run-Time Memory Organization

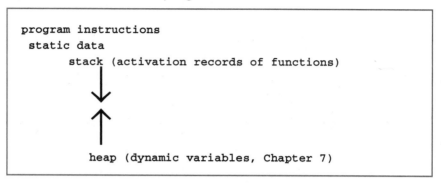

vation record is created for a function each time the function is invoked. The activation records are deleted when the function finishes execution and are recreated if the function is reentered another time. The activation record exists as long as the function has not exited by means of a **return** or by falling out the bottom since the actual **return** instruction ending a function is optional. An activation record continues to exist while another function, invoked by the current function, executes. For example, suppose function **main** calls **A**, **A** calls **B**. Activation records would exist for **main**, **A** and **B**. If **B** finishes and returns to **A** and then **A** calls **C**, we would have activation records for **main**, **A**, and **C**. **B**'s record will have been deleted when **B** finished and **C**'s record put in its place. These records are placed in memory in the stack space dedicated to the execution of this program. The contents of the activation records will be discussed momentarily.

The heap holds memory that has been dynamically created in any routine. This memory is not deleted when the function finishes since it is available through the address operator, thus not local to any routine. These concepts are discussed in Chapter 7.

Activation Records

Consider the stack area of memory that contains activation records. What information is placed here? An activation record is created for each function that is invoked and stores information listed in Figure 6.3.2. The activation records are dynamic, being created when a function is invoked and removed when the function finishes. Information in the activation record allows the operating system to maintain several invocations of a single function since an activation record is established each time the function is invoked. We now discuss the role of each item in the record.

Return Value   A function typically returns one value to the calling routine. Since the function might invoke itself, the return value is kept in the current activation record. After the function finishes, the return value is copied to a safe place and the invoking function copies the value from there.

Figure 6.3.2   Run-Time Activation Record

```
return value
actual parameters
access link
control link
machine status
local data (like int x)
temporaries
```

Actual Parameters   Since C passes all information to a function by *value,* a copy of the parameters passed is placed in the invoked function's storage. When doing call by address, the value of the address is passed. The value of the address is used to reference storage from the calling routine.

Access Link   The access link, dependent on the physical location of functions and blocks of code, determines the method of locating global variables. Figure 6.3.3 demonstrates a program where the access link is important to retrieve the current values of variables. The access link determines the function's values that are to be used when a variable is not within the current, executing function. In this case, the access link determines the **x** to use in function **sub1**; **x = 55** is the current **x** in Figure 6.3.3.

Control Link   The control link determines the address where control is to be given when the current function finishes its execution. The return address is local to the invocation of the function since many invocations can be active, due to recursion, at a particular time. Since a single function might be invoked several times, the return location is stored in the invoked activation record, rather than the invoking activation record.

Machine Status   This is information local to the particular manufacturer of a computer that may be required for support. It is beyond the scope of this text to discuss any details.

Local Data   This area is set aside for any *automatic* variable names, that is, those variables that are local to the function invoked. This memory is given to the function each time it is called and reclaimed when this instance of execution completes. If the function has an instruction like **int x;**, storage would be set aside for the **x** in this area when the function is entered and **x** is destroyed when the function completes.

Temporaries   Temporary variable names are created by the compiler when expressions are translated into executable code. For example, the expression

```
x = y * z + m / 2;
```

will be evaluated as

```
multiply y and z, store the result in t1
divide m and 2, store the result in t2
add t1 and t2, store the result in t3
assign t3 to x
```

The evaluation process required the creation of three temporary variables called t1, t2, and t3 in the example. These variables are not created by the programmer as part of the program itself, but are created by the compiler when the program is translated from C to an executable representa-

Figure 6.3.3 Scope of Functions and Blocks

```
1  #include <stdio.h>
2  int x=55; /* a global variable, known in main and sub1 */
3  main()
4  {
5     int x=5,/* this x will be used in main rather than x at line 2    */
6          y=6,
7           z=7;
   /* Start of a new block, with local x and y taking precedence over   */
   /* y at line 6 or x at line 5 or 2.                                   */
8      {
9          int x=3,   /*in this block, this x will be used              */
                      /*rather than line 5 or x at line 2               */
10              y=22; /*y is used in this block rather than y at line 6  */
11         printf("inside x = %d, y = %d, z = %d\n",x,y,z);
12      }
       /* code for main, x in line 5, y of line 6 and z of line 7 will be*/
       /* used since memory for x at line 9 and y at line 10 is already  */
       /* destroyed by the time program control enters here.            */
13      printf("outside x = %d, y = %d, z = %d\n",x,y,z);
14      sub1();
15 }
16 sub1()
17 {
18     int y = 17,   /* local to function sub1                         */
19          z = 22;   /* local to function sub1                         */
    /* Even though main is still active, but suspended, x and y in lines */
    /* 18 and 19 will be used rather than x in line 5 or y in line 6. The*/
    /* x and y of lines 9 and 10 are no longer an issue, since they were */
    /* destroyed when the block finished.                                */
20      printf("in function x = %d, y = %d, z = %d\n",x,y,z);
21 }
```

tion required by the computer. The temporaries are stored in the activation record when the function is invoked like other local variables. One can think of the temporaries as local variable names, the only minor difference is that they are not created by the programmer but rather by the compiler.

Scope

Scope refers to the concept of what variables will be known in which block or function. Global variables are known everywhere. Variables local to a function are known everywhere in that function and all contained blocks delimited by braces, { . . .}. If **x** is declared globally and redeclared locally, the local **x** takes precedence over the global **x**. The activation records, through the control link, are able to determine which **x** to use. As an example of scope consider Figure 6.3.3.

Try to determine the values the program in Figure 6.3.3 will print before reading on. The program output is

```
inside x = 3, y = 22, z = 7
outside x = 5, y = 6, z = 7
in function x = 55, y = 17, z = 22
```

Scope of a variable determines which name will be used when the variable is referenced. The scope is dependent on the physical location of the block of code in which the variable exists. Blocks of code, set off with braces, act like functions in that variables declared inside the block are considered to be *automatic*—they are given storage when the block is entered, and storage is reclaimed when the block is exited. This storage is the memory discussed in the activation record for local data. The major difference between a block and a function is that a block cannot be invoked; the program control must "fall" into the block through the normal execution sequence. In Figure 6.3.3, the **printf** starting with *inside* is executed first, it displays the **x** and **y** local to the block where the **printf** occurs and displays the **z** from the function surrounding the block. Thus, **x** = 3, **y** = 22, and **z** = 7 appear first. The second **printf** starting with *outside* displays the **x** and **y** from within the function **main** since the variables of the block are removed. Control has left the block, thus variables associated with it no longer exist. The third **printf**, from the invoked function **sub1**, prints the local values of **y** and **z**, and prints the global **x**. The *access* link in the control record determines where the current value of a variable is to be found.

▶ Exercises 6.3

6.3.1   What activation records will be present after the following sequence of function calls occur? Function **main** calls **A**, **A** calls **B**, **B** calls **C**.

6.3.2   What activation records will be present after the following sequence of function calls occur? Function **main** calls **A**, **A** calls **B**, **B** calls **A**.

6.3.3   What memory area will be exhausted if recursive calls do not stop, that is, if infinite recursion occurs?

6.3.4   What value of **x** will be printed in the following program?

```
#include <stdio.h>
int x = 6;
main()
{
int x = 5;
   {
   int x = 4;
      {
      int x = 3;
      }
   printf("x is %d\n",x);
   }
}
```

6.3.5   In exercise 6.3.4 what has happened to the **x** in **int x = 5** when the print executes?

6.3.6   In exercise 6.3.4 what has happened to the **x** in **int x = 3** when the print executes?

6.3.7   Why is it important to a programmer to understand operating system support features?

6.4 RECURSIVE SORTING AND SEARCHING

SECTION TOPICS

Quicksort

Binary Search

Divide and Conquer

Advantages and Disadvantages of Recursion

This section introduces two classic sorting and searching techniques using recursion. The first, quicksort, is typically implemented using recursion, while the second, binary search, is commonly implemented iteratively, but to emphasize recursion we will demonstrate the technique recursively. Both quicksort and binary search techniques are examples of the problem-solving method of "divide and conquer," which will be discussed at the end of the section.

Quicksort

The quicksort algorithm provides an elegant example of a recursive sorting algorithm.

▶ **PROBLEM** Write a computer program to implement the quicksort algorithm.

ANALYSIS The idea behind quicksort is to find a pivot that may be the first key, then partition the data so that all keys smaller than the pivot are on one side and all keys larger than the pivot are on the other side. The file to be sorted is partitioned so we need to concentrate only on sorting the remaining sections. The data could be a file of records containing a wide variety of information, but our goal is understanding the algorithm, so we will sort a set of integers.

DESIGN Initially, consider the file of integers as shown below by the line.

```
data
```

```
      ↑
    pivot
```

After the first pass through the data, the pivot will be correctly placed in its sorted position; all the smaller data will be on one side and all the larger data will be on the other side of the pivot as demonstrated:

```
data
```

```
    data smaller than      ↑       data larger than
    the pivot           pivot      the  pivot
```

After the data has been partitioned, we sort the smaller data and then the larger data, each of which is a smaller version of the initial problem, the necessary condition for recursion. The stopping point is when all the data has been sorted, that is, when all the intervals created by partitioning the data have each been sorted.

The goal is to place the integers in order. Overall efficiency is increased in quicksort, as compared to some sorting routines, since more numbers are placed nearer their final position after each pass through the data.

The details of the sorting procedure are now discussed. One number is chosen as the *pivot*. When placing the numbers in ascending order, all

Figure 6.4.1   Initial Quicksort

```
index:    0  1  2  3  4  5  6  7  8  9 10 11 12 13 14 15 16 17 18 19 20 21 22
number:  34 56 23 78 99 12 24 38 91 76 42 18 48 65 81 90 21 48 35 36 37 73 74
```

numbers smaller than the pivot are placed on the left, all numbers larger than the pivot are placed on the right, and the pivot is placed in its final position as a result of the first pass through the numbers. As an example consider Figure 6.4.1. The sort is invoked with the configuration in Figure 6.4.2.

Any number can be chosen as the pivot; initially, we choose the number at position 0 of the array. The variables **lft_bnd** and **rt_bnd** mark the left and right boundaries, respectively, of the interval to be sorted. You can see that **lft_ptr** begins at **lft_bnd** and moves to the right until it indexes a number greater than the pivot. Similarly, **rt_ptr** starts at **rt_bnd** and moves left until it indexes a number that is less than the pivot. When both **lft_ptr** and **rt_ptr** have stopped, the numbers are interchanged. Figure 6.4.3 demonstrates this condition.

After the exchange shown in Figure 6.4.3, the loop to move the **lft_ptr** to the right is reentered, causing the left pointer to stop at 78, the first number greater than the pivot. Then the loop to move the

Figure 6.4.2   Boundaries Quicksort

```
index:    0  1  2  3  4  5  6  7  8  9 10 11 12 13 14 15 16 17 18 19 20 21 22
number:  34 56 23 78 99 12 24 38 91 76 42 18 48 65 81 90 21 48 35 36 37 73 74
          ↑                                                                  ↑
        pivot                                                              rt_bnd
        lft_bnd                                                            rt_ptr
        lft_ptr
```

Figure 6.4.3   First Exchange

```
index:    0  1  2  3  4  5  6  7  8  9 10 11 12 13 14 15 16 17 18 19 20 21 22
number:  34 56 23 78 99 12 24 38 91 76 42 18 48 65 81 90 21 48 35 36 37 73 74
          ↑ 21                                             54               ↑
        pivot ↑                                            ↑              rt_bnd
        lft_bnd lft_ptr                                  rt_ptr
```

Figure 6.4.4 After Second Exchange

```
index:   0  1  2  3  4  5  6  7  8  9 10 11 12 13 14 15 16 17 18 19 20 21 22
number: 34 21 23 78 99 12 24 38 91 76 42 18 48 65 81 90 54 48 35 36 37 73 74
         ↑        18                      78                               ↑
        pivot     ↑                        ↑                            rt_bnd
        lft_bnd  lft_ptr                 rt_ptr
```

Figure 6.4.5 Completed First Pass

```
index:   0  1  2  3  4  5  6  7  8  9 10 11 12 13 14 15 16 17 18 19 20 21 22
number: 34 21 23 18 24 12 99 38 91 76 42 78 48 65 81 90 54 48 35 36 37 73 74
        12              34 ↑                                               ↑
         ↑               ↑ lft_ptr                                      rt_bnd
        pivot          rt_ptr
        lft_bnd
```

rt_ptr to the left is entered, moving this pointer to 18. A swap is performed exchanging 78 and 18. Figure 6.4.4 shows this result.

Again, the **lft_ptr** moves to the right and the **rt_ptr** moves to the left, exchanging as demonstrated. This process continues until the **rt_ptr** is one position to the left of the **lft_ptr**. The **pivot** is then exchanged with the value at the **rt_ptr**. This result is shown in Figure 6.4.5.

After the first pass, the pivot, 34, is in its final position. All numbers smaller than the pivot are left of the pivot, and all numbers larger than the pivot are right of 34, the pivot. This is the basic requirement of quicksort. We can now recursively complete the sorting process by invoking the quicksort routine with the boundaries of the data left of the correctly placed pivot, and invoke quicksort a second time with the boundaries right of the correctly placed pivot, that is, to recursively quicksort the data in the interval 0 to 4 and recursively quicksort the data between indices 6 and 22. The invoking instructions would be:

```
quicksort(a, lft_bnd, rt_ptr-1);/* sort left interval */
quicksort(a, rt_ptr+1, rt_bnd);/* sort right interval */
```

The **rt_ptr** has the index of the correctly placed element, so the interval to the left is **lft_bnd** to **rt_ptr-1** and the interval to the right is **rt_ptr+1** to **rt_bnd**. This program always sorts the left interval first, but this is not necessary. Efficiency can be improved if the interval containing the fewest numbers is sorted first. Figure 6.4.2 shows the initial

Figure 6.4.6 Next Invocation Conditions

```
index:     0  1  2  3  4  5  6  7  8  9 10 11 12 13 14 15 16 17 18 19 20 21 22
number:   12 21 23 18 24 34 99 38 91 76 42 78 48 65 81 90 54 48 35 36 37 73 74
           ↑           ↑
        pivot        rt_bnd
       lft_bnd       rt_ptr
       lft_ptr
```

conditions of the first recursive call. Can you determine the conditions of the next recursive call? They are listed in Figure 6.4.6.

CODE   The complete program is given in Figure 6.4.7.

Binary Search

We now revisit the binary search, which was first discussed in Chapter 4. Our discussion will provide a recursive implementation of this algorithm.

► PROBLEM   Given a sorted list of keys, use the binary search to find the position of the desired key.

ANALYSIS   Like the quicksort, we can partition the work to be done in binary search as follows:

>   If the element we are indexing is the desired element, we are finished.
>
>   Otherwise, search the upper or lower half as appropriate.

We have the necessary characteristics to write a recursive program that can do the searching, that is, a stopping point, and the ability to redefine the problem as a smaller case of itself. The program stops when it finds the element, and if the element is not found it looks in the appropriate half of the data, which is a smaller instance of the original problem.

DESIGN   The design was developed in detail in Chapter 4. You should compare the solution in Figure 6.4.8 with Figure 4.4.11 to see a comparison between a recursive and an iterative solution. It should be noted that while iteration and recursion are each easier to implement in a given situation, they are effectively equivalent. That is, what can be solved recursively can also be solved iteratively and vice versa. This section gives you a nice

Figure 6.4.7 Complete Quicksort

```
#include <stdio.h>
#define MAXNUMS 2000        /* maximum number of numbers              */
void quicksort (int *a, int lft_bnd, int rt_bnd);
void swap (int a[], int i, int j);
void print_arr (int a[], int nums);
main (int argc, char * argv[])
{
   char filenm[20];         /* the file of numbers to be sorted       */
   int dataarray[MAXNUMS];  /* program storage for numbers sorted     */
   int num_nums=0,i,eof;    /* number of numbers, end_of_file         */
   FILE *fopen(),*flpt;
   void print_arr(int dataarray[], int num_nums);
   /**********************************************************************/
   /* insure that the program has been invoked with a command line arg  */
   /* representing the program name and data file                       */
   /**********************************************************************/
   if (argc != 2)
   {
      printf("proper invocation: pgm datafile\n");
      exit(0);
   }
   flpt = fopen(argv[1],"r"); /* file opened properly ?                */
   if (flpt == NULL)
   {
      printf("Open failed, check data filename\n");
      exit(1);
   }
   /**********************************************************************/
   /* input the data file                                               */
   /**********************************************************************/
   eof = fscanf(flpt,"%d",&dataarray[num_nums]);
   num_nums = num_nums + 1;
   while (eof > 0)
   {
      eof = fscanf(flpt,"%d",&dataarray[num_nums]);
      num_nums = num_nums + 1;
      if (num_nums > 2000) /* check range of number of numbers          */
      {
         printf("too many numbers, increase array size and recompile\n");
         exit(2);
      }
   }
```

(continued)

275

Figure 6.4.7   Complete Quicksort (*continued*)

```
        num_nums = num_nums - 1;     /* number of numbers is one less      */
        printf("sorting %d numbers\n",num_nums);
        printf("the unsorted numbers are:");
        print_arr(dataarray,num_nums);
        quicksort(dataarray,0,num_nums-1); /* invoke the sorting routine    */
        printf("the sorted numbers are:");
        print_arr(dataarray,num_nums);
}
/***********************************************************************/
/* Quicksort the numbers by choosing the pivot at the left, putting    */
/* all numbers smaller than the pivot to the left and all numbers      */
/* greater than the pivot to the right. Then recursively sort the      */
/* left section, followed by recursively sorting the right section.    */
/***********************************************************************/
void quicksort (int*a, int lft_bnd, intrt_bnd)
        /*                                                              */
        /* a the array to be sorted                                     */
        /* lft_bnd the left bound of the interval to sort               */
        /* rt_bnd the right bound of the interval to sort               */
        /*                                                              */
{
    int i, lft_ptr,x, rt_ptr, pivot;
            /* i a dummy variable                                       */
            /* lft_ptr moves left to right through the interval         */
            /* x the value of the pivot                                 */
            /* rt_ptr moves right to left through the interval          */
            /* pivot the index of the pivot                             */
    void swap(int a[], int i, int j);
    if (lft_bnd >= rt_bnd) return; /* this interval has 0 elements      */
    pivot = lft_bnd;   /* the index of the element used as the pivot    */
    lft_ptr = lft_bnd; /* start the left pointer at the left bound      */
    rt_ptr = rt_bnd;   /* start the right pointer at the right bound    */
    x = a[pivot];      /* save the value of the pivot                   */
    while (lft_ptr < rt_ptr) /* there are still numbers to be considered */
    {
        while((a[lft_ptr] <= x) && (lft_ptr < rt_ptr))
            lft_ptr = lft_ptr + 1;/* move the left pointer to the right    */
        while(a[rt_ptr] > x)
            rt_ptr = rt_ptr - 1;/* move the right pointer to the left      */
        if (lft_ptr < rt_ptr)
            swap(a, lft_ptr, rt_ptr); /* swap elements if not finished      */
    }
```

(*continued*)

Figure 6.4.7 Complete Quicksort (*continued*)

```
/*************************************************************************/
/* These two instructions swap the last number with the pivot, insuring */
/* all numbers to the left of the pivot are smaller than the pivot value*/
/* and all numbers to the right of the pivot are larger than the pivot  */
/* value.                                                                */
/*************************************************************************/
   a[lft_bnd] = a[rt_ptr];
   a[rt_ptr] = x;

/*************************************************************************/
/* Recursively invoke the routine to sort the left interval and the     */
/* right interval.                                                       */
/*************************************************************************/
   quicksort(a, lft_bnd, rt_ptr-1);/* sort left interval              */
   quicksort(a, rt_ptr+1, rt_bnd);/* sort right interval             */
}

/*************************************************************************/
/* This routine swaps two elements in the array. It is called from       */
/* quicksort.                                                            */
/*************************************************************************/
void swap(int a[], int i, int j)
{
   int temp;
   temp = a[i];
   a[i] = a[j];
   a[j] = temp;
}

/*************************************************************************/
/* Since the array is printed twice, once unsorted and once sorted we    */
/* include a routine to do the printing.                                 */
/*************************************************************************/
void print_arr(int a[],int nums)
{
   int i;
   for(i = 0; i < nums; i=i+1)
   {
      if (i%10 == 0) printf("\n");
      printf("%3d ",a[i]);
   }
   printf("\n");
}
```

opportunity to compare the iterative solution with a very similar recursive solution.

CODE   The complete program with recursive function for binary search is given in Figure 6.4.8.

TEST   The data used is generated internally in the program and consists of even integers as follows:

```
index:    0  1  2  3  4  5  6  7  8  9 10 11 12 13 14 15 16 17 18 19 20 21 22 23 24
data:     0  2  4  6  8 10 12 14 16 18 20 22 24 26 28 30 32 34 36 38 40 42 44 46 48

index:   25 26 27 28 29 30 31 32 33 34 35 36 37 38 39 40 41 42 43 44 45 46 47 48 49
data:    50 52 54 56 58 60 62 64 66 68 70 72 74 76 78 80 82 84 86 88 90 92 94 96 98
```

```
A sample of the output is:
Desired Value = 14
looking in position 24
looking in position 11
looking in position 5
looking in position 8
looking in position 6
looking in position 7
the number 14 was found at index 7

Desired Value = 0
looking in position 24
looking in position 11
looking in position 5
looking in position 2
looking in position 0
the number 0 was found at index 0

Desired Value = 98
looking in position 24
looking in position 37
looking in position 43
looking in position 46
looking in position 48
looking in position 49
the number 98 was found at index 49
```

Note that to make the program search for different numbers you must change the #define DESIRED_VAL statement to reflect the new number and recompile. You should be able to modify the program to search for several different numbers in an execution without recompiling.

Figure 6.4.8   Recursive Binary Search

```
/*********************************************************************/
/* This program demonstrates the binary search concept using recursion. */
/*********************************************************************/
#include <stdio.h>
#define DESIRED_VAL 44    /* the desired value search for              */
#define ARR_SIZE 50       /* size of the search space                  */
int binsrch (int * arr, int lb, int up);
main()
{
    int arr[ARR_SIZE],     /* the array of numbers to search           */
        i,j,               /* loop control variables*/
        lower,             /* the lower index of the interval searched */
        upper,             /* the upper index of the interval searched */
        index;             /* the index of the desired number          */
    for(i = 0; i < ARR_SIZE; i=i+1) /* generate numbers for the array  */
        arr[i] = 2*i;           /* numbers must be ordered use these    */
    printf("Desired Value = %d\n",DESIRED_VAL);
    lower = 0;             /* initially the lower index                 */
    upper = ARR_SIZE-1;    /* initially the upper index                 */
    index = binsrch(arr,lower,upper);
    if(index >= 0)
        printf("the number %d was found at index %d\n", DESIRED_VAL, index);
    else
        printf("the number %d was not found\n", DESIRED_VAL);
}

/*********************************************************************/
/* This function implements the binary search routine. It is almost  */
/* identical to the while loop in Figure 4.4.11, with only a few of   */
/* the tests reversed.                                                */
/*********************************************************************/
int binsrch (int * arr, int lb, int up)
{
    int mid;              /* the index of the middle of the interval   */
    int index;           /* the index to return                        */
    mid = (up + lb)/2;            /* determine the middle value         */
    if(lb > up)
        return(-1);      /* value not found, return negative one       */
    printf("looking in position %d\n",mid);
    if(arr[mid] == DESIRED_VAL)
        return(mid);     /* found it!!!!                               */
    if(arr[mid] < DESIRED_VAL)  /* look in the lower half??????         */
    {                                                      (continued)
```

Figure 6.4.8 Recursive Binary Search (*continued*)

```
        return(binsrch(arr,mid+1,up));/* recursive call and look in the   */
   }                                  /* upper half. mid+1 since it is     */
   else                              /* not in mid                        */
   {
       index = binsrch(arr,lb,mid-1); /* look in the lower half           */
       return(index);
   }
}
```

It is interesting to consider how much "work" the computer has to do to find the desired number. Does the computer do the same number of comparisons every time, regardless of the desired number? Figure 6.4.9 shows a "search tree" that is used to demonstrate the work necessary to retrieve a particular number for a smaller data set of 20 numbers, 0 through 19.

Figure 6.4.9 shows that all searches begin by looking in position 9 of the array. If the number is smaller than 18 (the number at position 9), the next number compared is in position 4, shown in the left sub-tree. If the number is greater, then the right subtree is searched. The greatest number of comparisons is when the search gets to the bottom of the tree, as it does when searching for 6 (found at index 3), 16 (found at index 8), 26 (found at index 13), 32 (found at index 16), and 38 (found at index 19). The search tree demonstrates the number of

Figure 6.4.9 Binary Search Tree of Index Numbers

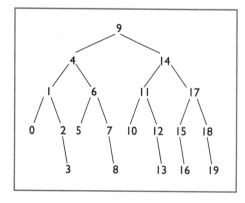

comparisons required for retrieving the numbers at the index. Numbers not in the array will require the maximum number of comparisons along one branch of the tree.

For example, to determine if 7 is in the tree, 7 is compared to 18 (the number at index 9 represented by the root of the tree). Since 7 is less than 18, the left branch is followed. Then 7 is compared to the number at position 4 (number 8) and again the left branch is followed. Now 7 is compared to the number at index 1 (which is 2) and the right branch is followed, since 7 is greater than the number in that array at index 2. Seven is compared to the number at position 2 and finally 3. But 7 is not found and there are no further places to look; 7 is not in the data. The maximum number of comparisons, 5 in this case, was required to determine 7 did not exist.

What is the greatest number of comparisons required to find a number in the array, using a binary search? The number of numbers from the top (root) of the tree to the bottom (leaf) represents the number of comparisons, since in our example, 7 was compared to numbers in positions 9, 4, 1, 2, and 3. Five comparisons were required, the maximum number of comparisons necessary to find any number in the array. So the search tree can be used to represent the number of comparisons for a particular algorithm to solve a problem that requires comparing numbers. You will see more of search trees and trees in general in classes such as Artificial Intelligence, Data Structures, and Analysis of Algorithms.

Divide and Conquer

The binary search and quicksort routines are examples of the problem-solving technique called *divide and conquer.* It is easier to sort or search through 50 numbers than 100 numbers, simply because it takes less time to sort or search 50 numbers as opposed to 100. So, to sort 100 numbers, quicksort tries to divide a list of numbers into two 50-number groups. To search 100 numbers, binary search tries to eliminate 50 numbers in the first query. Thus the name *divide and conquer,* because the program is dividing the data into smaller groups, making each group easier to solve.

Advantages and Disadvantages of Recursion

Section 6.3 discussed the operating system support of recursion. From that section we learned that function invocations require memory taken from the stack storage allocated to our program during run time. If a program enters infinite recursion, the stack storage will be consumed and the program will fail just as an infinite loop will cause the program to run forever. There is an additional problem with recursion not present in pro-grams without recursion. The program may be executing correctly and still exhaust the stack storage space. We know the return value, actual parameters, access link, local variables, etc., are stored each time the function is invoked; thus a program requiring much recursion—that is, many function invocations—may use up all the stack space even though it is executing correctly.

Often the elegance of recursive solutions outweighs the prospect of potential problems caused by using recursion. The programmer need only consider the program application. If the program is used in an area where the nature of the data is unknown and run-time errors are intoler-able, recursion should be avoided. On the other hand, if the program is used in a controlled environment, with the author of the program pres-ent, recursion is often the desirable paradigm. Recursive solutions are often shorter, easier to debug, and easier to understand than their itera-tive counter parts, so people who understand recursion can provide pro-gram maintenance and support easier with recursive solutions. Given large amounts of memory available in current computers, exhausting the stack is less likely to occur. The bottom line is to consider the use of the program and the amount of recursion necessary when planning the algo-rithm.

▶ Exercises 6.4

6.4.1   What is the maximum number of comparisons required when 64 num-bers are used in a binary search to retrieve any number?

6.4.2   What is the maximum number of comparisons required when 1000 num-bers are used in a binary search to retrieve any number?

6.4.3   In order to use a binary search, what arrangement of the data must be present?

6.4.4   Trace the execution of quicksort on 15 numbers.

6.4.5   Modify the quicksort algorithm so that it sorts in descending order.

6.4.6   Modify the quicksort algorithm so that it will sort an array of strings.

6.4.7   Use the quicksort algorithm to sort an array of size 1000 intergers ran-domly generated and count the number of comparisons required. Repeat the sort with 1000 numbers in reverse order. How many comparisons are required? Repeat the sort with 1000 numbers already in order. How many comparisons are required? Can you draw any conclusions?

▶ Key Words

base conversion	quicksort
binary search	recursion
binary search tree	recursive definitions
divide and conquer	scope
factorial	searching
greatest common divisor	sorting
identifier scope	stack data structure
operating system support	
(activation records, heap, stack)	

▶ Chapter Concepts

6.1   Recursion is the concept of a function invoking itself.

6.2   Direct recursion is when a function invokes itself from within itself.

6.3   Indirect recursion is a function being active more than once. That is, suppose function A calls B which calls C which calls A. A has been recursively called by C. Two instances of A exist.

6.4   Recursive definitions form the starting point for learning to program recursive functions.

6.5   All recursive definitions and functions require a stopping point and the redefinition of the problem as a similar instance of itself.

6.6   Recursion is simply the invocation of a function that is already active, and as such, it can be viewed as the invocation of a new function of the same name. This concept was demonstrated in Figure 6.1.6.

6.7   Scope is knowing where in a program a variable is present. Variables local to a function are declared in that function, whereas global variables are known everywhere in the program.

6.8   Binary search and quicksort demonstrate recursive solutions to common searching and sorting problems. These examples use the divide and conquer problem-solving methodology.

6.9   The concept used in analyzing algorithms of determining the amount of work required in a problem solution was shown by the recursive binary search.

▶ Programming Projects

6.1 Several computers and popular calculators use a postfix notation for arithmetic expressions rather than the common parenthesized infix. For example,

```
((2 + 3) * (4 + 5)) + 6
```

becomes

```
2 3 + 4 5 + * 6 +
```

in postfix. The advantage of postfix representation is the elimination of operator precedence or the need for parentheses. Since you are working for a micro/mini/large software house building a compiler, one of your tasks is to write the section that converts infix expressions to postfix. You can assume the data appears as it does in the above example, that is, one digit numbers in a correctly parenthesized expression. Your output should be the corresponding postfix expression. You are required to perform the conversion in a recursive function, but the input can be done in the **main** routine.

6.2 Since you did such a fine job on problem 6.1 your company now wishes to have you write the program that will evaluate the postfix expressions. Again, this evaluation process should be done by a recursive function. The input will appear as

```
2 3 + 4 *
```

and the output should correspondingly be

```
20
```

6.3 Permutations and combinations are used in combinatorics and a variety of other areas where counting is required. A permutation is defined as the number of reorderings possible with a list of numbers. For example, the permutation of three items, a,b,c, taken all three at a time, is six, as follows:

```
a,b,c    a,c,b
b,a,c    b,c,a
c,a,b    c,b,a
```

Permutations of three items taken two at a time are possible as follows:

```
a,b    b,a
b,c    c,b
a,c    c,a
```

The general equation for finding the number of permutations is

$$p = \frac{n!}{(n - r)!}$$

Write a program that uses a recursive function to compute the permutation of **n** items taken **r** at a time. Again, **n** in the above example would be 3 and **r** 3 in the first part, and **n** is 3 and **r** 2 in the second part.

6.4 The Towers of Hanoi is a classic problem that uses recursion in its solution. You are given three pegs. Peg 1 has five disks stacked from smallest to largest (top to bottom). Your task is to write a program that moves all the disks to another peg. The catch is that you cannot place a larger disk on top of a smaller disk. The figure demonstrates the initial and final configurations.

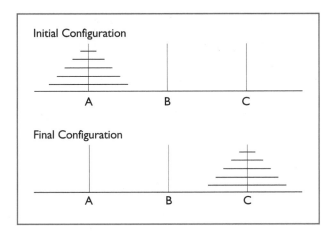

6.5 Square root can be calculated by guessing a number s_1. If s_1^2 is less than **n**, increase **s** by a certain amount, yielding s_2. If the new s_2^2 is greater than **n**, the square root of **n** lies between s_1 and s_2. Write a recursive function that will find an appropriate s_1 and s_2 given any **n**. Incorporate the function in a program that will read in the value of **n**, and report the s_1 and s_2 for the **n**. When the program is complete, $s_1 - s_2 < 1$.

6.6 Some programming languages do not provide a facility for computing exponentials. Write a recursive function to receive a base and an exponent which will compute the base raised to the exponent. Test your function by including it in a program which will read in the two numbers, invoke the function, and print the results.

6.7 Pattern matching and search, common to artificial intelligence, are represented by the following problem. Suppose there exists a 12 by 12 array containing blanks and X's. The X's represent block positions and the blanks are open positions. Starting at 0,0 you are to find a list of positions that will take you to position 11,11 (recall C starts out at 0). You can only move to an open position that is immediately above, below, left, or right. No moving on the diagonal. For example, the array shown here would have the following solution:

		X			X						X	
							X	X	X		X	
		X				X			X		X	
			X					X				X
		X	X	X	X		X			X	
		X							X			
		X			X	X		X			X
		X	X		X			X		X	X
		X		X			X			X	
	X									X	
			X	X	X						X
		X		X	X	X	X			X	

0,0 1,0   1,1 1,2 1,3 2,3 3,3 3,4   3,5   4,5 5,5 5,6 6,6

7,6 7,5   8,5 8,4 9,4 9,5 9,6 9,7   9,8   8,8 7,8 6,8 6,9

5,9 5,10   5,11 6,11 7,11 8,11 9,11 10,11 11,11

You are to write a recursive function that will find the path through the maze. Include the function in a program and test using various size mazes.

CHAPTER
7

Pointers and Dynamic Memory Allocation

INTRODUCTION

So far in our study of computing we have demonstrated problem solving using arrays and structures (as static storage) to store data. In both cases, we had to know how much data was to be stored and manipulated before the program ran since the number of the fields in the structure or the size of the array had to be written into the program before execution began. This limits some applications since it is not always possible to determine the size of an array or the number of fields required of a structure when the program begins execution. This chapter demonstrates how to overcome these problems by dynamically requesting the amount of storage during program execution and adding to that storage if it is found to be insufficient. C offers three basic ways of requesting storage during run time: `malloc`, `calloc`, and `realloc`. The function `malloc` is used for general storage requests, typically for structures; `calloc` stands for contiguous storage allocation and is used primarily for array applications; and `realloc` is used to reallocate an array that has been found too small without losing the data in the array. The instruction `free` gives back to the operating system memory requested by `malloc`, `calloc`, or `realloc`. The material on linked lists and trees provide examples of the use of dynamic storage.

7.1 DYNAMIC MEMORY ALLOCATION

SECTION TOPICS

Pointers to Structures—malloc

The Instruction free

Dynamic Array Allocation—calloc

Dynamic Array Allocation—realloc

Pointers to Structures—malloc

The basic instruction to request storage (memory) during run-time is `malloc`. Its form is:

```
pointer = (cast) malloc (number of bytes);
```

The *pointer* is the address of the memory received. Chapter 6 discussed run-time support of programs and indicated that this memory is provided from the *heap*, that portion of user-allocated run-time memory from which dynamic storage is provided. The only access we have to this dynamic memory is through the pointer. Since the function **malloc** is a C function that returns a pointer of type **NULL**, the pointer must be *cast* to the type of storage requested. The **sizeof** function is typically used to determine the number of bytes of memory requested. For example, consider the simple program shown in Figure 7.1.1.

Compare this program to the one in Figure 7.1.2. These two programs are similar but there is a significant difference. Figure 7.1.1 uses dynamic storage allocation and Figure 7.1.2 uses automatic storage allocation. You should be very familiar with the example in Figure 7.1.2 since it requests storage in the same manner we have used throughout the examples in previous chapters. The storage for **x** and **p** is allocated when the program is loaded into memory for execution. It exists for the duration of the program and is called automatic storage, storage that is given memory when the function is entered and removed when the function is finished.

Figure 7.1.1 allocates no storage until the **malloc** instruction is executed. This storage comes out of the heap rather than the stack that contains the activation record for the functions. Thus, the storage remains after the function executes—it is dynamic memory. The memory is ac-

Figure 7.1.1 First Look at malloc

```
/***********************************************************************/
/* This program allocates a simple integer, with p containing its     */
/* address. 5 is stored where p points and is then printed.           */
/***********************************************************************/
#include <stdio.h>
main ()
{
    int *p;         /* p is the name of storage capable of holding the  */
                    /* address of an integer                            */

    p = (int *) malloc (sizeof(int));
    *p = 5
    printf("the value at address p is %d\n",*p);
}
```

Figure 7.1.2 A Comparable Look at Storage

```
/************************************************************************/
/* This program allocates a simple integer x, makes p point to it,     */
/* places 5 in that storage and prints it.                             */
/************************************************************************/
#include <stdio.h>
main()
{
    int *p;  /* p holds the address of an integer                      */
    int x;   /* x holds the integer                                    */
    p = &x;  /* p receives the address of x                            */
    *p = 5;  /* put 5 in that storage address, same as x = 5           */
    printf("the value at address p is %d\n",*p); /* same value as      */
    printf("the value at x is %d\n",x);   /* this one!!!!!!            */
}
```

cessed only through the address, allowing other functions access to this memory if they know the address. Figure 7.1.3 provides a picture of the **malloc** instruction of Figure 7.1.1.

Typically, dynamic storage is not used to allocate just an integer—the programmer knows how many integer variables will be required in a program. While the storage allocated by **malloc** is not local to any one function, the variable holding the address of that storage is local to the function in which it is declared. That is, the pointer variable is *auto-*

Figure 7.1.3 The malloc Instruction

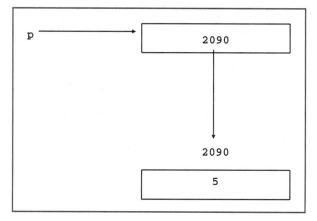

matic. To allow other functions to access the memory allocated by **malloc**, the pointer must be passed or returned to those functions. If the pointer is not passed, the memory taken from the heap will become unusable for the duration of this program's execution. Potentially much memory from the heap will be lost if this occurs frequently.

We have demonstrated the use of **malloc** to increase the amount of memory available for storing data values during execution of our program. The program in Figure 7.1.4 demonstrates the use of creating memory in one function and accessing it from another, showing that the memory allocated by **malloc** remains, and access to it is through the address passed as arguments of the function requesting the memory. Figure 7.1.4 also demonstrates the use of **malloc** to request storage for a structure. The structure contains one field that happens to be an integer, but could easily contain a variety of fields as demonstrated in previous discussions.

Figure 7.1.4 demonstrates that the memory allocated by **malloc** by the function **sub** stays even after **sub** finishes. Any data that is declared by **int**, **float**, or **char** is removed when a function finishes, but dynamic memory created by **malloc**, **calloc**, or **realloc** remains even after the function that allocated the memory finishes. The program in Figure 7.1.4 will print

```
value still in structure p -> x = 55
```

proving that the memory allocated has remained even after the function finished. It is not automatic memory. Of course, the variable containing the address of the memory is automatic and thus has to be passed for another routine to know the address of the **malloc**'d memory. This demonstrates that when control is returned to the **main** function, the structure still exists and that **p** contains its address. How does the operating system differentiate between automatic variables like **int x** and data that is **malloc**'d? The answer is that during run time, the operating system places the data in different sections of memory. The *automatic* variables are located in the *stack* portion of memory and *dynamic* storage (**malloc**) is taken from the *heap* portion of memory. The memory taken from the heap area is entirely under programmer control, through the address of the memory. The programmer requests memory through program instructions such as **malloc** and that memory remains available to the program until the program releases it by means of a **free** statement. Operating system courses will discuss techniques of maintaining the free area while compiler or system software courses discuss the run-time support package in general.

Figure 7.1.4 demonstrates several other features of C for accessing memory that has been **malloc**'d, namely, the way to access fields within

Figure 7.1.4   malloc'd Memory Address Passing

```
/***********************************************************************/
/* A program that allocates storage in a function for a structure and  */
/* accesses that storage in the main function of the program.          */
/* Structure templates used with malloc and parameter passing addresses */
/* are demonstrated by this example.                                   */
/***********************************************************************/
#include <stdio.h>

/***********************************************************************/
/* The structure template is written just as in any program requesting */
/* automatic data.                                                     */
/***********************************************************************/
struct data
{
    int x;     /* the structure contains one field, an integer         */
};
struct data *sub();  /* prototype the function since the default of int is */
                     /* not sufficient, it has to return an address     */
main()
{
    struct data *p;   /* p can contain the address of a structure data    */
    p = sub();        /* p receives the value returned from the function */
    printf("value still in structure p -> x = %d\n",p -> x);
}
struct data *sub()  /* this function returns the address of struct data */
{
    struct data *q;    /* q can contain the address of a structure data   */
    q = (struct data *) malloc (sizeof(struct data)); /* get a structure*/
    q -> x = 55;       /* put 55 in the data field of the structure       */
    return(q);         /* return the address of the structure             */
}
```

the structure. Since **p** has the address of the structure, C allows a field, **x**, to be accessed by a special notation, **p -> x**, where the **->** is two key strokes, - followed by >. It is read as **p** "pointing to" **x**. Since **p** has the address of the structure containing **x**, we say that **p** points to that structure, so the authors of C have adopted the ability to code the instruction as we say it, **p -> x** is **p** pointing to **x** or **p** containing the address of **x**. Using **p -> x** gives us the ability to access the value stored in **x**. Consider the following structure definition, first presented in Chapter 3:

```
struct x      /* x is the name of a structure template */
{
    int y;   /* y is a field in this structure          */
    float z; /* z is another field in this structure    */
} w;          /* w is automatic storage of one of these
                 structures                              */
```

To access each of the elements in the structure, we must write **w.y** or **w.z** for structure storage locations **y** and **z**. We now use the pointer notation to access fields in a structure when the only access to that structure is through its address. An equivalent substitute to the **->** notation is the dereferencing demonstrated in Figure 7.1.5.

The output generated by the program in Figure 7.1.5 is

```
value in field y is 5, value in field z is 12.200000
```

Figure 7.1.5 shows the equivalence of accessing the structure using the **.** notation and the **->** notation. Either can be used; it is solely up to the programmer since the notations perform exactly the same function. That is, **w -> y** is equivalent to **(*w).y**. The authors of C believed that **w -> y** is more intuitive than **(*w).y**, but the latter is consistent with the notation required in Chapter 3. Chapter 3 did not offer a choice of access notation since the structure was *automatic* rather than *dynamic* as we

Figure 7.1.5 Equivalence of * and ->

```
#include <stdio.h>

main()
{
    struct x
        {
        int y;
        float z;
        };
    struct x *w;
    w = (struct x *) malloc (sizeof(struct x));
    w -> y = 5;                 /* w pointing to field y receives a 5       */
    (*w).z = 12.2;              /* the value in storage addressed by w(the  */
                               /* address of the structure, field z receives*/
                               /* 12.2, same as w -> z = 12.2               */
    printf("value in field y is %d, value in field z is %f\n",(*w).y,w -> z);
}
```

have here. When addresses (pointers) are involved, we can use either notation. We will consistently use the pointer notation since it is believed to be clearer. In Figure 7.1.5, we have both notations, demonstrating that either notation can be used.

Consider now the problem of dynamic access to arrays. Consider Figure 7.1.6, which dynamically allocates a structure containing an array and stores randomly created numbers. We use **malloc** to request struc-

Figure 7.1.6   Dynamic Structure Containing an Array

```c
/**********************************************************************/
/* This program will create a structure containing an array and fill the */
/* array with randomly generated integers. It then prints those integers. */
/* The goal of the program is to demonstrate how dynamic structures    */
/* containing arrays are accessed.                                     */
/**********************************************************************/
#include <stdio.h>

main()
{
   struct x          /* x is the name of a structure template containing */
   {                 /* an array of 10 elements called arr              */
      int arr[10];
   };

   struct x *p;      /* p has the ability to hold the address of a      */
                     /* structure x                                     */
   int i;            /* index variable for a loop                       */
   p = (struct x *) malloc (sizeof(struct x)); /* get one structure     */

/**********************************************************************/
/* Now fill the structure with random integer data.                   */
/**********************************************************************/
   for(i = 0; i< 10; i=i+1)
   {
      p -> arr[i] = rand();/* simply subscript the array normally,access*/
   }                       /* the field of the structure through p      */
/**********************************************************************/
/* Now print the array of random numbers                              */
/**********************************************************************/
   for(i = 0; i< 10; i=i+1)
   {
      printf("p -> arr[%d] = %d \n",i,p -> arr[i]); /* to print, we     */
   }                       /* access as we did to fill the array        */
}
```

ture storage with array fields as opposed to `calloc`, which will be used for storage requests of arrays, either arrays of integers, floats, characters, or structures.

The results of Figure 7.1.6 might be the following, depending on the computer system used. An IBM-compatible computer using Turbo C generated the following output:

```
p -> arr[0] = 346
p -> arr[1] = 130
p -> arr[2] = 10982
p -> arr[3] = 1090
p -> arr[4] = 11656
p -> arr[5] = 7117
p -> arr[6] = 17595
p -> arr[7] = 6415
p -> arr[8] = 22948
p -> arr[9] = 31126
```

Notice the array subscript was inserted into the print statement to display the index of the position of the array being printed. The numbers actually displayed, if you run this program, will depend on the computer used.

The Instruction free

As you construct programs using `malloc`, situations will arise when requested storage is no longer needed. The instruction `free` is used to return dynamic memory to the heap and therefore make that memory available to be used for other purposes later in the program. The method of giving the storage back is to `free` the pointer to that storage. The form of the instruction is:

```
free(pointer variable);
```

This instruction does not destroy the value stored in the variable, but simply allows the storage addressed through this variable to become available for other purposes. When `malloc` is called upon for new storage, the memory just released might be used. Figure 7.1.7 demonstrates this principle.

The output of the program is:

```
y's field has 5, z's field has A
y's field has 10, z's field has B
with q y's field has 10, z's field has B
```

The output generated by the last two lines of the program warrant some explanation. Even though the storage pointed to by `p` was `free`'d, `p` still retained the address of that memory, the memory was marked by the operating system as "available for use." When `q` received memory

Figure 7.1.7   The free Instruction

```
/***********************************************************************/
/* This program demonstrates the use of free to return storage back to */
/* the heap when the program no longer requires that memory. After the */
/* first malloc and free, the program malloc's again and assigns new   */
/* data into the just received storage. q points to the new data and   */
/* p still points to the area.                                         */
/***********************************************************************/
#include <stdio.h>

main()
{
   struct x      /* the structure template                            */
   {
      int y;     /* the structure has field y                         */
      char z;    /* and field z                                       */
   } *p,*q;      /* p and q can point to one of these structures       */

   p = (struct x *) malloc (sizeof(struct x)); /* p has the address    */

   p -> y = 5;  /* put 5 in one field just for fun!                    */
   p -> z = 'A';/* put an A in the other field just for fun            */
            /* print the field to see that the data is there           */
   printf("y's field has %d, z's field has %c\n", p -> y, p -> z);

/***********************************************************************/
/* Now make the storage available for other uses with free            */
/***********************************************************************/
   free(p); /* Simply free the pointer—does away with                 */
            /* the storage. The pointer can again point to the         */
            /* same kind of storage if another malloc were executed.   */

   q = (struct x *) malloc (sizeof(struct x)); /* q has the address    */
            /* of maybe the same storage area that p had since p's     */
            /* area has been free'd                                    */
   q -> y = 10;
   q -> z = 'B';
   printf("y's field has %d, z's field has %c\n", p -> y, p -> z);
   printf("with q y's field has %d, z's field has %c\n", q -> y, q-> z);
}
```

from **malloc** it obtained the address of the same memory still pointed to by **p**. Thus, when we assigned new values to the memory in **q**'s address, we effectively changed **p**'s values as well. Figure 7.1.8 demonstrates the sequence of events.

Figure 7.1.8 More on malloc

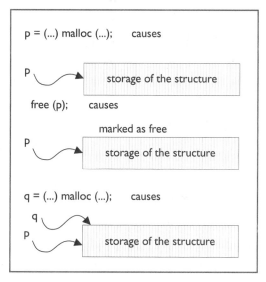

Figure 7.1.8 demonstrates that while **p** has been **free**'d, the address stored at **p** is not destroyed. The memory that **p** referenced is really marked for reuse. When **q** received memory, it just happened that **q** received the same memory that had been given to **p**. This certainly doesn't have to be the case — the operating system routine that monitors the heap determines where the next block of memory will be given for a **malloc**. This program was executed on a PC compatible, a Sequent Symmetry, and a Sun 386i, all of which gave the same results.

When requesting many structures or storage locations with **malloc**, it is possible to exhaust the heap. If there is no additional storage in the heap, the programmer must free some storage before continuing. C will alert the program by assigning **NULL** to the variable receiving the address. To ensure the program does not fail, each request by **malloc** should be followed by a test to determine if the address is valid. For example, the above programs should have the instructions:

```
p = (struct x *) malloc (sizeof(struct x));
                    /* p has the address                    */
if (p == NULL)
{
   printf("malloc failed!\n");
   exit(1);        /* the error message prints and the
                        program stops                       */
}
```

The above code tests for successful execution of the `malloc` instruction. If `malloc` fails, `p` will be `NULL` and the program will print an error message and stop. When you construct your program, you will decide the appropriate action to take if `malloc` fails.

We now demonstrate a comparable dynamic memory allocation used for requesting array storage during run time.

Dynamic Array Allocation—calloc

The term `calloc` is an acronym for *continuous allocation,* which is the storage used for arrays. The general form of `calloc` is:

> array pointer = (cast) `calloc`(number of elements in the array, `sizeof` each element);

For example, to allocate a 20-element array of integers, we would code:

```
p = (int *) calloc (20, sizeof(int));
```

where `p` is the array name, which you recall is the address of the first element of the array. Like `malloc`, `calloc` returns a pointer of type `void` so we must change the type, using the cast, to be a pointer of the appropriate type—`int` in this case. The 20 is the number of elements of the array and the `sizeof` is the amount of space required for each element. Figure 7.1.9 demonstrates a complete program using `calloc`.

The output generated using a PC-compatible computer is:

```
the randomly generated numbers in p are:
p[0] = 346
p[1] = 130
p[2] = 10982
p[3] = 1090
p[4] = 11656
p[5] = 7117
p[6] = 17595
p[7] = 6415
p[8] = 22948
p[9] = 31126
```

The output generated on a Sequent Symmetry is:

```
the randomly generated numbers in p are:
p[0] = 1103527590
p[1] = 377401575
p[2] = 662824084
p[3] = 1147902781
p[4] = 2035015474
```

Figure 7.1.9 Dynamic Arrays Using calloc

```
/******************************************************************/
/* This program will demonstrate the use of calloc to dynamically  */
/* allocate a 10 element array of integers.                        */
/******************************************************************/
#include <stdio.h>

main()
{
    int *p;    /* p will contain the address of the first element  */
    int i;     /* index control variable for filling the array     */

    p = (int *) calloc (10, sizeof(int));
    if (p == NULL)
    {
        printf("calloc failed\n");
        exit(1);
    }

    for (i = 0; i < 10; i=i+1)
        p[i] = rand();

    printf("the randomly generated numbers in p are:\n");
    for (i = 0; i < 10; i=i+1)
        printf("p[%d] = %d\n",i,p[i]);
}
```

```
p[5] = 368800899
p[6] = 1508029952
p[7] = 486256185
p[8] = 1062517886
p[9] = 267834847
```

We note that the output from these example programs is the same except for the numbers generated by the **rand()** function. The access to the dynamically created array is precisely the same as the automatic array of Chapter 3 and again in Chapter 5. The function **calloc** is very similar to **malloc**; it is used to dynamically request continuous storage. We will provide another example of dynamically allocating storage for an array of structures. This is similar, in a way, to Figure 7.1.6, which dynamically allocated a structure containing an array using **malloc**. Figure 7.1.6 was one structure containing an array, where Figure 7.1.10 is effectively many structures—an array of structures.

Figure 7.1.10   Using calloc for a Structure

```
/*************************************************************************/
/* This program will demonstrate the use of calloc to dynamically       */
/* allocate a 10 element array of structures.                           */
/*************************************************************************/
#include <stdio.h>

struct arr
{
   int m;/* one integer field in the structure                         */
};

main()
{
   struct arr *p; /* p will contain the address of the structure        */
   int i;   /* index control variable for filling the array             */
          /* allocate a structure                                       */
   p = (struct arr *) calloc (10, sizeof(struct arr));
   if (p == NULL)
   {
      printf("calloc failed\n");
      exit(1);
   }

   for (i = 0; i < 10; i=i+1)
      p[i].m = rand();      /* fill the array, standard array of structure*/
                        /* reference                                    */
   printf("the randomly generated numbers in p are:\n");
   for (i = 0; i < 10; i=i+1)
      printf("p[%d].m = %d\n",i,p[i].m);
}
```

Again, the use of the dynamically allocated array is precisely like the automatic array demonstrated in Chapter 3 and again in Chapter 5. The only advantage to this method is that the size of the array can be determined while the program is executing, and if it is not large enough, the array can be increased in size without affecting the data already stored. The output generated on one computer from the program in Figure 7.1.10 is:

```
the randomly generated numbers in p are:
p[0].m = 346
p[1].m = 130
p[2].m = 10982
p[3].m = 1090
```

```
p[4].m = 11656
p[5].m = 7117
p[6].m = 17595
p[7].m = 6415
p[8].m = 22948
p[9].m = 31126
```

Dynamic Array Reallocation—realloc

Now we consider **realloc**, which is used to allocate more memory to an array when the initial allocation is found to be insufficient. The **realloc** instruction does not destroy the data already present in the array; it merely adds more memory to the end of the array. Its general form is:

```
pointer=(cast)realloc((cast)pointer,number_of_elements*
sizeof(data));
```

For example, we might code the following line to increase the size of the array **p** from Figure 7.1.9.

```
p = (int *) realloc ((int *)p, 15*sizeof(int));
```

The instruction **realloc** simply increases the size of memory allocated by **calloc**. A sample program is shown in Figure 7.1.11. The output of this figure is:

```
the randomly generated numbers in p are:
p[0] = 346
p[1] = 130
p[2] = 10982
p[3] = 1090
p[4] = 11656
p[5] = 7117
p[6] = 17595
p[7] = 6415
p[8] = 22948
p[9] = 31126
the expanded array with old and new data
p[0] = 346
p[1] = 130
p[2] = 10982
p[3] = 1090
p[4] = 11656
p[5] = 7117
p[6] = 17595
p[7] = 6415
p[8] = 22948
```

Figure 7.1.11   realloc

```
/***********************************************************************/
/* This program will demonstrate the use of calloc to dynamically      */
/* allocate a 10 element array of integers and then use realloc to     */
/* increase the size of the array to 15 elements.                      */
/***********************************************************************/
#include <stdio.h>

main()
{
   int *p;  /* p will contain the address of the first element        */
   int i;   /* index control variable for filling the array           */

   p = (int *) calloc (10, sizeof(int));
   if (p == NULL)
   {
      printf("calloc failed\n");
      exit(1);
   }
/***********************************************************************/
/* Fill the first 10 elements of the array with random numbers.        */
/***********************************************************************/
   for (i = 0; i < 10; i=i+1)
      p[i] = rand();

/***********************************************************************/
/* Print the numbers.                                                  */
/***********************************************************************/
   printf("the randomly generated numbers in p are:\n");
   for (i = 0; i < 10; i=i+1)
      printf("p[%d] = %d\n",i,p[i]);

/***********************************************************************/
/* Now allocate more memory to the array and print the resulting array. */
/***********************************************************************/
   p =   (int *) realloc ((int *)p, 15*sizeof(int));
   if  (p == NULL)
   {
      printf("realloc failed\n");
      exit(1);
   }
```

(continued)

Figure 7.1.11 realloc (*continued*)

```
/**************************************************************** */
/* Now fill the rest with data.                                  */
/**************************************************************** */
   for (i = 10; i<15; i=i+1)
      p[i] = rand();

/**************************************************************** */
/* Now print it all, demonstrating more data received and original data */
/* not destroyed.                                                */
/**************************************************************** */
   printf("the expanded array with old and new data \n");
   for (i = 0; i < 15; i=i+1)
      printf("p[%d] = %d\n",i,p[i]);
}
```

```
p[9]  = 31126
p[10] = 9004
p[11] = 14558
p[12] = 3571
p[13] = 22879
p[14] = 18492
```

The first 10 elements of the array were not changed when the additional array positions were received. While the program is executing, when additional space in the array is required, **realloc** can be used to increase the size of the array without modifying the existing data.

C has the unique ability to create a two-dimensional array where the second dimension varies. That is, for each row of the array, the number of columns may vary in contrast to other languages where the second dimension is the same for all rows. Traditional languages work like C's declaration

```
int two_dim_array [10][20]
```

that requests automatic storage for 400 integers formed in 10 rows and 20 columns. Figure 7.1.12 illustrates this concept.

We realize that array names in C contain the address of the first element of the array. In the case of a two-dimensional array, we first allocate a single-dimensioned array of addresses. Each address in this first array contains the address of a row (the second dimension) of the

Figure 7.1.12   Array Allocation

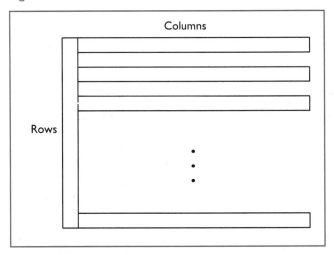

array. In this way, the number of elements in that second dimension (row) can vary from one row to the next. Figure 7.1.13 illustrates this concept.

To make Figure 7.1.13 happen, we **calloc** the first dimension of the array and then **calloc** each of the second dimensions separately. Figure 7.1.14 shows the program that accomplishes the task.

Figure 7.1.14 establishes a single-dimension array of 10 entries, each capable of holding the address of the address of a character. The second

Figure 7.1.13   Ragged Array

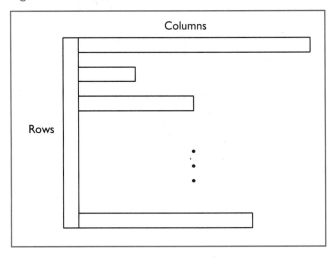

Figure 7.1.14   Two-Dimension Array calloc

```
/**********************************************************************/
/* This program will calloc twice to create a two dimensioned array  */
/* where the second dimension can be of different size for each of    */
/* the first dimensions. We will store lists of names as the data     */
/* which will be read from the keyboard.                              */
/**********************************************************************/

#include <stdio.h>

main()
{
   int i;           /* index variable for loops                       */
   char **names;    /* the two dimensioned array of characters for    */
                    /* names. Double pointer for two dimensions.      */
   char tempname[50];/* place the name in here initially to deter-    */
                    /* mine its length, then we will create an array  */
                    /* size to hold this name.                        */
   int eof;         /* An integer used to indicate when the program   */
                    /* is finished reading and requesting storage.    */
   int name_length;/* the length of each name which will be the       */
                    /* size of the second dimension.                  */
   int number_of_names = 0;
                    /* The count of the number of names to be stored. */
   int total_number_of_names = 0;/* Count the total number of names.  */
/**********************************************************************/
/* Now the program starts by reading in the first name, then          */
/* entering the big loop to create all the storage and save the       */
/* names in that storage.                                             */
/**********************************************************************/

/**********************************************************************/
/* Assume there are 10 names to be entered, if more use               */
/* realloc to increase the size of the array.                         */
/**********************************************************************/
   names = (char **) calloc (10, sizeof(char *));

   printf("Please enter the first name\n");
   eof = scanf("%s",tempname); /* read in the first name              */

/**********************************************************************/
/* Now enter the big loop that will read in all the names, allocate   */
/* the second dimension and reallocate more space if the initial      */
/* 10 is not enough. The program assumes there will be at least       */
/* one name.                                                          */
/**********************************************************************/
   while (eof > 0)    /* we haven't gotten all the names yet.         */
   {
```

(continued)

Figure 7.1.14   Two-Dimension Array calloc (*continued*)

```
      total_number_of_names=total_number_of_names+1; /* total names    */
      number_of_names=number_of_names+1;
      if (number_of_names >= 10) /* we must increase the size of      */
      {                          /* the first dimension.              */
          names = (char **) realloc ((char **)names,
                      (10+total_number_of_names)*sizeof(char *));
                              /* increase the size by another 10      */
          number_of_names = 0;     /* reset the name counter          */
      }
/****************************************************************/
/* Find the length of the name to be stored in this dimension      */
/* and calloc the space necessary, then copy the name into         */
/* that space.                                                     */
/****************************************************************/
      name_length = strlen(tempname) + 1; /* +1 for the '/0' end of  */
                                      /* string marker.               */
      names[total_number_of_names]=(char *)calloc(name_length,sizeof(char));
      strcpy(names[total_number_of_names],tempname);

      printf("Please enter the next name or ^z (dos) or ^d (unix) to
              end.\n");
      eof = scanf("%s",tempname);    /* read in the next name        */
      }                              /* end of the while loop        */

/****************************************************************/
                                                                  /*  */
/* Print out the names.                                            */
/****************************************************************/
    printf("The entered names are:\n");
    for(i = 1; i <= total_number_of_names; i=i+1)
       printf("the %d name is %s\n",i, names[i]);
}
```

dimension is the character string containing the name of a person. All arrays in C are addresses, so the first dimension (each row) addresses the second dimension holding the names. We will demonstrate for the following data:

```
Please enter the first name
Eno
Please enter the next name or ^z (dos) or ^d (unix) to end.
Moss
```

```
Please enter the next name or ^z (dos) or ^d (unix) to end.
Susan
Please enter the next name or ^z (dos) or ^d (unix) to end.
Pete
Please enter the next name or ^z (dos) or ^d (unix) to end.
George
Please enter the next name or ^z (dos) or ^d (unix) to end.
^z
The entered names are:
the 1 name is Eno
the 2 name is Moss
the 3 name is Susan
the 4 name is Pete
the 5 name is George
```

The storage organization created by the preceding run is illustrated in Figure 7.1.15.

Line 32 requests storage for the first dimension of the array where each element contains the address of the second dimension. Initially 10 positions are requested. If this is found to be insufficient, the **realloc** of line 48 requests an additional 10 positions. At most 9 character addresses would be wasted by this program since a new block of 10 is requested each time more space is needed. The new block of 10 would not be requested unless a name had to be stored. As many names can be stored as necessary with this program since the array is expanded by 10 as each set of 10 is filled. Line 60 requests storage for the second dimension, as required by the number of characters in the name. Only the exact amount of storage is given for each name, as demonstrated by Figure 7.1.15.

Figure 7.1.14 represents a method of storing a list of names where the number of names is unknown and the number of characters of each name is unknown. The program will efficiently use memory, allocating just the amount necessary to hold the characters of each name.

Figure 7.1.15   Memory Allocated by Figure 7.1.14

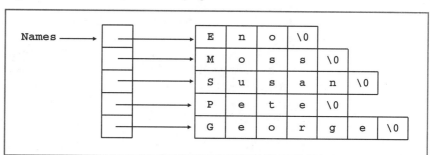

▶ Exercises 7.1

7.1.1   Write the storage request instruction using **malloc** to request sufficient storage for a character.

7.1.2   Suppose **r** is a variable containing the address of storage. How can we cause the storage to become available for other use?

7.1.3   What is the "type" of the address returned by **malloc**?

7.1.4   Write the instructions to provide a storage structure for the character name, integer street number, character city, character state, and integer zip code.

7.2 LINKED LISTS

SECTION TOPICS

Singly Linked List

Insertion in a Linked List

Ordered Linked Lists

This section discusses creating linked lists as an alternative to arrays for storing data. There are several types of linked lists including singly linked lists, doubly linked lists, and circular linked lists. Singly linked lists will be discussed and implemented. The remaining types of lists will be left to the exercises. Linked lists are standard data structures that can be implemented with dynamic storage using **malloc**.

Singly Linked List

The concept of a singly linked list is to dynamically allocate data storage areas and make each area contain the address of the next area. For example, the structure in Figure 7.2.1 might represent a node in the list.

The number of data fields in a node depends on the nature of the problem being solved. Figure 7.2.2 demonstrates the representation of a linked list as it is created in memory. Here we have only one data field and the *address of next node* is represented by arrows to that node, just as we have done with pointers in the past.

The variable **head** contains the address of the first node in the list. Each node contains, in addition to the data, the address of the next node,

Figure 7.2.1 Possible Single Node of a Linked List

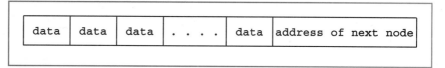

Figure 7.2.2 Singly Linked List

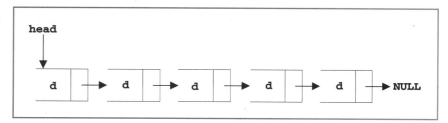

and the last node's address field contains the keyword NULL, indicating there are no more nodes in the list.

▶ **PROBLEM** Consider the problem of receiving a number of weights. We would like to store the weights in highest to lowest order, but they will be received in random order.

ANALYSIS If we stored the weights in an array, each time a new weight was received all the weights less than the newest would have to be moved down in the array. Instead we use a linked list, which allows the addition of a node in the middle of the list without moving the remaining nodes.

   Figure 7.2.3 demonstrates that we must find the correct location for inserting the new node into the list, modify the address of its preceding node, and make its address field contain the address of the next node. No other modifications of the list are necessary; there is no moving of data.

DESIGN Three conditions require consideration: a node inserted at the front of the list, a node inserted in the middle of the list, and a node inserted at the end of the list. We can identify the first condition if the value to be inserted is greater than the value of the node addressed by **head**. To identify and insert a node in the middle of a list, we need two variables that will identify the node before and the node after the position for inserting the new node. We will call these variables **lead** and **follow** as shown in Figure 7.2.4. Of course we need the address of the node to be inserted. The set of conditions is shown in Figure 7.2.4,

Figure 7.2.3   Insertion in a Linked List

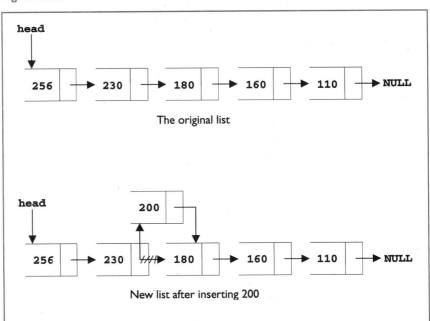

The original list

New list after inserting 200

Figure 7.2.4   Insertion in a Linked List

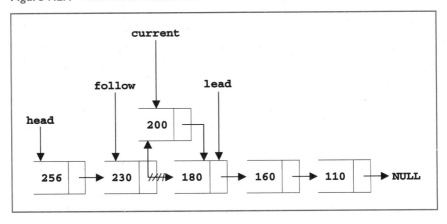

where **current** contains the address of the node to be inserted. We can recognize a node to be inserted at the end of the list if **lead** becomes **NULL**.

CODE   Figure 7.2.5 shows the code to make all this happen.

Figure 7.2.5 Ordered Linked List

```
/************************************************************************/
/* This program will create a single linked list inserting integer     */
/* number weights into the list in order, large to small.              */
/************************************************************************/
#include <stdio.h>

struct node * insert(struct node *,int); /* the function prototype      */
                            /* the function that will do the insertions */
void print(struct node *); /* the function prototype                    */
struct node                /* the node to be inserted into the list     */
{
   int weight;          /* the data to be held in the node              */
   struct node *next;   /* the field to hold the address of the next node*/
};
                        /* returns a pointer to the node structure       */
main()
{
   struct node *head;   /* to hold the address of the head of the list  */
   int eof;             /* used to detect end-of-file                   */
   int data;            /* temporary storage for weight                 */

   head = NULL;         /* the list is initially empty                  */
   printf("enter a weight, ^z (dos) ^d (unix) to end\n");
   eof = scanf("%d",&data); /* read weights into "data"                 */
   while (eof > 0)
   {
      head = insert(head,data); /* invoke the function to insert data   */
      printf("enter a weight, ^z (dos) ^d (unix) to end\n");
      eof = scanf("%d",&data); /* read weights into "data"              */
                      /* into the list addressed by head                */
   }
   print(head);         /* invoke the function to print the list         */
   return(0);           /* return good completion to the system          */
}                       /* end of "main"                                 */
/************************************************************************/
/* The insert function will insert a node at the proper place in the list. */
/************************************************************************/

struct node * insert(struct node * head, int data)
                   /* head is the address of the first node of list     */
                   /* data is the data to be inserted into the list     */
{
```

(continued)

Figure 7.2.5　Ordered Linked List (*continued*)

```
   struct node *lead;    /* to hold the address of the node after   */
   struct node *follow;  /* to hold the address of the node before  */
   struct node *current; /* to hold the address of the node inserting */

/****************************************************************/
/* Put in the first node if the list is empty and return the head of the */
/* list to main.                                                */
/****************************************************************/
   if (head == NULL)         /* the list is empty             */
   {
      head = (struct node *)malloc(sizeof(struct node));/* request a node */
      head -> weight = data;  /* put the data in the node      */
      head -> next = NULL;    /* this is the end of the list   */
      return(head);           /* finished, go back to main     */
   }

/****************************************************************/
/* check to see if the node is larger than the first           */
/****************************************************************/
   if (head -> weight < data)    /* insert in the very front    */
   {
      current = (struct node *)malloc(sizeof(struct node)); /* get a node */
      current -> next = head;     /* make this node address old head  */
      current -> weight = data;   /* put data in                   */
      head = current;             /* move head to current node     */
      return(head);               /* finished putting node in front */
   }

/****************************************************************/
/* check where to put the node, maybe in the middle or maybe at the end */
/****************************************************************/
   lead = head -> next;  /* make lead point to the next node    */
   follow = head;        /* and follow point to the current node */
   while (lead != NULL)  /* move down the list until we get to the end */
   {
      if (lead -> weight < data)  /* lead is just past where to insert */
      {                           /* insert the node here           */
         current=(struct node *)malloc(sizeof(struct node));/* get a node */
         current -> weight = data; /* put the weight in the node    */
         follow -> next = current;/*make the previous node address current */
         current -> next = lead;/* current node addresses the lead node */
         return(head);            /* node has been inserted        */
      }
```

(*continued*)

Figure 7.2.5   Ordered Linked List (*continued*)

```
        follow = lead;          /* move the follow pointer down the list    */
        lead = lead -> next;  /* move lead down the list                    */
    }

/********************************************************************************/
/* If control gets here, the node is to be inserted at the end of the list.*/
/* Work to be done is the same as insertion in the middle of the list.    */
/********************************************************************************/
    current = (struct node *) malloc (sizeof(struct node));/* get a node */
    current -> weight = data;    /* put the weight in the node           */
    follow -> next = current;    /* make the previous node address current */
    current -> next = lead;      /* current node addresses the lead node   */
    return(head);                /* node has been inserted                 */
}



/********************************************************************************/
/* Use this function to print the list.                                   */
/* Note that head is being passed by value and therefore will remain at */
/* the head of the list when finished and control is back in main.      */
/********************************************************************************/
void print(struct node * head)
{       /* head is the head of the list to be printed                    */
    while (head != NULL)
    {
        printf("%d \n",head -> weight);    /* print the data in the node   */
        head = head -> next;               /* move to the next node        */
    }
}
```

TEST   The data given to this program is as follows:

                    300
                    250
                    200
                    275
                    225
                    110
                    325

The exact execution of the program is as follows:

```
enter a weight, ^z (dos) ^d (unix) to end
300
enter a weight, ^z (dos) ^d (unix) to end
250
enter a weight, ^z (dos) ^d (unix) to end
200
enter a weight, ^z (dos) ^d (unix) to end
275
enter a weight, ^z (dos) ^d (unix) to end
225
enter a weight, ^z (dos) ^d (unix) to end
110
enter a weight, ^z (dos) ^d (unix) to end
325
enter a weight, ^z (dos) ^d (unix) to end
^z
325
300
275
250
225
200
110
```

The set of data causes nodes to be inserted in all possible positions (before the first, in the middle, and after the last) in the list. When 300 was inserted, the node was put in an empty list, 250 was placed at the end of the list, 200 also at the end, 275 was placed after the first node, 225 was put near the middle, 110 again at the end, and 325 at the very beginning. Thus, the data values were ordered by their position in the list so when the data is printed by traversing the list, all data is in order.

This is a rather complicated program, but with careful analysis, design, and implementation, programs of this type are well within your reach. This is an example of the level of difficulty required by most programs that accomplish meaningful tasks.

▶ Exercises 7.2

7.2.1 Given a sorted (linked) list of 20 data items, how many comparisons are necessary to find the value of the last item?

7.2.2 Compare the advantages and disadvantages of storing data in a dynamic linked list as opposed to an array.

7.2.3 A doubly linked list has a pointer field containing the address of the next node, like a singly linked list, and a pointer field containing the address of the previous node. Write the structure declaration statement to allow this to happen.

7.2.4 Write the **malloc** instruction to allocate a node for the doubly linked list described in exercise 7.2.3.

7.2.5 Given the following doubly linked list and pointers as shown, write the instructions to request a third node and insert it between these two.

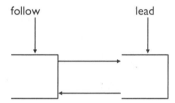

7.2.6 Given an array of 20 sorted items, how many comparisons are necessary to find the last item?

7.2.7 Describe the work required to insert a number into an array where the value of the number is the median of the largest and smallest numbers in the array.

7.2.8 A circular list modifies the single list by making the address portion of the last node contain the address of the first node rather than **NULL**. Suppose **head** contains the address of the first node and **last** contains the address of the last node. Write the instructions necessary to make the list be circular. Assume the address field of the node is called **next**.

7.2.9 Create a list-management program. The program must be menu driven and must contain the following modules:

create, add beginning, add end, add after, delete first, delete last, delete node, traverse, quit

The node contained in the list may be a simple structure, such as

```
struct node
{
        char data[40];
        struct node *next;
}    NODE;
```

Each of the modules in your list management system must be documented, must be C functions, and must receive and return appropriate values. If you decide to do anything unique, make sure it is documented.

7.3   TREES

This section demonstrates the use of a binary tree for storing data. Data access is slightly more efficient when stored in trees than in lists, but more memory is required to represent a tree.

Definition of a Tree

A tree is a directed acyclic graph. This simply means that we can represent data in a tree structure rather than an array or list. A tree is similar to the trees that grow in the forest; that is, they have a single root, branches, and leaves. Consider the example of a tree shown in Figure 7.3.1.

This figure demonstrates that 50 is the root; there can be only one. All lines connecting numbers are branches and all numbers across the bottom are leaves. Notice the tree grows down and no nodes connect to nodes at the same level or above them. There are no cycles. We consider an implementation of trees using **malloc** to dynamically allocate the nodes of the tree.

▶ PROBLEM   We are interested in storing the weights of the previous section. But when we consider the list representation required to traverse the whole list to get

Figure 7.3.1   Tree Notation

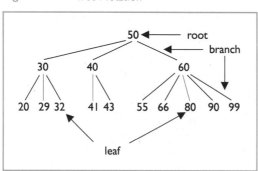

Figure 7.3.2 Binary Tree

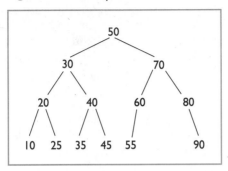

to the last element, we are interested in a more efficient method of storing data. The more efficient method will store the data in a binary search tree. In a binary tree, each node has only 0, 1, or 2 children or nodes below it. The tree in Figure 7.3.1 is a general tree, one where nodes can have several children. We use a search tree where the first node is placed at the root and all successive nodes are placed to the left or right of the root, depending on the data stored in that node. That is, numbers smaller than the root are stored on the left and numbers larger than the root are stored on the right. This pattern is continued at each level. Figure 7.3.2 demonstrates.

At each level, a node with a value smaller than the value in the current node is placed on the left and a node with a value larger than the current node's value is placed on the right. If the data values are distributed evenly, causing the tree to be balanced, search time for a particular weight is reduced compared to a linked list, since only the *height of the tree* number of comparisons is required to find the data in the worst case, whereas the complete list had to be traversed. The height of a tree is defined to be the number of nodes in the path from the root to the farthest leaf. The height of the tree in Figure 7.3.2 is 4. However, if the data is not received randomly, the tree can degenerate into the list. That is, assuming the numbers come in order, the tree will result in a list with all the nodes down one side.

ANALYSIS   We need a data structure that will allow two addresses to be stored in each node, one for the left child and one for the right child. Again, each node will contain one piece of data as it did in the linked list program. We have two possibilities for insertion into the tree: inserting into an empty tree and inserting into a tree containing nodes with data. If the tree is empty, a variable **head** will contain **NULL**, in which case we simply need to create a node and insert the data. If **head** is not **NULL**, we need to traverse down the tree, left or right, depending on the value in the node as compared to the value being inserted.

DESIGN   We will use a structure to represent the nodes containing two address fields, one for the left child and one for the right child, and a data field. When a new piece of data is received, we will look on the left for a place to put the new node if the data is smaller and on the right if the data is larger. Thus, we will search for a place to insert the node depending on the value of the data.

CODE   Figure 7.3.3 shows the complete program for insertion into a binary tree. The print routine has changed significantly from the list traversal of the previous section. It is a recursive routine that prints the data at the root, then moves down the left branch printing weights as it goes. When the left is exhausted, the right branches are pursued, again printing weights as it goes.

TEST   A sample run of the program in Figure 7.3.3 follows:

```
enter a weight, ^z (dos) ^d (unix) to end
50
enter a weight, ^z (dos) ^d (unix) to end
30
enter a weight, ^z (dos) ^d (unix) to end
80
enter a weight, ^z (dos) ^d (unix) to end
40
enter a weight, ^z (dos) ^d (unix) to end
10
enter a weight, ^z (dos) ^d (unix) to end
60
enter a weight, ^z (dos) ^d (unix) to end
45
enter a weight, ^z (dos) ^d (unix) to end
90
enter a weight, ^z (dos) ^d (unix) to end
55
enter a weight, ^z (dos) ^d (unix) to end
65
enter a weight, ^z (dos) ^d (unix) to end
^d
50
30
10
40
45
80
60
55
65
90
```

Figure 7.3.3 Binary Search Tree

```
/***********************************************************************/
/* This program will create a binary search tree, insert integer numbers */
/* representing weights, and traverse the tree, printing each data item */
/* in preorder.                                                         */
/***********************************************************************/

#include <stdio.h>
struct node *insert(struct node *, int);   /* the function prototype    */
                      /* the function that will do the insertions       */
void preprint(struct node *);
                   /* the field to hold the address of the left node    */
                   /* function to do the printing                       */
struct node            /* the node to be inserted into the list         */
{
   int weight;         /* the data to be held in the node               */
   struct node *left;  /* the field to hold the address of the left node */
   struct node *right; /* the field to hold the address of the right node */
};
                       /* returns a pointer to the node structure       */
main()
{
   struct node *head;  /* to hold the address of the head of the tree   */
   int eof;            /* used to detect end-of-file                    */
   int data;           /* temporary storage for weight                  */

   head = NULL;        /* the list is initially empty                   */
   printf("enter a weight, ^z (dos) ^d (unix) to end\n");
   eof = scanf("%d",&data); /* read weights into "data"                 */
   while (eof > 0)
   {
      head = insert(head,data); /* invoke the function to insert data   */
      printf("enter a weight, ^z (dos) ^d (unix) to end\n");
      eof = scanf("%d",&data); /* read weights into "data"              */
                       /* into the list addressed by head               */
   }

   preprint(head);     /* invoke the function to print the tree         */
   return(0);          /* return good completion to the system          */
}                      /* end of "main"                                 */
```

(continued)

Figure 7.3.3   Binary Search Tree *(continued)*

```
/*********************************************************************/
/* The insert function will insert a node at the proper place in the tree. */
/*********************************************************************/

struct node * insert(struct node * head,int data)
                    /* head is the address of the first node of tree  */
                    /* data is the data to be inserted into the tree  */
{
   struct node *current;  /* to hold the address of the node inserting  */
   struct node *search;   /* to hold the address of the node searching  */
   struct node *follow;   /* to hold the address of the node following  */
/*********************************************************************/
/* Put in the first node if the tree is empty and return the head of the  */
/* tree to main.                                                          */
/*********************************************************************/

   if (head == NULL)   /* the tree is empty                           */
   {
      head = (struct node *)malloc(sizeof(struct node));/* request a node  */
      head -> weight = data;  /* put the data in the node              */
      head -> left = NULL;    /* the left child does not exist         */
      head -> right = NULL;   /* the right child does not exist        */
      return(head);           /* finished inserting the root, return main */
   }

/*********************************************************************/
/*check to see where to put the node, left or right, head stays at the top */
/*********************************************************************/
   search = head;
   while(search != NULL)
   {
       follow = search;          /* always points one node behind        */
      if (data > search -> weight)  /* insert to the right              */
          search = search -> right;   /* go right if data is greater    */
        else
          search = search -> left;/*go left if data is less or equal    */
   }
```

Figure 7.3.3 Binary Search Tree (*continued*)

```
/*******************************************************************/
/* Search is null so follow is addressing the parent node, we are ready */
/* to actually attach the node to the tree.                    */
/*******************************************************************/
   current = (struct node *) malloc (sizeof(struct node)); /* get a node */
   current -> weight = data;     /* put data in                 */
   if (data > follow -> weight)  /* insert the node on the right    */
       follow -> right = current;
   else                          /* otherwise put the node on the left */
       follow -> left = current;
   return (head);                /* return head even though it hasn't chg */
}



/*******************************************************************/
/* Use this function to print the tree.                        */
/* Note that head is being passed by "value" and therefore will remain at */
/* the head of the list when finished and control is back in main. */
/*******************************************************************/
void preprint(struct node *head)
                    /* head is the address of the root of the tree.  */
{
   if (head != NULL)
   {
      printf("%d \n",head -> weight); /* print the data in the node    */
      preprint(head -> left);         /* go down the left side         */
      preprint(head -> right);        /* go down the right side        */
   }
}
```

The program doesn't really show the construction of the tree since only data is stored and printed, but not the actual structure. Figure 7.3.4 shows the stages as each value is inserted.

Each tree in Figure 7.3.4 represents the status just after the node has been inserted into the tree. The **search** variable moves through the tree, locating the point to insert the new node, and **follow** just trails one node behind **search** to identify the node where the new node is to be attached. After **follow** is established, we attach the new node on the left or the right depending on the value of the data in the new node. Again, when inserting a data value, the left or right branch of the tree is followed if the data is smaller or larger, respectively, than the value of the data in the node being considered.

Figure 7.3.4 Insertion in a Binary Tree

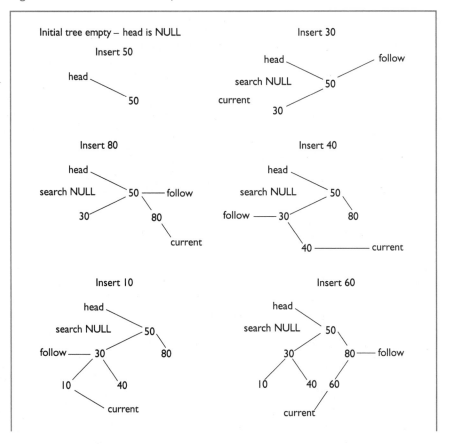

As we see from these examples, **calloc**, **realloc**, and **malloc** are general-purpose storage request instructions that add considerable flexibility to the execution of a program. A great deal or a small amount of data can be handled without wasting large amounts of memory using these tools.

▶ Exercises 7.3

7.3.1 Draw the search tree required for searching any 15 numbers.

7.3.2 Trace the path in the previous problem required to find the number in position 7 of the data array.

Figure 7.3.4 Insertion in a Binary Tree (*continued*)

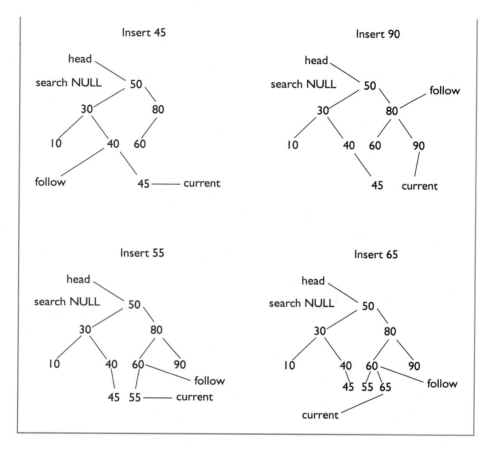

7.3.3 Trace the path in the previous problem required to find the number in position 6 of the data array.

7.3.4 What is the maximum number of comparisons necessary to search for a number not in the array in the previous problem.

7.3.5 Write a general expression for the number of comparisons required to search for a number in an array containing **n** numbers.

7.3.6 What is the maximum number of comparisons when 64 numbers are used in a binary search to retrieve any number?

7.3.7 What is the difference in data structure between a doubly linked list and a tree?

▶ Key Words

automatic storage	node
binary tree	NULL
branch	pointers
calloc	ragged array
cast	realloc
dynamic memory	root
free	search tree
heap	stack
leaf	storage request
linked list	tree
malloc	two-dimensional array

▶ Chapter Concepts

7.1   The function **malloc** allocates a block of space in memory consisting of a specified number of bytes. The space allocated by **malloc** is not initialized. The address of the allocated space is returned after a successful call to **malloc**, or **NULL** for an unsuccessful call.

7.2   The function **calloc** allocates contiguous space in memory for an array. The space allocated by **calloc** is initialized to all bits zero. The address of the allocated space is returned after a successful call to **calloc**, or **NULL** for an unsuccessful call.

7.3   The function **realloc** changes the size of a block of memory pointed to by a pointer. Values in the previously allocated space are unchanged. Any new space is not initialized. A successful call returns the address of the newly allocated space, or **NULL** if the call to **realloc** was unsuccessful.

7.4   A call to the function **free** causes the space pointed to by a pointer to be deallocated—making the space available for subsequent calls to **malloc**, **calloc**, or **realloc**. If the pointer is not **NULL**, it must have been the address of space allocated by a previous call to **malloc**, **calloc**, or **realloc**. If the pointer is **NULL** this function has no effect.

7.5   Dynamic memory refers to memory that is allocated from the heap at run time.

7.6 Dynamic memory allocation techniques may be used to allocate two-dimensional (and higher) arrays as well as ragged arrays.

7.7 A two-dimensional ragged array is an array in which not all rows are the same length.

7.8 A singly linked list is a list that is processed sequentially. Each node in the list contains as one of its entries the address of the next node in the list to be processed.

7.9 Some of the basic operations to be performed on singly linked lists include creating a list, looking up an element, adding a node and inserting an element, and deleting a node.

7.10 A binary tree is a linked data structure in which each node has two links (addresses), one for the left branch of the tree and one for the right branch.

7.11 Data may be stored efficiently in a binary search tree. Retrieving data from a binary search tree requires a minimum number of "looks" at the data. On average, significantly fewer comparisons are required to retrieve information from a binary search tree than from a singly linked list.

▶ Programming Projects

7.1 Write a complete program that will provide the user with a menu driven linked-list management system. Your package must contain functions that will create a list, add a node at the beginning of the list, add a node at the end of the list, add a node before a given node in the list, add a node after a given node in the list, delete a node from the list, display the number of entries in the list, and search the list for a particular data item. You may make up any data structure you wish to store in the list.

7.2 Write a complete program that will provide the user with a menu-driven binary-tree management system. Your package must contain functions that will create a tree, add a node to the tree, delete a node from the tree, search the tree for a particular data item, traverse the tree visiting each node of the tree using preorder traversal, postorder traversal, and inorder traversal.

7.3 Since a singly linked list contains a data item and a pointer (the address of the next item in the list), a singly linked list may be processed in one direction only, the direction of the pointers. Generalize the concept of a singly linked list to include a pointer not only to the next item in the list, but also a pointer to the previous item in the list, so that the list may be processed in both directions. Such a "doubly linked" list provides additional difficulty when we attempt to insert a new node or delete an existing node. Write iterative functions which will perform insertion and deletion in a doubly linked list.

7.4   Assuming that the data stored in a binary search tree is numeric, program a function that will find the sum of all of the data elements stored in such a tree.

CHAPTER
8

Files and File Processing

INTRODUCTION

The goals of this chapter include introducing sequential and random files, including discussing the capability of a computing language to access, manipulate, create, and destroy external files, and to explore standard file algorithms, including searching and sorting techniques.

In previous chapters we have been concerned mainly with input from the keyboard and output displayed on the screen. For many applications, this method of gathering information to be processed by the computer is acceptable and appropriate, while for other applications it is not possible to enter all the information to be processed from the keyboard. For example, perhaps a large amount of information has been gathered electronically by accessing a computing network, and this information is to be used as input to our program. We must develop methods and techniques for accessing data files stored on electronic media and develop capabilities for writing information from our computer program to electronic-media secondary storage.

In this chapter, we will discuss the capability of the C programming language for reading and writing sequential data files and random data files. The standard input/output library **stdio** contains many functions that have been written and added to the C programming language specifically for file processing. We will study many of these functions and discuss several applications of file usage.

8.1 SEQUENTIAL FILES

SECTION TOPICS

Sequential File Handling Functions

Error Conditions

Searching Sequential Files

Sequential File Update

Sequential File Handling Functions

We may think of a data file of information much like a filing cabinet that could be found in any office. In order to put information into the filing cabinet, the file drawer must be opened, the information must be placed in an appropriate location in the file, and the file drawer must be closed. A data file on electronic-storage media may be conceptualized similarly. To place information into a file, the file must be opened, written, and closed. To retrieve information from a file, the file must be opened, the information retrieved, and the file closed.

A file is a *sequential* file if it is designed to be read one element at a time, from beginning to end. If a file is accessed sequentially, then one may not read the second element from the file without reading the first. In order to read the **n**th element of the file, regardless of what the elements on the file are, one must read past the first **n**–1 elements of the file.

As an example, consider an ordinary cassette tape recorder. If you insert your favorite music cassette and wish to listen to the songs in order, you simply press "play" and sit back and enjoy the music. On the other hand, if you wish to listen to your favorite song, and it happens to be the tenth song on the cassette, you must fast forward the cassette past the first nine songs on the tape in order to get to the tenth song. The songs have been written on the cassette in a sequential manner. We might also say that a cassette tape is sequential-access media. It is not possible to go directly to the tenth song without moving the storage medium past the first nine selections.

If it were possible to immediately access the tenth song without moving past the first nine, then we would say that we have *direct* access, or random-access capability. A cassette is not a direct-access storage medium. (Here we are ignoring the distinction between the storage medium and the file stored on that storage medium. It is possible to access a file sequentially even though it is stored on random-access media.)

As an example of random-access media, consider a compact disk containing music you would like to hear played on your compact disk player. If we wish to hear the tenth selection, we simply enter that information, and the player will (almost) immediately begin playing the tenth selection. Enough information is included on the compact disk to enable the player to find and play the tenth selection without examining the first nine selections. In this way, we might identify a compact disk as random-access storage. Similarly, an ordinary floppy disk which is used on your personal computer can be thought of as random-access storage media. There is, however, a certain amount of overhead associated with random-access storage. The compact disk, for example, must contain information concerning the location of the selection, whereas on the cassette tape, no information concerning the location of the selection is required. To find the tenth selection, we must listen to the first nine.

We now consider sequential files in C. Files on auxiliary storage are opened and closed by using the file handling functions **fopen()** and **fclose()** found in the standard input/output library. In order to access a file, we refer to the file by using a pointer of type **FILE**. The identifier **FILE** is defined in **<stdio.h>** as a particular structure of information with members that carry information about various aspects of the file in question. The reader need not be concerned at this moment with the specifics of this structure. Information may be read from and written to a file by using the file versions **fscanf()** and **fprintf()** of the ordinary input/output functions **scanf()** and **printf()**.

▶ **PROBLEM**   Consider the problem of duplicating a file. Suppose a file called "input" contains the first few lines of Lincoln's Gettysburg address:

> **Four-score and seven years ago our forefathers brought**
> **forth on this continent a new nation, conceived in**
> **liberty and dedicated to the proposition that all men are**
> **created equal.**

We wish to duplicate this file, writing the copy to a file called "output."

ANALYSIS   Several possibilities exist for solving this problem. We may read the file character by character, writing each character to the output file, and stop when we run out of characters in the input file. An acceptable alternative might be to read the file a sentence at a time (if that is possible) and write each sentence to the output file, stopping when we run out of sentences. We will read the file character by character.

DESIGN   The steps in the process include the following:

1. Open the input file for reading.
2. Open the output file for writing.
3. Read a character from the input file.
4. **while** we are not at the end of the input file, perform each of the following.
5. Write a character to the output file.
6. Read a character from the input file.
7. End **while**.
8. Close the input file.
9. Close the output file.

Since this program is fairly simple, no further refinement of the process is needed before we proceed to the coding phase of the problem-solving process.

CODE   The complete program for duplicating a file is contained in Figure 8.1.1.

TEST   To test this program, prepare a file containing the desired text and save the file with the name "input" as suggested. Do not prepare a file called "output." Enter and execute the program presented in Figure 8.1.1. Whereas no file called "output" exists before the execution of the program, after the execution of the program, check your active directory and find that now there is a file called "output," which was created for you by the execution of the program.

Because this is the first program we have written concerning reading and writing external data files, we offer a few words of explanation of the features of the program.

First, we must include the standard input/output library, since the functions we use for opening the file, reading the file, writing the file, and closing the file, as well as the special structure **FILE** and the constant **EOF**, are defined in this library.

Second, the file pointers **inptr** and **outptr** are pointers of type **FILE**, which are used to establish communication with the external data files. Usually, communication with an external file is done through the use of a file pointer. The names **inptr** and **outptr** are appropriate vari-

Figure 8.1.1   File Duplication

```c
#include <stdio.h>

main()
{
        FILE
                *inptr, *outptr;

        int
                c;

        inptr = fopen ("input", "r");
        outptr = fopen ("output", "w");

        c = getc(inptr);
        while (c != EOF)
        {
                putc(c,outptr);
                c = getc(inptr);
        }
        fclose(inptr);
        fclose(outptr);

}
```

able names. The call to the function **fopen()** establishes the value of the file pointer and determines whether the file will be read, written, or updated. The first argument of the **fopen()** function contains a string that is a description of the file to be accessed. The second argument of the **fopen()** function is also a string that contains a description of the activity to be performed on the file, as shown in Figure 8.1.2.

Figure 8.1.2   File Modes

ARGUMENT	DESCRIPTION
`"r"`	read
`"w"`	write
`"a"`	append

The statement

```
inptr = fopen ("input", "r");
```

causes the file "input" to be opened in "read" mode, while the statement

```
outptr = fopen ("output", "w");
```

causes the file "output" to be prepared for writing. Note that if the file "output" does not exist it is created, and if it does exist it is destroyed in favor of the new information. If we wish to add information to the end of an existing file without destroying the current content of the file, the file must be opened with descriptor **"a"** for append. The statement

```
c = getc(inptr);
```

reads a single character from the file pointed to by **inptr**. If this character is not an end-of-file character, then the **while** loop which follows

```
while  (c != EOF)
{
        putc(c,outptr);
        c = getc(inptr);
}
```

will continue to read and write characters until an end-of-file is detected. Note that when we read the last character of the file, the end-of-file character is not returned. We must attempt to read *past* the end of the file in order for the end-of-file character to be returned. The actual character returned by the **getc()** function when it attempts to read past the end of the file may vary from installation to installation, but generally is defined to be (-1). Since (-1) is an integer (and because we already know we can store character values in integer storage locations), the variable **c** was defined as an integer in this program. The final two statements

```
fclose(inptr);
fclose(outptr);
```

close the files pointed to by **inptr** and **outptr** and the program terminates.

Consider now the possibility of reading the file an entire sentence at a time. One might think that using a **scanf()** function to read from the file might work, particularly if the **%s** conversion character was used to modify the input. If we enter the program shown in Figure 8.1.3, we may be startled by the results.

This program reads the input file

```
Four-score and seven years ago our forefathers brought
forth on this continent a new nation, conceived in
liberty and dedicated to the proposition that all men are
created equal.
```

and produces the following output file:

Figure 8.1.3   Use of fscanf( )

```
#include <stdio.h>

main()
{
      FILE
            *inptr, *outptr;

      int
            c;

      char
            sentence[80];

      inptr = fopen ("input", "r");
      outptr = fopen ("output", "w");

      c = fscanf(inptr,"%s",sentence);
      while (c != EOF)
      {
            fprintf(outptr,"%s",sentence);
            c = fscanf(inptr,"%s",sentence);
      }
      fclose(inptr);
      fclose(outptr);
}
```

```
Fourscoreandsevenyearsagoourforefathersbroughtforthonthis
continentanewnation,conceivedinlibertyanddedicatedtothe
propositionthatallmenarecreatedequal.
```

Why did this occur? The answer is, of course, because the function **fscanf()**, like its cousin **scanf()**, will not read white-space characters. When a space, tab, newline, etc., character is encountered, the function **fscanf()** stops reading and returns a successful conversion. The remaining calls to the function **fscanf()** in the **while** loop continue reading from where the previous call to **fscanf()** left off. As a result, neither the spaces between the words nor the newline characters at the end of the lines were read or included in the output. The function **fscanf** is an inappropriate function to use when attempting to read the file a sentence at a time. If this is so, what other functions included in our library may be used? Consider the program shown in Figure 8.1.4, which makes use of some additional file-handling functions.

Figure 8.1.4   Use of fgets( )

```c
#include <stdio.h>

main()
{
        FILE
                *inptr, *outptr;

        char
                *c;

        char
                sentence[80];

        inptr = fopen ("input", "r");
        outptr = fopen ("output", "w");

        c = fgets(sentence,80,inptr);
        while (c != NULL)
        {

                fprintf(outptr,"%s",sentence);
                c = fgets(sentence,80,inptr);
        }
        fclose(inptr);
        fclose(outptr);

}
```

In this example, the function **fgets()** reads a sentence of up to 80 characters long from the file pointed to by **inptr**. The function **fgets()** will read until it has acquired 79 characters (**n**–1) or until it detects a newline character, in which case no additional characters are read from the file. A **NULL** character is written to the end of the string to terminate the process. The newline character is preserved and included in the string. This function returns a pointer as its return value. When the end-of-file is encountered, this function returns a **NULL** pointer.

Executing the program on the input file

```
Four-score and seven years ago our forefathers brought
forth on this continent a new nation, conceived in
liberty and dedicated to the proposition that all men are
created equal.
```

produces the desired output file, which is identical to the input file.

As an alternative to the call to the **fprintf()** function

```
fprintf(outptr,"%s",sentence);
```

in the example, the statement could have been replaced by the statement

```
fputs(sentence, outptr);
```

with identical results.

▶ **PROBLEM**   An external file called "numbers" contains a collection of integers. We wish to read the file and find the sum and average of the integers on the file.

ANALYSIS   Since the problem description did not contain any information about how many numbers were on the file, we must assume that one of our program's responsibilities will be to determine how many numbers exist on the file. We must accumulate the sum of the numbers as well as the number of numbers on the file. We shall continue to read the file until **EOF** is encountered.

DESIGN   The tasks that must be performed include the following:

1. Initialize the accumulators.
2. Open the file.
3. Read an integer.
4. **while** we are not at the end of the file.
5. Add the integer to the sum.
6. Count the integer.
7. Read the next integer.

8. Continue from step 4.

9. When end-of-file occurs, close the file.

10. Calculate the average.

11. Display the results.

The function **fscanf()** is an appropriate tool to use to read the integers from the file, since we are not concerned about white-space characters. We assume that the integers are separated by spaces, newlines, or perhaps tab characters.

CODE   The complete program to read a file of integers and find the sum and average of those integers is contained in Figure 8.1.5.

TEST   Assume a file called "numbers" contains the following:

Figure 8.1.5 A File of Integers

```c
#include <stdio.h>

main()
{
        FILE
                *inptr;

        int
                c, n, count, sum, average;

        count = 0;
        sum = 0;
        inptr = fopen ("numbers", "r");
        c = fscanf(inptr,"%d",&n);
        while (c != EOF)
        {
                sum = sum + 1;
                count = count + 1;
                c = fscanf(inptr,"%d",&n);
        }
        fclose(inptr);
        average = sum/n;
        printf("The file contained %d integers\n",count);
        printf("The sum of these integers is %d\n",sum);
        printf("The average of the integers is %d\n",average);

}
```

```
23
44
56  77  12   3
66      22       88
11      23       34      45
1
2
3
```

Note that sometimes the integers are separated by spaces, sometimes by newline characters, and sometimes by tab characters. The input function `fscanf()` does not care, since we expect it to read until it has encountered **EOF**. The output from the program would appear similar to the following:

```
The file contained 16 integers
The sum of these integers is 510
The average of the integers is 170
```

Notice that what was calculated was an *integer* average. If the file had contained float values, the sequence of operations would have been the same, but we would have had to handle the calculations differently.

Error Conditions

When interacting with files, several possible conditions may arise that could cause a program abnormal termination. It is primarily the responsibility of the programmer to trap these situations and inform the user if and when they occur. For example, in the program of Figure 8.1.5, what would the program have responded if the file "numbers" had not been present? What does the function `fopen()` return if it attempts to open a nonexistent file? The answer to this question is that the behavior of the program will be unpredictable, since the pointer of type **FILE** will not be assigned an appropriate address. As a result, when the program attempts to access the file through this pointer, the program will probably crash.

To trap this condition, we need to realize that the `fopen()` function returns a value, which will be **NULL** if the file does not exist. Therefore, we must check for this condition. Consider the modification in Figure 8.1.6 of the program in Figure 8.1.5. It is possible that a sophisticated error handling routine might be developed to allow processing to continue. In this example, we have caused the program to terminate execution with a message indicating the nature of the difficulty.

Other possible error conditions are handled in the exercises.

Figure 8.1.6   Error Handling

```
#include <stdio.h>
main()
{
        FILE
             *inptr;

        int
             c, n, count, sum, average;

        count = 0;
        sum = 0;
        inptr = fopen ("numbers", "r");
/****************************************************************/
/***************** error handling routine ******************/
/****************************************************************/
        if (inptr == NULL)
        {
               printf("Error opening file... \n");
               exit(1);
        }
/****************************************************************/
        c = fscanf(inptr,"%d",&n);
        while (c != EOF)
        {
               sum = sum + n;
               count = count + 1;
               c = fscanf(inptr,"%d",&n);
        }
        fclose(inptr);
        average = sum/n;
        printf("The file contained %d integers\n",count);
        printf("The sum of these integers is %d\n",sum);
        printf("The average of the integers is %d\n",average);
}
```

Searching Sequential Files

Many times a file consists of a collection of records. Records may be further subdivided into fields. A record may contain, for example, the information on a particular individual. Records may be simple or quite complex. When we think of a record, we may think of a structure in the C sense. Records may be homogeneous (contain all the same kind of information) or heterogeneous (contain information of mixed types).

We now consider the problem of searching a sequential file for the occurrence of particular records.

▶ **PROBLEM**   A file called "payrates" contains a collection of information organized by employee number, employee last name, and employee hourly pay rate. Each record corresponds to an employee, while each record contains three fields: one for employee number, one for employee name, and one for employee pay rate. The employee number is a three-digit integer, the employee name is a character string, and the pay rate is a float value, similar to the following:

> 112   Eggen   11.25

This record indicates that employee Eggen has employee number 112 and is currently earning $11.25 per hour. Our problem is to find the average hourly rate for employees with employee numbers between 100 and 199, and to write each of these employees to a new file called "onehundreds."

ANALYSIS   Several questions must be answered before we proceed to the design phase of the problem-solving methodology. Specifically, what should be used to read the records? How do we separate each of the individual portions of the record? How do we find the desired records on the file? To answer these questions, we shall assume that, as in the example record, the fields in the record are separated by at least one space. Knowing that, we may use the **fscanf()** function to read the information from the file. We need to make sure that we perform the correct number of reads to gather the information correctly. Once the record has been read and we have the three fields of the record, it is a straightforward matter to determine whether the record is one of the desired records by checking its employee number. Finding the average hourly pay rate will be similar to previous averaging problems.

DESIGN   The steps in the process include the following:

1. Open the input file.
2. Open the output file.
3. Read a record.
4. **while** we are not at the end of the file.
5. **if** the record is one of the desired records.
6. Increment the counter.
7. Add the pay rate to the sum of pay rates.

8. Write the record to the output file.

9. Read the next record.

10. End **while**.

11. Calculate the average.

12. Display the results.

CODE Figure 8.1.7 illustrates the file search for this problem.

TEST If the program were executed on the file "payrates," which has contents shown below, then the output would be as indicated and the output file would be as shown.

Assume the file "payrates" has the following content:

```
112   eggen 11.25
115   smith 10.50
200   jones 6.50
300   flores 8.25
166   jordan 23.55
339   bird 4.25
```

The screen output would be:

```
The average pay rate for the individuals in the one-
hundreds is $ 15.10
```

The file "onehundreds" would be:

```
112   eggen    11.25
115   smith    10.50
166   jordan   23.55
```

Note that the file "onehundreds" contains only those records that have employee number between 100 and 199, inclusive.

The program illustrated in Figure 8.1.7 is admittedly quite simple and straightforward. However, it illustrates the fundamental principle behind a sequential search. Fundamentally, one must look at the first record. If it has the desired characteristics, keep it; otherwise look at the second record. If it has the desired characteristics, keep it; otherwise look at the third record, and continue processing the file until all of the records have been examined. There is no way, when using a sequential search, to examine the **n**th record directly. In order to examine the **n**th record, one must examine the first **n-1** records before examining the **n**th record.

Other standard sequential file search problems are given in the exercises. Common problems include finding the "largest" element on a file, finding the "second largest" element on a file, finding the smallest element on a file, and so on.

Figure 8.1.7 Simple File Search

```
#include <stdio.h>

main()
{
        FILE
                *inptr, *outptr;
        int
                c,count,empno;
        float
                pay, sum, average;
        char
                empname[20];

        count = 0;
        sum = 0;

        inptr = fopen("payrates", "r");
        if (inptr == NULL)
        {
                printf("Problem opening file \"payrates\" \n");
                exit(1);
        }
        outptr = fopen("onehundreds","w");

        c = fscanf(inptr,"%d %s %f",&empno, empname, &pay);
        while (c != EOF)
        {
                if (empno >= 100 && empno <= 199)
                {
                        /* desired record found */
                        count=count+1;
                        sum += pay;
                        fprintf(outptr, "%d %s %6.2f\n",empno,
                                empname, pay);
                }
                c = fscanf(inptr,"%d %s %f",&empno, empname,
                        &pay);
        }
        average = sum/count;
        printf("The average pay rate for the individuals");
        printf(" in the one-hundreds is \$%6.2f\n",average);
}
```

Sequential File Update

Consider now the problem of updating a sequential file.

► **PROBLEM**   Suppose for the moment that the "payrates" file of the previous example is to be processed in another way. The company foreman has decreed that each person on the file is to receive a 5 percent pay raise across the board. We are to update the existing file, but each record on the file is to include a 5 percent increase in the field that represents that individual's pay rate.

ANALYSIS   It would be nice if we could just go to the appropriate location on the file, read the information, update it, and write it back to the file. Unfortunately, in C, as in many other languages, sequential files may not be opened for reading and writing at the same time. So how are we to handle this problem with the tools we have developed so far? One possible answer is to create an additional file. We will read the existing file, create a new file with the updated information, then destroy the old file and rename the new file with the old file name. In this way, it will be transparent to the user that an additional file was used. In fact, the only way this could cause a problem is if the file were so large that there was insufficient time to accomplish the task, or worse yet, if there were insufficient auxiliary storage space to hold the additional file.

DESIGN   The steps necessary to perform the given task include the following:

1. Open the files.
2. Read records from the first file.
3. Update the pay field.
4. Write the records to the second (temporary) file.
5. Close the files.
6. Destroy the outdated file.
7. Rename the temporary file with the appropriate name.

This design may seem unduly cumbersome, but it points out the capabilities and the limitations of sequential file access. Perhaps there is another file access technique that will let us do what we wish—to read and write a file at the same time? Indeed there is—direct access files are discussed in the next section.

CODE   In order to increase an individual's pay by 5 percent, we must multiply by 1.05. Referring to Figure 8.1.8, observe that the functions **fscanf** and **fprintf** work exactly like their screen counterparts

Figure 8.1.8 Sequential File Update

```c
#include <stdio.h>
main()
{
     FILE
          *inptr, *outptr;
     int
          c,empno;
     float
          pay;
     char
          empname[20];
     /***************************************************************/
     /*open the input and the temporary files, with error checking  */
     /***************************************************************/
     inptr = fopen("payrates", "r");
     if (inptr == NULL)
     {
          printf("Problem opening file \"payrates\" \n");
          exit(1);
     }
     outptr = fopen("tempfile","w");
     if (outptr == NULL)
     {
          printf("Problem opening output file...\n");
          exit(1);
     }
     /***************************************************************/
     /*read the file, update the pay field, write to the temp file  */
     /***************************************************************/

     c = fscanf(inptr,"%d %s %f",&empno, empname, &pay);
     while (c != EOF)
     {
          pay = pay*1.05;
          fprintf(outptr,"%4d %20s %6.2f\n",empno,empname,pay);
          c = fscanf(inptr,"%d %s %f",&empno, empname, &pay);
     }
```

(continued)

Figure 8.1.8 Sequential File Update (*continued*)

```
/******************************************************************/
/* make sure you close the files, otherwise remove and rename    */
/* will not work correctly.                                      */
/******************************************************************/
fclose(inptr);
fclose(outptr);
/******************************************************************/
/* remove the old "payrates" file, rename "tempfile" "payrates"  */
/* note the error checking.                                      */
/******************************************************************/
if((remove("payrates")) == -1)
{
        printf("remove didn't work...\n");
}
if((rename("tempfile","payrates")) != 0)
{
        printf("rename error...\n");
}
}
```

scanf and **printf**. In particular, note that the output file contains the formatting characteristics presented by its formatting string. The specification **"%20s"** indicates that 20 character spaces will be used for the output string, and that the output string will be right justified in this field.

The function **remove()** will delete the file presented as its argument. This function returns 0 if the file was successfully deleted and −1 if an error in deleting the file occurred. The function **rename()** is similar. A prototype for this function is

```
int rename(oldfilename, newfilename);
```

where **oldfilename** and **newfilename** are character pointers. This function returns 0 if the files were successfully renamed and nonzero if an error occurred. The most common cause for error in using these functions is if one attempts to remove or rename a file that has not been closed, or perhaps if the file is in another directory.

TEST We execute the preceding program on the file "payrates":

```
112 eggen 11.25
115 smith 10.50
200 jones 6.50
300 flores 8.25
166 bush 23.55
339 quayle 4.25
```

The final appearance of the "payrates" file will be as follows:

```
112          eggen      11.81
115          smith      11.02
200          jones       6.82
300          flores      8.66
166           bush      24.73
339          quayle      4.46
```

Note that the formatting characteristics are included in the file, and that the values in the first two fields are uneffected. The values in the "pay" field are all increased by 5 percent.

▶ Exercises 8.1

Assume that "integers" is a sequential file containing an unknown number of integers in your current (active) directory.

8.1.1 Write a program that will find the largest integer on the file.

8.1.2 Write a program that will find the smallest integer on the file.

8.1.3 Write a program that will find the second-largest integer on the file. Assume that "nameandage" is a file with an unknown number of records containing an individual's name, followed by at least one space, followed by that person's age, as in the following:

eggen 39

smith 22

jones 12

etc.

8.1.4 Write a program that will find the number of persons on the file over 30 years of age.

8.1.5 Write a program that will find the number of individuals who are exactly 20 years of age.

8.1.6 Write a program that will find the number of records containing the name "eggen." (Do you remember how to compare strings?)

8.1.7   Write a program that will find the average age of the persons on the file.

8.1.8   Three years have passed since the file was created. Write a program that will increase all of the ages on the file by three.

8.1.9   Write a program that will find the average age of the persons on the file whose names begin with the letter "e."

8.1.10   Error conditions. What other situations may cause a program interacting with external files to terminate abnormally? Develop error handling routines for these situations.

8.2 RANDOM-ACCESS FILES

SECTION TOPICS

The Need for Direct-Access Files

Facilities for Handling Direct-Access Files

The Need for Direct-Access Files

As the previous section pointed out, there are situations where sequential files are restrictive in the sense that certain applications require us to be able to change selected fields of a file. That is, it is desirable to read a selected entry from a file, change it, and replace it on the file. We must be able to read and write the file directly in order to do this simple operation. As we recall, sequential access files may be opened—"r" for reading, "w" for writing, but not both.

When we consider direct-access files, additional file modes are present in C, as shown in Figure 8.2.1. When a file is opened for update (+ present in the mode string), then the corresponding stream may be used

Figure 8.2.1   File Modes

FILE MODE	ACTION
`"r"`	Open text file for reading
`"w"`	Open text file for writing
`"a"`	Open text file for append
`"rb"`	Open binary file for reading
`"wb"`	Open binary file for writing
`"ab"`	Open binary file for append
`"r+"`	Open existing file for update
`"w+"`	Open existing file for update, or create if it does not exist
`"a+"`	Open existing file for append, or create if it does not exist, for update

for both reading and writing. However, a read operation may not be followed directly by a write operation without an intervening call to **fseek()**, **ftell()**, or **rewind()**. These will be explained shortly.

Facilities for Handling Direct-Access Files

In order to access a file, whether direct access or sequential access, whether text or binary, the file must be opened and closed in the usual way, with calls to **fopen()** and **fclose()**. Beyond that, functions are needed to handle the "position in the file" indicator, which tells where subsequent reads and writes are going to take place. If we can successfully locate the position in the file indicator, it is possible to access any byte of a file. The following three functions can help locate the position in the file indicator: **ftell()**, **fseek()**, and **rewind()**.

The function **ftell()** gives the current position of the file position indicator. The value returned is a number representing the number of bytes from the beginning of the file, starting with 0. Whenever a character (byte) is read from the file, this value is incremented by 1. A prototype for this function is

```
long ftell(FILE *);
```

Note that this function returns a long **int**, and requires a **FILE** pointer as its argument.

The function **fseek()** is used to set or locate the file position indicator. This function takes three arguments: a file pointer, an offset, and a place. The file pointer indicates the file in question, the offset indicates the number of bytes from the place to position the file indicator, and place may be 0, 1, or 2, where 0 indicates the beginning of the file, 1 indicates the current indicator position, and 2 indicates the end of the file. A function prototype for **fseek()** is

```
int fseek(FILE *, long, int);
```

Note that the return value is an integer, which will be 0 if **fseek()** was successful, nonzero otherwise. In **<stdio.h>** we find the definitions

```
#define SEEK_SET        0
#define SEEK_CUR        1
#define SEEK_END        2
```

which are commonly used with the **fseek()** function.

The function **rewind()** moves the position in the file pointer to the beginning of the file. The call to

```
rewind(filepointer);
```

is equivalent to the call

```
fseek(filepointer, 0L, SEEK_SET);
```

▶ **PROBLEM**   As an example of the use of these functions, consider the problem of writing a file backwards. This exercise has little practical value, but provides an example of the use of `fseek()`.

ANALYSIS   The strategy for writing a file backwards will be to move the position in the file indicator to the end of the file, back up one character, read that character, write it to the screen, back up two characters (the one we read and the one to its left, which is to be read next), read the next character, and so on, until we get to the first character in the file as indicated by `ftell()`. We must be careful not to attempt to position the file indicator before the beginning of the file since this will cause an error on most systems. However, many systems will allow you to position the file indicator past the end of the file, which will effectively increase the size of the file.

DESIGN   The steps in the process are as follows:

1. Get the desired filename from the user.
2. Open the file.
3. Position the indicator at the end of the file.
4. Back up one character.
5. `while` we are not at the beginning of the file.
6. Read a character.
7. Write the character.
8. Back up two characters.
9. End of `while`.
10. Close the file.

CODE   Note that the file in Figure 8.2.2 is opened using the "rb" mode. The only other thing to note in this example is the line `if (c == 13) c = 10;` which will change any return characters encountered to newline characters so the file will appear correctly on the screen.

TEST   The input file is:

```
Four-score and seven years ago our forefathers brought
forth on this continent a new nation, conceived in
liberty and dedicated to the proposition that all
men are created equal.
```

The output will be:

```
Please enter a file name: input
The file name you entered was input
```

Figure 8.2.2 Reading a File Backwards Using ftell( ) and fseek( )

```c
#include <stdio.h>

main()
{
      char
            filename[100];
      int
            c;
      FILE
            *inptr;
      printf("\nPlease enter a file name: ");
      scanf("%s",filename);
      printf("The file name you entered was %s\n",filename);
      inptr = fopen(filename,"rb");
      if(inptr == NULL)
      {
            printf("problems opening file...\n");
            exit(1);
      }
/************************************************************/
/*    position file pointer at the end of the file         */
/************************************************************/
      fseek(inptr,0L,2);
/************************************************************/
/*    back up one character                                */
/************************************************************/
      fseek(inptr,-1L,1);
      while(ftell(inptr) >= 0)
      {
            c = getc(inptr);
            if (c == 13) c = 10;
            printf("%c",c);
            if(fseek(inptr,-2L,1) != 0)
            {
                  printf("\nfseek failed...\n");
                  exit(1);
            }
      }
}
```

```
.lauqe detaerc era nem
lla taht noitisoporp eht ot detacided dna ytrebil
ni deviecnoc ,noitan wen a tnenitnoc siht no htrof
thguorb srehtaferof ruo oga sraey neves dna erocs-ruoF
fseek failed...
```

The message **"fseek failed ..."** appears on the screen at the end of the process since the last call to **fseek()** attempts to move the position indicator one character before the beginning of the file, which is impossible.

As noted above, in **<stdio.h>** we find the definitions

```
#define SEEK_SET        0
#define SEEK_CUR        1
#define SEEK_END        2
```

which are commonly used with the **fseek()** function. To position the file indicator at the end of the file the command **fseek(inptr, 0L, SEEK_END)** might have been used. Note the use of the **L** modifier to make sure the compiler treats the second argument of the **fseek()** as a long integer.

▶ **PROBLEM** Consider now the problem of updating a file in place. Suppose we have sent away for a mailing list, but for some records in the list the trailing four digits on the nine-digit zip codes are question marks, similar to the following record:

eggen   4731 misty run   san antonio   texas   78217-????

Our task is to look through the records and change these question marks to 0's, which make better numbers than question marks do.

ANALYSIS We assume that it is known that each record contains 15 characters for the name, 20 characters for the address, 15 characters for the city name, and 15 characters for the state name. We also observe that the zip code is 10 characters (with 1 character for the dash). Thus, the total record length is 75 characters. Assuming that each record contains a return at the end, the total record length is 76 characters. We must locate the position in the file indicator at the 71st character of each consecutive record, read 4 characters, check to find out whether they are question marks, and replace them with 0's if they are.

DESIGN The steps in the process include the following:

1. Get filename from user.

2. Calculate the size of the file and the number of records in the file.

3. For each record, read the 71st through 75th characters.

4. Check to see if these characters are question marks.

5. If they are question marks, replace these characters with 0's.

6. Repeat until all records have been processed.

CODE The complete program for updating a direct-access file in place is given in Figure 8.2.3.

TEST Assume that the input file appears as follows:

```
eggen       4731 misty run      san antonio  texas   78217-1129
clinton     1600 pennsylvania   washington   dc      00001-????
superman    9999 misty way      milky way    galaxy  98765-????
spiderman   123 mary ann        his city     ohio    12345-1234
batman      200 dark alley      gotham city  ny      22222-????
gore        1601 pennsylvania   washington   dc      33333-????
```

Figure 8.2.3 Update a File in Place

```c
#include <stdio.h>

main()
{
    char
        filename[100],ch1,ch2,ch3,ch4;
    int
        i,bytesinfile, records;
    FILE
        *inptr;
    long int
        fileposition;

    printf("\nPlease enter a file name: ");
    scanf("%s",filename);
    printf("the file name you entered was %s\n",filename);
    inptr = fopen(filename,"rb+");
    if(inptr == NULL)
    {
        printf("problems opening file...\n");
        exit(1);
    }
    /***********************************************/
    /* calculate the number of records in the file    */
    /***********************************************/
```

(continued)

Figure 8.2.3   Update a File in Place (*continued*)

```
    fseek(inptr, 0, SEEK_END);
    bytesinfile = ftell(inptr);
    records = bytesinfile/76;
    printf("number of records is %d\n",records);
    /***************************************************/
    /* Position the file indicator at the first        */
    /* zip code...                                      */
    /***************************************************/
    fileposition = 71;
    if (fseek(inptr, fileposition, SEEK_SET) != 0)
    {
        printf("\nfseek failed...\n");
        exit(1);
    }
    for (i=0;i<records;i=i+1)
    {
        /***************************************************/
        /* Read the characters and see if question marks  */
        /***************************************************/
        fscanf(inptr, "%c%c%c%c", &ch1,&ch2,&ch3,&ch4);
        if(ch1 == '?' && ch2 == '?' && ch3 == '?' && ch4 == '?')
        {
            printf("Yes...\n");
            fseek(inptr, -4, SEEK_CUR);
            fprintf(inptr, "%c", '0');
            fprintf(inptr, "%c", '0');
            fprintf(inptr, "%c", '0');
            fprintf(inptr, "%c", '0');
        }
        else
        {
            printf("no...\n");
        }
        fileposition = fileposition + 76;
        if (fseek(inptr, fileposition, SEEK_SET) != 0)
        {
            printf("\nfseek failed...\n");
            exit(1);
        }
    }
    fclose(inptr);
}
```

The screen will contain the following output:

```
Please enter a file name: data
The file name you entered was data
number of records is 6
no . . .
Yes . . .
Yes . . .
no . . .
Yes . . .
Yes . . .
```

The output file will be transformed into the following:

eggen	4731 misty run	san antonio	texas	78217-1129
clinton	1600 pennsylvania	washington	dc	00001-0000
superman	9999 misty way	milky way	galaxy	98765-0000
spiderman	123 mary ann	his city	ohio	12345-1234
batman	200 dark alley	gotham city	ny	22222-0000
gore	1601 pennsylvania	washington	dc	33333-0000

We note that all of the question marks have been changed into 0's, and that the remainder of the file has been left unchanged.

Several interesting features are presented by this example. First consider the following lines:

```
fseek(inptr, 0, SEEK_END);
bytesinfile = ftell(inptr);
records = bytesinfile/76;
printf("number of records is %d\n",records);
```

The first of these lines moves the position indicator to the end of the file. The `ftell()` function calculates the number of bytes from the beginning of the file, effectively calculating the total number of bytes in the file. Since we know the number of bytes in each record is 76, dividing by 76 will tell the number of records present. We can use this information to tell us the number of times we have to loop to process each record.

The only reason for the screen output is so we know the program is doing what it is supposed to. This output is unnecessary and would have to be eliminated if the file size were large.

One more important point must be discussed. The file was opened with the mode `"rb+"`. This means the file may be updated—read and written. The only requirement that C imposes on this operation is that between each read and write operation, there must be an intervening call to `fseek()`.

In the previous example, if we wished to read and write the information contained in the records on the file, it is probably advisable to store the information for each record in a structure. A possible structure declaration for the information might be similar to the following:

```
struct info
{
        char name[15];
        char address[20];
        char city[15]
        char state[15];
        char zip[10];
}
```

▶ **Exercises 8.2**

8.2.1 Write a program that will perform the update function of Figure 8.2.3, only your program must use a structure (record) to store the information from the file. What modifications must be made to the program to accomplish this?

8.2.2 Write a program that will search a direct-access file similar to the file used in Figure 8.2.3 for all of the records for which the last name is Eggen. Is your searching algorithm based on sequential access? Why or why not? What characteristics must a file contain in order for us to use direct-access capabilities?

8.2.3 A file has record length 80, with a newline character at the end of each record. Each of the fields in the record has record length 20. Write a collection of **fseek** commands that will locate the file position indicator at the beginning of the fourth field of the fifteenth record of the file.

8.2.4 A file has record length 45 with a newline character at the end of each record. Assume that the file position indicator is at the end of the file. Write commands that will position the file indicator at the beginning of the fifth record.

8.2.5 A file has record length 59 with a newline character at the end of each record. Write a sequence of commands that will tell the number of records on the file.

8.2.6 Assume that we may not use the **fseek** command, and that the file position indicator is at the end of the file. Based on these assumptions, write code that will tell the number of records on the file.

8.3 SORTING

Earlier in this text we addressed the issue of sorting algorithms and the computer's ability to sort and maintain extensive collections of data. In this section we will continue to explore sorting, but this time from a new point of view. Suppose the information to be sorted is too extensive to be contained in memory all at once.

Internal Sorting versus External Sorting

In the case where the information to be sorted can be contained in the random-access memory of the computer, several very efficient algorithms for sorting are known and well studied. However, in certain situations, we must ask the computer to sort collections of data so large that the data cannot be contained in random-access memory at the same time. Yet our application requires a file that contains the information in sorted order. How may we accomplish the sort?

Two possible answers should come to mind. In the first case, perhaps we can read from the file as much data as random-access memory will hold, sort this, write it to a file, read in another portion, sort, write, and so on. In this way, several portions of the file will be sorted, but not the entire file. If we could develop some way of putting together the sorted portions of the file, then the problem would be solved.

A second possible approach may involve using a direct-access file to store the data to be sorted. If we could use a random-access file like we use random-access memory, perhaps modifications of sorting algorithms used previously could be used in this situation.

We must be aware that if the file to be sorted contains so much data that it will not fit in internal memory, there is effectively no limit on the size of the data file. We must be concerned with issues of efficiency of algorithms. Not just any algorithm can be used, since the overhead associated with accessing the data file itself is costly and must be considered in the overall efficiency of the algorithm.

Sorting by Merging

Many algorithms are called "merge" sort. Talking to computer science professionals may yield several different answers to the question "what is a merge sort?" The algorithm we will present has the advantage of being relatively simple, and yet solves the problem of sorting files of arbitrarily large size.

▶ **PROBLEM**   A file contains an unknown number of integers, possibly a very large number. These integers may be thought of as pointers, tags, indices, or something similar. If they were pointers, locations, or some sort of tag, then the algorithm given may be modified to produce an algorithm capable of sorting arbitrary structures or records of information which may be stored on a random-access file. We must put the integers into ascending order.

ANALYSIS   To solve this problem, we need two additional files. We will distribute the integers onto the two files, then merge the files back together, then distribute again, then merge, etc., until the file becomes sorted. We assume that the file of integers is sufficiently large so that it cannot all be contained in the computer's random-access memory. A file-sorting algorithm is necessary.

Suppose the original file is DATA and the two additional files are ONE and TWO. The distribution phase consists of the following:

1. Integers are written from DATA to ONE if they are less than or equal to the previous item from DATA.

2. Integers are written from DATA to TWO if they are greater than the previous item from DATA.

The merge phase of the algorithm proceeds by comparing the first element from ONE with the first element from TWO. The smaller one is written to DATA. If it came from ONE, then the position indicator in ONE is advanced, and the next element from ONE is compared with the first element from TWO. The smaller number is written to DATA. If the smaller number came from TWO, then the position indicator in TWO is advanced, and the next element from TWO is compared with the number from ONE. Continue comparing and writing the smaller number to DATA until one of the files is exhausted. The elements from the remaining file are then copied to DATA, and we then return to the distribution phase.

We continue the distribution-merge until all of the numbers are distributed on just one of the temporary files, ONE or TWO. Then we know the file is in order.

DESIGN   The steps necessary to implement the above algorithm include the following:

1. Repeat steps 2 through 9.
2. Open the file DATA and the temporary files ONE and TWO.
3. Distribute the numbers from DATA to ONE and TWO.
4. Close the file DATA and the files ONE and TWO.
5. Open the file DATA and the temporary files ONE and TWO.
6. Merge the elements from ONE and TWO to DATA.
7. Close the file DATA and the files ONE and TWO.
8. Until ONE or TWO is empty.
9. Examine the files.

The sorting process is a repeated application of the "distribute-merge-distribute-merge . . ." process that continues until all elements are distributed to one of the temporary files, indicating that the original file is sorted. The sorting process involves considerable file access, but if a situation arises where not all of the file to be sorted will fit into random-access memory, the user has no choice but to consider a file-sorting algorithm.

It is clear that some additional detail is necessary in the preceding design. In particular, steps needed to perform the distribution include:

3a. Read an element 'previous' from the file DATA.

3b. Write the element to file TWO.

3c. Do until end of file DATA.

3d. Read an additional element 'next' from DATA.

3e. If 'next' is less than 'previous' write 'next' to file ONE, else write 'next' to file TWO.

3f. Replace 'previous' with 'next'.

3g. End of do.

To perform the merging of the two files back to a single file, the steps include

6a. Read an element 'a' from file ONE.

6b. Read an element 'b' from file TWO.

6c. Do while both of ONE and TWO are not empty.

6d. If a < b then write 'a' to DATA and read another element 'a' from file ONE.

6e. Else write 'b' to DATA and read another element 'b' from file TWO.

6f. If file ONE empties first, copy the remaining elements from TWO to DATA.

6g. If file TWO empties first, copy the remaining elements from ONE to DATA.

You need to do some hand checking to be convinced that this method does indeed put the elements of the file in order, perhaps before you attempt to write your own code, or study the code provided in Figure 8.3.1.

CODE   The method is simple and rather easy to code, which makes it worthwhile to consider. Unfortunately, it is rather slow since considerable file access is required.

Figure 8.3.1   Merge Sort

```
#include <stdio.h>
/*****************************************
   program to perform a merge sort
   written by M. Eggen
*****************************************/

main()
{
       int
              i,ctr,ctone,cttwo,done,previous,next,
              posone,postwo,a,b,passes;
       FILE
              *data,*one,*two;
       passes=0;

       done = 1;
       while (done == 1)
       {
              printf("%d\n",passes=passes+1);
              /*********************************************
              We have three files, DATA, ONE, and TWO. We
              must first distribute the elements from DATA
              to the files ONE and TWO.
              *********************************************/
              ctone=0;cttwo=0;ctr=0;
              data = fopen("DATA","r");
```
(continued)

Figure 8.3.1 Merge Sort *(continued)*

```
one = fopen("ONE","w");
two = fopen("TWO","w");
fscanf(data,"%d",&previous);
ctr=ctr+1;
fprintf(two,"%d\n",previous);
cttwo=cttwo+1;
while((fscanf(data,"%d",&next) != EOF))
{
      ctr=ctr+1;
      if(next < previous)
      {
            fprintf(one,"%d\n",next);
            ctone=ctone+1;
      }
      else
      {
            fprintf(two,"%d\n",next);
            cttwo=cttwo+1;
      }
      previous=next;
}
fclose(data);fclose(one);fclose(two);
/************************************************
At this point we are done with the distribution.
If one or other of the files is empty, then all
were distributed to one file, meaning the
original is already in order. If not, then we
merge the two files together and go back to the
distribution again.
************************************************/
if((ctone == 0) || (cttwo == 0)) done = 0;
data = fopen("DATA","w");
one = fopen("ONE","r");
two = fopen("TWO","r");
posone = fscanf(one,"%d",&a);
postwo = fscanf(two,"%d",&b);
while ((posone != EOF) && (postwo != EOF))
{
      if(a < b)
      {
```

(continued)

Figure 8.3.1 Merge Sort (*continued*)

```
                                fprintf(data,"%d\n",a);
                                posone = fscanf(one,"%d",&a);
                        }
                        else
                        {
                                fprintf(data,"%d\n",b);
                                postwo = fscanf(two,"%d",&b);
                        }
                }
                if(posone == EOF)
                {
                        while(postwo != EOF)
                        {
                                fprintf(data,"%d\n",b);
                                postwo = fscanf(two,"%d",&b);
                        }
                }
                else
                {
                        while(posone != EOF)
                        {
                                fprintf(data,"%d\n",a);
                                posone = fscanf(one,"%d",&a);
                        }
                }
                fclose(data);fclose(one);fclose(two);
        }
        printf("passes %d\n",passes);
}
```

TEST To test the algorithm, construct a file DATA containing an arbitrary number of elements. For example, construct a file of 1000 randomly generated integers and ask the algorithm given in the figure to sort them into order. Most of the time taken by the algorithm involves file access. Tests done by the authors indicate that a file of 1000 randomly generated integers takes approximately 30 distribute-merge passes to perform the sort.

Random-Access File Sorting

As a final example of sorting, consider the problem of sorting a random-access file. Essentially our thoughts are that, since we are able to access any byte of the file individually, we should be able to handle an external random-access file in much the same way as we would handle an array. As we have learned, an array is a direct-access data structure, which means that we are able to access any element of the array by using its index in the array. If we can keep track of the position in a direct-access file, we should be able to manipulate it as we would an array.

▶ **PROBLEM** A direct-access file contains a number of records. We wish to sort the records into ascending order.

ANALYSIS For this particular problem, a number of sorting methods are possible, some of which are suggested in the exercises. In addition, a number of different record entities could be sorted. Rather than cloud the issue, which is sorting, we choose to sort a file of integers. The algorithm chosen is also not very efficient or elegant, but illustrates direct file access. The algorithm is a modification of the bubble sort, which was studied earlier. We compare adjacent elements in the file and interchange them if they are out of order. We continue to compare and interchange elements in the file until no interchanges are made, in which case the file is in order. We note that the algorithm would work equally well if more complex records were involved. We would need to know the record length of the records involved, and would need functions that read one record from the file and write one record to the file. Otherwise, the program illustration could remain as presented.

DESIGN A pseudocode design for the solution to the sorting problem follows:

1. Get the name of the file to be sorted from the user.
2. Open the file.
3. Calculate the number of records in the file, knowing the record length.
4. Set switches flag to true.
5. While switches flag is true perform the following:
6. Set switches flag to false.
7. Compare adjacent elements of the file.
8. Switch if not in order and set switches flag to true.
9. Display messages to the user.

The design presented is acceptable, but hides the details of random file access. Study the code presented in Figure 8.3.2 for these details. Look in the exercises for suggestions of other sorting techniques to use.

CODE   The complete program for our direct-access bubble sort is contained in Figure 8.3.2.

Figure 8.3.2   Direct File Sort

```c
#include <stdio.h>

/***********************************************************
The purpose of this exercise is to accomplish a sort using
a direct access file. While the activity is merely sorting
a file of integers, the methods and techniques illustrated
can be used in a variety of environments. We choose an
ordinary bubble sort algorithm as our illustration. We shall
assume that the file contains integers between 100 and 999,
one integer per record. The record length is four bytes,
one byte for each digit of the integer, and one byte for the
newline at the end of the record.
***********************************************************/

#define RECORD_LENGTH           4
#define SEEK_SET                0
#define SEEK_CUR                1
#define SEEK_END                2
void PrintFile(char filename[20]);

main()
{
      char
            filename[20];
      int
            i, firstnumber, secondnumber, switches, records, bytesinfile;
      long int
            PlaceInFile;
      FILE
            *input;


      /*******************************************
      get the name of the file to be sorted
      from the user and open the file
      *******************************************/
```

(continued)

Figure 8.3.2 Direct File Sort *(continued)*

```
printf("Please enter the name of the file to be sorted: ");
scanf("%s", filename);
printf("The file name you entered was: %s\n", filename);
input = fopen(filename, "r+");
if (input == NULL)
{      printf("problems opening file...\n");
       exit(1);
}
printf("The unsorted file is:\n\n");
PrintFile(filename);
/*****************************************
calculate the number of records in the file
*****************************************/

fseek(input,0,SEEK_END);
bytesinfile = ftell(input);
printf("bytes in file %d\n",bytesinfile);
records = bytesinfile/RECORD_LENGTH;
printf("number of records %d\n",records);

/*****************************************
Locate the "position in the file pointer" at
the beginning of the file and begin the sort
*****************************************/
fseek(input,0,SEEK_SET);
switches = 1;
while (switches == 1)
{
       switches = 0;
       PlaceInFile = 0;
       for (i=0;i<records-1;i=i+1)
       {
              fseek(input,PlaceInFile,SEEK_SET);
              fscanf(input,"%d",&firstnumber);
              fseek(input,PlaceInFile + RECORD_LENGTH,SEEK_SET);
              fscanf(input,"%d",&secondnumber);
              if (firstnumber > secondnumber)
              {
                     /*******************************
                     numbers not in order, switch them
                     *******************************/
```

(continued)

Figure 8.3.2   Direct File Sort *(continued)*

```
                                fseek(input,PlaceInFile,SEEK_SET);
                                fprintf(input,"%d",secondnumber);
                                fseek(input,PlaceInFile + RECORD_LENGTH,SEEK_SET);
                                fprintf(input,"%d",firstnumber);
                                switches = 1;
                        }
                        PlaceInFile = PlaceInFile + RECORD_LENGTH;
                }
        }
        fclose(input);
        printf("\nThe file should be in order\n");
        PrintFile(filename);
}
void PrintFile(char filename[20])
{
        FILE
                *input;
        int
                x,ctr=0;

        input = fopen(filename,"r");
        while ((fscanf(input,"%d",&x)) != EOF)
        {
                printf("%4d",x);
                ctr=ctr+1;
                if (ctr%10 == 0) printf("\n");
        }
        fclose(input);
}
```

TEST   We created a file with 100 random integers in it and tested it on our local UNIX system. Following are the results:

```
[62]% a.out
Please enter the name of the file to be sorted: DATA
The file name you entered was: DATA
The unsorted file is:

 161 191 101 180 635 997 313 716 994 245
 730 653 400 895 912 547 519 879 725 702
```

```
454 194 339 904 106 478 957 982 452 150
500 149 686 712 948 770 706 312 588 483
911 145 858 542 777 815 118 704 181 215
367 917 939 151 229 346 540 586 412 985
517 705 376 694 461 885 814 117 105 181
880 564 493 802 769 486 654 389 870 570
792 573 225 617 436 917 486 758 521 833
122 113 886 569 163 622 128 850 520 404
bytes in file 400
number of records 100

The file should be in order
101 105 106 113 117 118 122 128 145 149
150 151 161 163 180 181 181 191 194 215
225 229 245 312 313 339 346 367 376 389
400 404 412 436 452 454 461 478 483 486
486 493 500 517 519 520 521 540 542 547
564 569 570 573 586 588 617 622 635 653
654 686 694 702 704 705 706 712 716 725
730 758 769 770 777 792 802 814 815 833
850 858 870 879 880 885 886 895 904 911
912 917 917 939 948 957 982 985 994 997
[63]%
```

Searching a Direct-Access File

The searching techniques developed to this point were all designed based on sequential file access. What advantages can be gained searching a file if the file can be accessed using the direct-access file techniques discussed above?

▶ **PROBLEM**   A direct-access file contains a collection of records, sorted in ascending order. We wish to search the file for a particular record, and report to the user whether or not the record exists in the file. Of particular interest is developing a searching technique which will allow us to determine whether the record exists in as few "looks" into the file as possible.

ANALYSIS   There are several interesting things to consider here. First, if the file were a sequential-access file of size **NumberOfRecords**, then it is possible we would have to look into the file **NumberOfRecords** times to determine whether a particular record did or did not exist on the file. The desired record may in fact be the last record in the file. On the other hand, if the file is direct or random access, then we may look at the record in the middle of the file. If the desired record is less than the middle record, we may discard the upper half of the file. If the desired record is greater than the middle record, we may discard the lower half of the file. Then we look at the middle record of the portion of the file that remains, and again discard half of the remaining file, depending on whether the record is less than or greater than the sought-after record. This binary search algorithm was discussed when we studied arrays, and applies equally well to the problem of searching a random-access file. For the sake of discussion and illustration, suppose we have a file of 3-digit integers containing `NumberOfRecords` records. Suppose also that this file has been sorted into ascending order. We shall attempt to answer the question, "How many looks into the file are necessary to determine whether a particular integer is or is not on the file?"

To be certain, if we throw away half the file with each look, we can easily calculate the number of looks necessary to either find the desired record or conclude that the record is not on the file. For example, if a file contains a thousand records, then we are certain that 10 looks into the file will be sufficient for that determination, since $2^{10} = 1024$, and $1024 > 1000$. More generally, if a file contains n elements, we wish a value k such that $2^k \geq n$, or such that $k \geq \log_2 n$. From the calculus we know that $\log_2 n = \log_e n / \log_e 2$. Thus, if we are considering a file of size n records and we have not found the desired number after `ceil(log_e n/log_e 2)` looks, we may return a message saying that the number cannot be found on the file.

DESIGN   Four major tasks are associated with this problem:

1. Prompt the user for the name of the file to be searched.
2. Open the file.
3. Search the file for the desired integer.
4. Report to the user whether the integer is on the file, and report the number of file seeks required.

Of course, step 3 needs some refinement (left as an exercise).

CODE   The complete program for the direct-access binary search is contained in Figure 8.3.3.

TEST   A sample execution of the program might produce output similar to the following:

```
Please enter the name of the file to be searched: DATA
desired file is DATA
```

```
101 105 106 113 117 118 122 128 145 149
150 151 161 163 180 181 181 191 194 215
225 229 245 312 313 339 346 367 376 389
400 404 412 436 452 454 461 478 483 486
486 493 500 517 519 520 521 540 542 547
564 569 570 573 586 588 617 622 635 653
654 686 694 702 704 705 706 712 716 725
730 758 769 770 777 792 802 814 815 833
850 858 870 879 880 885 886 895 904 911
912 917 917 939 948 957 982 985 994 997
Please enter the number you would like to search for: 122
I will try to find 122
bytes in file 400
number of records 100
middle of file is 50
middle record 564
maxlooks is 7
top is 50
bottom is 0
current x is 339
top is 25
bottom is 0
current x is 161
top is 12
bottom is 0
current x is 122
number 122 found in 4 looks
```

Perhaps it is not appropriate in all situations to print as much as we have in this example, but for the sake of understanding the process some additional program tracking is nice to see. When the program is prepared for production, we can remove all of the extra print. Of course, to fully test the program we must use files of varying sizes, and must test in situations where the number to be found is not in the file. Additional testing includes testing the "boundary," that is, trying to find the lowest and highest, the second lowest and second highest, and trying to find a record that is out of range of the current records in the file. Our program should respond correctly in all of these cases.

The basic structure of the binary file search is presented in Figure 8.3.3. To search in the cases where more general records are involved, the "read" routine would have to be altered and the comparison criterion investigated. However, if the file is sorted as shown, the routines can be used with the changes indicated.

Figure 8.3.3 Direct-Access Files, Binary Search

```c
#include <stdio.h>
#include <math.h>

#define RECORD_LENGTH 4
#define SEEK_SET 0
#define SEEK_CUR 1
#define SEEK_END 2

void GetFileName(char filename[20]);
void GetNumberToFind(int *n);

main()
{
    int
        numbertofind, bytesinfile, records,x,bottom,top,counter,maxlooks;
    long int
        place;
    FILE
        *input;
    char
        filename[20];

    GetFileName(filename);
    printf("desired file is %s\n",filename);
    GetNumberToFind(&numbertofind);
    printf("I will try to find %d\n",numbertofind);
    input = fopen(filename, "r+");
    if (input == NULL)
    {     printf("problems opening file...\n");
          exit(1);
    }
    /*********************************************
    calculate the number of records in the file
    *********************************************/
    fseek(input,0,SEEK_END);
    bytesinfile = ftell(input);
    printf("bytes in file %d\n",bytesinfile);
    records = bytesinfile/RECORD_LENGTH;
    printf("number of records %d\n",records);

    /*********************************************
    begin the search...
    *********************************************/
```

(continued)

Figure 8.3.3 Direct-Access Files, Binary Search (*continued*)

```
        bottom = 0;
        top = records;
        place = (bottom + top)/2;
        printf("middle of file is %ld\n",place);
        fseek(input,place*RECORD_LENGTH,SEEK_SET);
        fscanf(input,"%d",&x);
        printf("middle record %d\n",x);
        counter = 1;
        maxlooks = ceil(log(records)/log(2));
        printf("maxlooks is %d\n",maxlooks);

        while ((x != numbertofind) && (counter <= maxlooks))
        {
                if (x > numbertofind)
                        top = place;
                else
                        bottom = place;
                printf("top is %d\n",top);
                printf("bottom is %d\n",bottom);
                place = (bottom + top)/2;
                fseek(input,place*RECORD_LENGTH,SEEK_SET);
                fscanf(input,"%d",&x);
                counter=counter+1;
                printf("current x is %d\n",x);
        }
        if (counter <= maxlooks)
                printf("number %d found in %d looks",numbertofind, counter)
        else
                printf("number %d not found on file\n",numbertofind);

}
void GetFileName(char filename[20])
{
    printf("Please enter the name of the file to be searched: ");
    scanf("%s",filename);
    return;
}

void GetNumberToFind(int *n)
{
    int x;
    printf("Please enter the number you would like to search for: ");
    scanf("%d",n);
    return;
}
```

▶ Exercises 8.3

8.3.1   Explain the difference between an internal sort and an external sort. What are the advantages of each? What are the disadvantages?

8.3.2   Generalize the merge-sort algorithm so that it will sort an arbitrary number of records of the form

```
struct family_info
        {
        char fathers_name;
        char mothers_name;
        int number_of_children;
        };
```

by **number_ of_children** in the family and by **mothers_name**.

8.3.3   How many passes (distribute-merge) would be required to sort a file that was already in order?

8.3.4   How many passes (distribute-merge) would be required to sort a file that was exactly in reverse order?

8.3.5   What "arrangement" of elements of a file do you think represents a worst case for the merge-sort algorithm presented, in the sense that the arrangement will require the most distribute-merge passes?

8.3.6   Modify the merge-sort algorithm so that it will sort in descending order.

8.3.7   The merge-sort algorithm presented contains one method of deciding how to perform the distribution of the original file into the two files. Can you suggest other possible ways to perform the distribution that might speed up the sort?

8.3.8   Modify the direct-access file sort algorithm of Figure 8.3.2 so that it uses a modified insertion sort to perform the sort.

8.3.9   Modify the direct-access file sort algorithm of Figure 8.3.2 so that it uses a modified quicksort algorithm to perform the sort.

8.3.10   What advantages are realized by using direct-access file access techniques and a binary search to find information in a file?

8.3.11   What are the disadvantages of using direct access and binary search?

8.3.12   Modify the program given in Figure 8.3.3 so that it does a random search rather than a binary search. Specifically, the program in Figure 8.3.3 calculates the average of bottom and top, and looks at that place in the file. Modify the program so that it selects a random value between bottom and top and looks at that location in the file, discarding the interval where the sought-after number cannot lie. What are the advantages and the disadvantages of this method of searching?

8.3.13   Provide appropriate pseudocode for the algorithm of Figure 8.3.3.

▶ Key Words

append	file sorting
binary search	fopen
direct-access file search	fprintf
direct-access file update	fputs
direct (random) access	fscanf
direct (random) file	fseek
EOF	ftell
external sorting	read
fclose	rewind
fgets	sequential access
file	sequential file
file mode	sequential file search
file organization	sequential file update
FILE pointer	sorting by merging
file processing	write

▶ Chapter Concepts

8.1   Sequential files are files which are expected to be processed one element at a time, from beginning to end.

8.2   In order to access the **n**th element of a sequential file, we must read past the first **n-1** elements of the file.

8.3   A sequential file may be opened for input or opened for output, but may not be opened for both input and output at the same time.

8.4   In C, files are opened with the **fopen()** function and closed with the **fclose()** function. Files are accessed in C by means of a **FILE** pointer.

8.5   A direct-access (random-access) file is a file from which the **n**th record is accessible without examining the first **n-1** records. By keeping track of the size of the records stored in the file, and by using the functions `fseek()`, `ftell()`, and `rewind()`, we may position the "position in the file pointer" at any record of the file.

8.6 Data may be read from an external file using the functions `fscanf`, `fgetc`, or `fgets`.

8.7 Data may be written to a file by using the functions `fprintf`, `fputc`, or `fputs`.

8.8 External sorting algorithms are necessary to sort information if not all the information will fit into the computer's primary memory.

8.9 Since any record of a direct-access file is reachable, many of the sorting algorithms for sorting arrays may be adapted for sorting direct-access files. An array is a direct-access data structure.

▶ Programming Projects

8.1 Write a program that will examine a text file and count the number of words in the file. You may assume that words are separated by one or more spaces, by newline characters, or by tab characters.

8.2 Write a program that will examine a text file and count the word lengths in the file. Your program should report the number of one-letter words, the number of two-letter words, etc. You may assume that the words are separated by one or more spaces, by newline characters, or by tab characters. You must not count punctuation characters when determining word lengths. For example, if a comma follows a word, like *word*, just presented, it must be counted as a four-letter word, not a five-letter word.

8.3 An input file has been transmitted to your workstation with multiple spaces in several instances in the file. Write a program to replace each occurrence of multiple spaces with a single space.

8.4 Several input text files have been provided as input to your program. Write a program that will combine these files into a single file.

8.5 An input text file and an integer **n**, **n < 80**, are provided as input. Write a program that will format the file so that the line length is less than or equal to **n**. You must be careful with wordwrap. You may not break a word—words that make the line length greater than **n** must be moved to the next line.

Appendix A
Standard Headers

stdio.h

The input and output functions, types and macros defined in stdio.h constitute the largest of the libraries.

```
#define SEEK_SET    0
#define SEEK_CUT    1
#define SEEK_END    2

int remove(char *filename);
int rename(char *oldfilename,char *newfilename);
FILE *tmpfile(void);
char *tmpnam(char *string);
int fclose(FILE *stream);
int fflush(FILE *stream);
FILE *fopen(char *filename,const char *mode);
FILE *freopen(char *filename, char *mode, FILE *stream);
void setbuf(FILE *stream, char *buffer);
int setvbuf(FILE *stream, char *buffer, int mode, size_t size);
int fprint(FILE *stream, const char *, ...);
int fscanf(FILE *,char *format, ...);
int printf(char *format, ...);
int scanf(char *format, ...);
int sprintf(char *string, char *format, ...);
int sscanf(char *string, char *format, ...);
int vfprintf(FILE *stream, char *format, void *arg);
int vprintf(char *format, void *arg);
int vsprintf(char *string, char *format, void *arg);

int fgetc(FILE *stream);
char *fgets(char *string, int n, FILE *stream);
int fputc(int c, FILE *stream);
int fputs(char *string, FILE *stream);
int getc(FILE *stream);
int getchar(void);
```

```
char *gets(char *string);
int putc(int c, FILE *stream);
int putchar(int c);
int puts(char *string);
int ungetc(int c, FILE *stream);

size_t fread(void *ptr, size_t size, size_t n, FILE *stream);
size_t fwrite(void *ptr, size_t size, size_t n, FILE *stream);

int fgetpos(FILE *stream, fpos_t *pos);
int fseek(FILE *stream, long offset, int n);
int fsetpos(FILE *stream, fpos_t *pos);
long ftell(FILE *stream);
void rewind(FILE *stream);

void clearerr(FILE *stream);
int feof(FILE *stream);
int ferror(FILE *stream);
void perror(char *string);
```

ctype.h

```
int isalnum(int c);
int isalpha(int c);
int iscntrl(int c);
int isdigit(int c);
int isgraph(int c);
int islower(int c);
int isprint(int c);
int ispunct(int c);
int isspace(int c);
int isupper(int c);
int isxdigit(int c);
int tolower(int c);
int toupper(int c);
```

string.h

```
void *memcpy(void *string1, void *string2, size_t n);
void *memmove(void *string1, void *string2, size_t n);
char *strcpy(char *string1, char *string2);
char *strncpy(char *string1, char *string2, size_t n);
char *strcat(char *string1, char *string2);
char *strncat(char *string1, char *string2, size_t n);
int memcmp(void *string1, void *string2, size_t n);
```

```
int strcmp(char *string1, char *string2);
int strcoll(char *string1, char *string2);
int strncmp(char *string1, char *string2, size_t n);
void *memchr(void *string, int c, size_t n);
char *strchr(char *string, int c);
size_t strcspn(char *string1, char *string2);
char *strpbrk(char *string1, char *string2);
char *strrchr(char *string, int c);
size_t strspn(char *string1, char *string2);
char *strstr(char *string1, char *string2);
char *strtok(char *string1, char *string2);
void *memset(void *string, int c, size_t n);
char *strerror(int n);
size_t strlen(char *string);
```

math.h

```
double atan(double x);
double cos(double x);
double exp(double x);
double fabs(double x);
double log(double x);
double sin(double x);
double sqrt(double x);
double tan(double x);
double acos(double x);
double asin(double x);
double atan2(double x, double y);
double ceil(double x);
double cosh(double x);
double floor(double x);
double fmod(double x, double y);
double frexp(double x, int *exp);
double log10(double x);
double modf(double x, double *ptr);
double pow(double x, double y);
double sinh(double x);
double tanh(double x);
```

stdlib.h

```
#define RAND_MAX
double atof(char *ptr);
int atoi(char *ptr);
```

```
long atol(char *ptr);
double strtod(char *ptr, char **ptr);
long strtol(char *ptr, char **ptr, int base);
unsigned long strtoul(char *ptr, char **ptr, int base);
int rand(void);
void srand(unsigned seed);
void *calloc(size_t n, size_t size);
void free(void *ptr);
void *malloc(size_t size);
void *realloc(void *ptr, size_t size);
void abort(void);
int atexit(void (*function) (void));
void exit(int n);
char *getenv(char *string);
int system(char *string);
int abs(int n);
div_t div(int numer, int denom);
long labs(long n);
ldiv_t ldiv(long numer, long denom);
```

assert.h

```
void assert(int expression);
```

time.h

```
clock_t clock(void);
double difftime(time_t time1, time_t time0);
time_t mktime(struct tm *ptr);
time_t time(time_t *ptr);
char *asctime(struct tm *ptr);
char *ctime(time_t *ptr);
struct tm *gmtime(time_t *ptr);
struct tm *localtime(time_t *ptr);
size_t strftime(char *string, size_t size, char *format,
     struct tm *ptr);
```

Appendix B

ASCII Character Codes

DECIMAL	OCTAL	HEXADECIMAL	CHARACTER
0	0	0	Ctrl l
1	1	1	Ctrl A
2	2	2	Ctrl B
3	3	3	Ctrl C
4	4	4	Ctrl D
5	5	5	Ctrl E
6	6	6	Ctrl F
7	7	7	Ctrl G
8	10	8	Ctrl H
9	11	9	Ctrl I
10	12	A	\n
11	13	B	Ctrl K
12	14	C	Ctrl L
13	15	D	Return
14	16	E	Ctrl N
15	17	F	Ctrl O
16	20	10	Ctrl P
17	21	11	Ctrl Q
18	22	12	Ctrl R
19	23	13	Ctrl S
20	24	14	Ctrl T
21	25	15	Ctrl U
22	26	16	Ctrl V
23	27	17	Ctrl W
24	30	18	Ctrl X
25	31	19	Ctrl Y
26	32	1A	Ctrl Z
27	33	1B	Escape
28	34	1C	Ctrl <
29	35	1D	Ctrl /
30	36	1E	Ctrl =
31	37	1F	Ctrl −
32	40	20	Space
33	41	21	!
34	42	22	"
35	43	23	#
36	44	24	$
37	45	25	%

DECIMAL	OCTAL	HEXADECIMAL	CHARACTER
38	46	26	&
39	47	27	'
40	50	28	(
41	51	29	)
42	52	2A	*
43	53	2B	+
44	54	2C	'
45	55	2D	_
46	56	2E	.
47	57	2F	/
48	60	30	0
49	61	31	1
50	62	32	2
51	63	33	3
52	64	34	4
53	65	35	5
54	66	36	6
55	67	37	7
56	70	38	8
57	71	39	9
58	72	3A	:
59	73	3B	;
60	74	3C	<
61	75	3D	=
62	76	3E	>
63	77	3F	?
64	100	40	@
65	101	41	A
66	102	42	B
67	103	43	C
68	104	44	D
69	105	45	E
70	106	46	F
71	107	47	G
72	110	48	H
73	111	49	I
74	112	4A	J
75	113	4B	K
76	114	4C	L
77	115	4D	M
78	116	4E	N
79	117	4F	O
80	120	50	P
81	121	51	Q
82	122	52	R
83	123	53	S
84	124	54	T
85	125	55	U
86	126	56	V
87	127	57	W
88	130	58	X

DECIMAL	OCTAL	HEXADECIMAL	CHARACTER
89	131	59	Y
90	132	5A	Z
91	133	5B	[
92	134	5C	\
93	135	5D	]
94	136	5E	^
95	137	5F	_
96	140	60	'
97	141	61	a
98	142	62	b
99	143	63	c
100	144	64	d
101	145	65	e
102	146	66	f
103	147	67	g
104	150	68	h
105	151	69	i
106	152	6A	j
107	153	6B	k
108	154	6C	l
109	155	6D	m
110	156	6E	n
111	157	6F	o
112	160	70	p
113	161	71	q
114	162	72	r
115	163	73	s
116	164	74	t
117	165	75	u
118	166	76	v
119	167	77	w
120	170	78	x
121	171	79	y
122	172	7A	z
123	173	7B	{
124	174	7C		
125	175	7D	}
126	176	7E	~
127	177	7F	Delete

Appendix C
Operators and Precedence Table

This table presents (almost) all C operators, in order from highest to lowest precedence. The operators at the top of the table have a higher precedence than those at the bottom. Operators in each grouping have the same precedence and would be executed according to the associativity indicated at the right.

( )	function call	left to right
[ ]	array subscript	
->	structure pointer	
.	structure member	
++	increment	right to left
--	decrement	
-	unary minus	
!	logical negation	
&	address	
*	dereference	
*	multiplication	left to right
/	division	
%	modulus	
+	addition	left to right
-	subtraction	
<<	left shift	left to right
>>	right shift	
<	less than	left to right
<=	less than or equal to	
>	greater than	
>=	greater than or equal to	
==	equal to	
!=	not equal to	
&	bitwise AND	left to right
^	bitwise exclusive OR	
|	bitwise inclusive OR	
&&	logical AND	
||	logical OR	

? :	conditional	right to left
=	assignment	right to left
+=	add assignment	
−=	subtract assignment	
*=	multiply assignment	
/=	divide assignment	
%=	modulus assignment	
<<=	left shift assignment	
>>=	right shift assignment	
&=	bit and assignment	
^=	bit exclusive or assignment	
|=	bit inclusive or assignment	
,	comma	left to right

Appendix D
Reserved Words in C

The following words are reserved by most compilers. These words are called key words or reserved words. These words may not be used as function or variable names without generating compiler errors on most C compilers.

auto	break	case	char
const	continue	default	do
double	else	enum	extern
float	for	goto	if
int	long	register	return
short	signed	sizeof	static
struct	switch	typedef	union
unsigned	void	volatile	while

Note that some C compilers also reserve the use of the words asm, cdecl, far, Fortran, huge, interrupt, near, and Pascal.

Appendix E
Brief C Reference

This apprendix summarizes C programming constructs for quick reference by the beginning C programmer.

Scalar Data Types

TYPE	SAMPLE
char	char character;
int	int number;
short int	short int number;
long int	long int number;
unsigned int	unsigned int number;
float	float value;
double	double value;

Aggregate Data Types

Array: An array is a collection of elements of the same data type. In C the first element of an array has index zero.

```
int numbers[5];
float values[10];
char name[20];
float matrix[2][3];
```

Structure: A structure (or a record) is an aggregate data type of mixed information. Not all members of a structure need be the same data type.

```
struct student_record
    {
        char name[20];
        long int id;
        char address[25];
        float tuition_owed;
    } student;
```

Here **student_record** is a structure tag, and **student** is a structure variable of type **student_record**.

Comments

Internal documentation may be included in your C source code by enclosing those comments within /* and */. Note that comments may not be enclosed within other comments with most C compilers.

```
/* this is a valid comment */
/* this is an /* invalid */ comment */
```

Statements

STATEMENT	EXAMPLE

simple if

```
if (condition) statement;
```

```
if (age < 40)
    printf("in your prime!");
```

if ... else ...

```
if (condition)
    statement;
else
    statement;
```

```
if (age > 21)
    printf("legal age");
else
    printf("too young");
```

block if

```
if (condition)
{
    compound statements;
}
```

```
if (char == 'y')
{
    printf("message");
    printf("new message");
    x = x + 1
    /* calculations and
        statements */
}
```

block if ... else ...

```
if (condition)
{
    statements;
}
else
{
    more statements;
}
```

```
if (disc < 0)
{
    printf("no real roots\n");
    printf("please try again\n");
}
else
{
    root1 = (-b + sqrt(disc))/(2*a);
    root2 = (-b - sqrt(disc))/(2*a);
}
```

for loop

```
for (initial; termination; modification)
{
    body of loop;
}
```

```
for (i=0;i<10;i=i+1)
{
    printf("%4d %4d\n",i,i*i);
}
```

STATEMENT	EXAMPLE

while loop (pretest)

```
/* initialization */

while (condition)
{
     body of loop;
}
```

```
i=0;

while (i<10)
{
    printf("%4d %4d\n",i,i*i);
    i=i+1;
}
```

do (repeat) loop (posttest)

```
do
{
     body of loop;
} while (condition);
```

```
i=0;
do
{
    printf("%4d %4d\n",i,i*i);
    i=i+1;
} while (i<10);
```

Index